COMPILED BY ADELAIDE TAMBO
FOREWORD BY NELSON MANDELA

H

Hansib Publications Limited, 2004
London: PO Box 34621, London E17 4GL
Hertfordshire: Orchard Road, Royston, Hertfordshire SG8 5HA

www.hansib-books.com

ISBN 1 870518 94 2 (paperback)
ISBN 1 870518 95 0 (hardback)

First published in 1987 by Heinemann Educational Books Ltd
in the African Writers Series

Cover photographs (back and front) courtesy of
International Defence Aid Fund

We would like to thank Executive Mayor, Duma Nkosi, Ekurhuleni
Metropolitan Municipality, and Mayor Steve Bullock, London Borough
of Lewisham, for their co-operation with this title

We are grateful to Harcourt Education Ltd for their permission to
reprint this book

The reprinting of this book is to commemorate
ten years of Freedom in South Africa

Supported by:

Ekurhuleni Metropolitan Municipality
The London Borough of Lewisham
Hansib Publications Limited

To all those who made the supreme sacrifice
in the fight to eradicate our country of the
scourge of apartheid, to our leaders in gaol,
to our people — the struggling masses
of our nation

Amandla Ngawethu   Matla Ke A Rona
Power to the People

CONTENTS

LIST OF PHOTOGRAPHS

(above) Oliver Tambo with Nelson Mandela in the 1950s.
(below) Nelson Mandela's foreword to *Oliver Tambo Speaks*, which was smuggled out of Pollsmoor Prison.

FOREWORD BY NELSON MANDELA

I am a member of the African National Congress. I have always been a member of the African National Congress and I will remain a member of the African National Congress until the day I die. Oliver Tambo is much more than a brother to me. He is my greatest friend, and comrade for nearly 50 years. If there is any one amongst you who cherishes my freedom, Oliver Tambo cherishes it more, and I know that he would give his life to see me free. There is no difference between his views and mine.'

It is an extraordinary exercise for a man to write an introduction to a book he has not seen, an exercise which may degenerate into inaccurate generalizations. All that I know is that the book is a collection of Oliver's speeches and, at the moment of writing, I have not even the barest information as to exactly where and when the speeches were made, the actual issues discussed and the title of the book. He is a banned person, and in terms of South African law what he says may not be published. For this reason it has not been possible to keep track of his speeches during the 26 years in which he has been in exile.

But we live in abnormal times and our own actions must inevitably be influenced by the circumstances in which we have to carry out our political tasks. There are many areas of activity in which our responses must depart from the accepted norms and usual practice, and this introduction is one of them.

Fortunately the task is made relatively easy by the fact that the theme and quality of Oliver's speeches are fairly predictable. As a student, school teacher and lawyer, he established a solid reputation as a clear thinker and accomplished speaker, a reputation which became a valuable asset when he turned politician.

His speeches and writings will in all probability include a

detailed review of the current political situation in South Africa, the kind of society for which the people are fighting, the unity of the people, the preservation of an alliance between the ANC and SACP, the combination of legal and illegal struggle, the mapping out of the short- and long-term goals of the ANC, the strength and weaknesses of the organization and enemy, the prosecution of the armed struggle, tribute to the brave heroes who have fallen in the battlefield and who have been captured by the enemy and those who are operating inside the country against heavy odds, the importance of sanctions against South Africa, mass mobilization, violence amongst the people, negotiation with the government, the significance of the successive South African delegations to Lusaka, relations with our neighbouring states and the rest of the world.

Although Oliver may not be quoted in South Africa, the government has been unable to silence either comment on his leadership qualities or the warm praise he is receiving from a wide variety of sources. Here we can only mention but a few of these. Tom Lodge, one of South Africa's leading political commentators, writing in the October 1985 issue of *South Africa International,* describes Oliver's political style as low key, and adds that the success the ANC has had in maintaining its unity and purpose in 25 years of exile is attributable in no small part to his personal qualities. John Battersby writes from London: 'Mr Tambo is on an international mission to win friends and influence people on behalf of the ANC, and is having considerable success.' The rousing reception he received at the Bournemouth Labour Party Conference in 1985 illustrates the formidable impact his speeches have made on the British people.

All these tributes occurred in just one year and form part of the countless compliments which have been and which continue to be showered on him. In the early sixties when he addressed a session of the United Nations, he even received praise from quite an unexpected corner. In reply to that speech Mr Eric Louw, then South African Minister of Foreign Affairs, sought to defend the policy of his government by pointing out that it was the very South Africa which was under attack which had produced a man of Oliver's calibre.

The wide-ranging interview published by the *Cape Times* in November 1985, in which he gave a brilliant exposition of the policy of the ANC on several important issues, was widely welcomed in the country and considerably fuelled the demand for the lifting of his ban so that South Africans of all political persuasions could become acquainted with his views on the critical questions confronting the country.

The ANC is enjoying unprecedented public exposure; Oliver has become one of the best-known freedom fighters in the world, and his speeches will be read with interest in almost all these countries, bringing the message of the ANC to fighters for human rights in those distant lands, and winning powerful friends for the struggle. In South Africa, the collection, in spite of the difficulties that will inevitably accompany its distribution, will constitute another milestone in the development of the ANC. It will not only serve to refute the wild and sinister government propaganda against the organization, but it will also help to mould the thinking of the youth and to galvanize the masses of the people behind the anti-apartheid struggle.

His speeches, even though they reach us through comments by others, have been of particular significance to political prisoners, especially those serving long terms of imprisonment. Our confidence in him as an individual, in the dynamic and committed men and women around him, their immense commitment to the principle of collective action, and unfailing sensitivity to the needs of their fellow men, has inspired us beyond words, and put the entire freedom struggle firmly on a new dimension.

PREFACE

This book is the result of the persistent pleas of many friends in the struggle against apartheid who have urged for years that a record be made of the contribution of Oliver Tambo to the cause. All his life has been spent in the political struggle for the liberation of the black people of South Africa and for the establishment of a non-racial South African nation. Yet, little of his life's work has been publicized. This is largely because of his self-effacing character; he has no desire to be seen as some kind of hero. These pages show that he has dedicated his life to his country and to his colleagues in the liberation struggle.

It has taken many years to collect Oliver's speeches. My family and friends pressed me to have them published, and four years ago I prepared to do so but for some reason procrastinated. However, with Oliver's 70th birthday approaching I felt that a book of his speeches would be a fitting birthday present. By producing this book, our three children and I salute him in the name of our people, . We owe this book to those compatriots who have paid the supreme price in the liberation struggle, to those in prison, to those in exile and to those who are carrying on the struggle inside South Africa.

In the light of impending success in our liberation struggle, the whole world now looks to the African National Congress and assesses its role and its policies. It is only natural that the President also be judged. I hope that these speeches will show him both as a political leader and as a man.

There are several people to thank:
my children, Tembi and Martin Kingston, Dalindlela Tambo and Tselane Tambo, Daphne and Mahlubi Kumalo;
Ben Turok, Director of the Institute For African Alternatives, who edited the speeches and without whose help this book would not have been realized;
E.S.Reddy, former Secretary of the UN Unit Against Apartheid, helped me collect Oliver's UN speeches;
Professor Tom Karis for helping us find some speeches;

Michael Seifert and Helen Searle for their legal advice with difficult and finer points of law.

Finally I must thank my family for their continuing support and encouragement. I have benefited a great deal from their young lives.

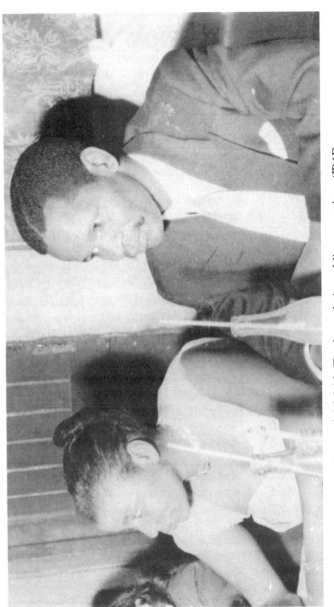

Oliver and Adelaide Tambo at their wedding reception. *(IDAF)*

NOTE ON TERMINOLOGY

Different people in South Africa are classified by the apartheid system into four discrete population groups: 'White' for European settlers or their descendants; 'Coloured' for those of mixed descent; 'Indian'(or Asian) for descendants of Asian indentured labourers and traders who arrived in South Africa in the nineteenth century; and 'African' for members of Bantu-speaking groups. 'Non-European' and 'Bantu' were official classifications in the 1950s and 1960s but are no longer part of apartheid discourse. All these apartheid terms have given offence and when capitalized in the text they are used merely for descriptive purposes. The term 'black' is preferred in popular usage today when referring to the oppressed people of South Africa.

1
FREEDOM IN OUR LIFETIME

Introduction

Oliver Tambo was born into a modest peasant household in Bizana in the Transkei on 27 October 1917. He began his education at mission schools in the area of Flagstaff and with missionary sponsorship went on to St. Peter's Secondary School in Johannesburg, matriculating with a first class pass in 1938. Awarded a scholarship, he studied at Fort Hare University College, a forcing ground for the training of African leaders in South Africa and abroad. It was there that Tambo first met Nelson Mandela, one year his senior. They cut their teeth in student politics and formed a close relationship that was to lead to a legal partnership in Johannesburg in 1952. Tambo graduated with a B.Sc.in 1941, but stayed on for a Diploma in Education only to be expelled during a students' strike in 1942. This did not prevent him from taking a post as a science and mathematics teacher at St Peter's, his old school (1943-47). There he became acquainted with three fellow teachers who were to play important roles in the African National Congress: Lembede, Mbatha, and Mda. He also renewed his friendship with Mandela, who had moved to Johannesburg to study law. In 1944 they became, with others including Walter Sisulu, founder members of the ANC Youth League.

Tambo, Mandela and Sisulu were the most prominent founding members of the ANC Youth League and all went on to hold leading posts in the ANC. In December 1949 Tambo and seven other Youth Leaguers — including Walter Sisulu who became Secretary-General — were first elected to the National Executive. This group shaped ANC philosophy and direction in important ways. It was the Youth League's 'Programme of Action', adopted as the ANC's policy in 1949, that prepared the way for civil disobedience against the apartheid regime in the 1950s. It was their leadership that directed the Defiance Campaign in 1952 as a result of which over 8,000 volunteers were imprisoned for defying six selected apartheid laws. It was their shift from an exclusive African nationalism that prepared the ground for the Congress Alliance (with its symbol of a wheel with four spokes) of the four organizations: African National Congress (ANC), South African Indian Congress (SAIC), South African Coloured People's Organization (SACPO) and South African Congress of Democrats (SACOD). And it was the ANC's guiding principles that created the mass movement represented by some 3,000 delegates at the Congress of the People at Kliptown on 25-26 June 1955.

When the Freedom Charter was adopted at Kliptown, Tambo was the Acting Secretary-General of the ANC. He had become Acting Secretary-General in August 1954, when Sisulu was served with a banning order and required to resign from the ANC. Although Tambo was restricted at the same time to the magisterial districts of Benoni and Johannesburg for two years and prohibited from attending gatherings, he was not required to resign and was able to guide the ANC in the campaigns against the Western Areas removals and the introduction of Bantu Education. In December 1955 Tambo was formally elected Secretary-General, a post he held until 1958.

After the Congress of the People the Congress Alliance gained a mass following and an organized presence in every African township throughout the country. It now faced state repression on a new scale and in a new form. In December 1956, 156 leaders of all races were arrested and charged under the Suppression of Communism Act with a treasonable conspiracy to overthrow the government. Tambo was amongst them. The preliminary examination in the Treason Trial began in January 1957, but charges were dropped in stages against the majority of the accused until only 30 remained on trial. Charges against Tambo were withdrawn on 17 December 1957. The trial dragged on for four and a half years, as the prosecution tried and failed to show the policy of the ANC to be one of violence. The final 30 accused were acquitted on all counts in March 1961.

During the period of the trial the state enforced its own form of institutional violence against the movement and indeed all protesters. There was repression in 1957 when Bantu authorities were enforced in Zeerust and women were ordered to carry passes. There was more repression in 1958 with the enforcement of cattle culling in Sekhukhuneland, in 1959 when the people of Cato Manor protested against pass raids, and in 1960 when the Government attempted to impose Bantu authorities in Pondoland. And as the defence was about to begin presenting its case in March 1960, the trial was disrupted by massive police action at the time of the Sharpeville shootings and the declaration of a State of Emergency.

In December 1958 Luthuli was elected President-General of the ANC for a third time, Tambo was elected to the post of Deputy President-General and Duma Nokwe became Secretary-General. But a group of separatist nationalists emerged in the organization. Their leader, Robert Sobukwe, argued that the only people who really wanted change in South Africa were Africans, whose material conditions were the worst of all. Consequently, in his view, co-operation with whites was unwarranted. He also rejected any form of association with communists, alleging that their influence in the Congress Alliance had led to the watering down of the 1949 Programme of Action. The emergence of this group led to the formation of the Pan-Africanist Congress (PAC) in April 1958.

The ANC decided to launch a campaign against passes on 31 March 1960, but they were upstaged by the PAC who began their campaign ten days earlier. The state reacted with more violence. In the Sharpeville massacre 69 were killed and 180 wounded. The ANC called a nation-wide protest strike for 28 March. The state responded by declaring a State of Emergency on 30 March and detaining Luthuli and 2,000 other activists, a detention which lasted for five months. Some evaded the police and core groups of the ANC and SACP were established underground which rebuilt an active national network. Ruth Mompati, Moses Kotane, Michael Harmel and Ben Turok amongst others survived intensive police searches. Meanwhile, Oliver Tambo slipped across the Bechuanaland border to rouse world-wide protest. He was in Accra, Ghana, on 8 April when he heard that both the ANC and the PAC had been banned.

Mandela summed up the politics of the 1950s in these words:

> During the last ten years the African people in South Africa have fought many freedom battles, involving civil disobedience, strikes, protest marches, boycotts and demonstrations of all kinds. In all these campaigns we repeatedly stressed the importance of discipline, peaceful and non-violent struggle. We did so, firstly, because we felt that there were still opportunities for peaceful struggle and we sincerely worked for peaceful changes. Secondly, we did not want to expose our people to situations where they might become easy targets for the trigger-happy police of South Africa. But the situation has now radically altered.
>
> South Africa is now a land ruled by the gun.
>
> (N.Mandela, *No Easy Walk to Freedom*, 1965, p.119)

The stormy 1950s tested the ANC leadership fully. It was a decade of transition from protest politics to mass resistance which had to be guided skillfully by a leadership itself undergoing profound change. Tambo's steady rise to the most senior positions was indicative of his responsiveness to the increasingly serious political crisis in the country and a recognition of growing confidence in his calm but committed leadership.

1.1 THE NATURE OF OUR STRUGGLE
*('Passive Resistance in South Africa' published in J.A.Davis and J.K.Baker, **Southern Africa in Transition,** Frederick A.Praeger, New York, 1966)*

Oppressed people in South Africa have always associated the history of the United States with the great name of Abraham Lincoln. There was an issue involving human rights in his day — an issue that challenged the principles enshrined in the Declaration of Independence. To the honour of his name, his people, and his country, Abraham Lincoln translated these great principles into concrete action.

The US Government has made some forthright statements of policy in condemnation of such practices as apartheid in South Africa, where black men and women are held in bondage in violation of the principles enunciated in the Universal Declaration of Human Rights. What puzzles and worries Africans, however, is the opposition persistently offered by the White House to any action intended to put an end to this bondage.

In its historical development, 'passive resistance' in South Africa has been closely associated with the late Mahatma Gandhi and his philosophy. As early as 1907, he led the Indian community in South Africa in acts of passive resistance. In later years there were further passive-resistance campaigns by the Indian community. Mahatma believed in the effectiveness of what he called the 'soul force' in passive resistance. According to him, the suffering experienced in passive resistance inspired a change of heart in the rulers. The African National Congress , on the other hand, expressly rejected any concepts and methods of struggle that took the form of a self-pitying, arms-folding, and passive reaction to oppressive policies. It felt that nothing short of aggressive pressure from the masses of the people would bring about any change in the political situation in South Africa. As a counter measure to Mahatma Gandhi's passive resistance, the African National Congress launched, in 1952, the Campaign for the Defiance of Unjust Laws, or the 'Defiance Campaign'.

Before they were finally defeated and subjugated by sheer force of superior arms, our forefathers had been engaged in many bitter struggles against the white foreign invaders and colonial conquerors, both Boer and British. With spears and battle-axes their only weapons, and with shields their sole means of protection against bullets, Africans fought grimly in defence of their land and their national independence. The armed struggle was carried on intermittently for 127 years. In the end, however, the Africans were defeated, totally disarmed, and then shepherded into what are known as reserves. These reserves, 260 in number, are usually in the poorest parts of the country and are utterly inadequate for their large populations.

But wounds could not be licked indefinitely. If the British and the Boers, despite the bitterness of a hard-fought war, could come together in a united front against the African people, why could not the Africans unite and face their common problems and enemy, no longer as individual and separate tribes but as a united people? The answer was found on 8 January 1912, when African chiefs, intellectuals, clergymen, workers, and peasants from every tribe in South Africa met in Bloemfontein and formed the African National Congress. The organization turned out to be more than a negative reaction to the formation of a union of white foreigners and conquerors. It became the symbol of African unity and gave our people a sense of nationhood that has survived the most determined applications of the policy of divide-and-rule over a period of more than 50 years. Seeing in this organization a serious threat to their continued political and economic domination of the country — an evil force to be fought and destroyed by all means — the white rulers of South Africa and their successive governments employed a variety of measures to eradicate it. They intimidated and victimized chiefs, teachers, and governmental employees who supported the organization; they engaged the services of informers and *agents provocateurs*; they engineered groundless quarrels among members of the organization; and they encouraged the foundation of splinter and opposition groups to confuse the people, to undermine their struggle for national emancipation, and, in that way, to perpetuate oppression and exploitation.

At the time of the formation of the ANC, there was no question of relying on armed force as a means of struggle. Only ten or so years previously, the Boers had tried that method against the British and failed. Bambata had resorted to arms in 1906 and also failed. Deputations, petitions, demonstrations, and conference resolutions were the order of the day. Besides, the Africans had been forcibly disarmed. The ANC, therefore, led the people into essentially peaceful and non-violent forms of action. It was not unusual for governments of the pre-apartheid era to take some notice of African demands and hold out some promise of possible concessions. In some cases, political pressure in the form of public meetings and protest demonstrations yielded favourable results. Although the overall political and economic situation of the Africans remained consistently intolerable, there was always hope for securing some redress of grievances through peaceful means. The African was not denied such rights as freedom of assembly, speech, organization, the press, and movement — all of which have since completely vanished.

The pattern of legislation passed by successive governments was distinctly discriminatory against the African people and aimed at establishing and perpetuating a servant-and-master relationship between black and white. Thus, Africans employed by white farmers were treated like serfs and worked from dawn to dusk for a mere pittance; the poor and hunger-stricken inhabitants of the overcrowded and arid reserves were subjected to heavy taxation; and, in the urban areas, Africans were harassed by laws requiring passes and were chased from pillar to post by the police.

During World War Two, Hitler became the hero, and Nazism the faith, of hundreds of Afrikaners. The fanaticism of the SS was a virtue to be emulated. As the Jews had been shown their place in Hitler's Germany, so would the Kaffirs in South Africa. But the Africans, heartened by the Allies' promise of a post-war world in which the fundamental rights of all men would be respected, became increasingly impatient with their lot. Institutions such as the Advisory Boards, the Natives' Representative Council, the Transkeian Bunga, and the 'Native Parliamentary Representatives' — an insignificant handful of whites representing Africans in the South African Senate and House of Assembly — were all attacked by Africans as dummy bodies, and agitation for their boycott was started. Anti-pass campaigns were launched in urban areas where the Africans were most affected by the pass system, protests against poor housing and low wages mounted, and the rural population resisted Government schemes that interfered with their rights to land and that sought to limit their livestock.

The war ended, but repression continued unabated. In 1946, the African mine workers in Johannesburg and the Reef went on strike. The strike was ruthlessly repressed and several Africans were killed. The Natives' Representative Council, a dummy African parliament, which, since its establishment in 1937, had struggled in vain to prevent the enactment of discriminatory legislation, adjourned indefinitely in protest. In the same year, the South African Indians launched a passive-resistance campaign against a law restricting their right to land ownership. In the meantime, the growing African National Congress continued protesting against various forms of segregation. The Government, on the other hand, adopted more repressive legislation.

It was in this atmosphere of discontent and expectation that the black cloud of reaction and brutal repression descended on South Africa: Dr Malan's Nationalist Party seized political power in May 1948. These were the disciples of Hitler. One year later, the shape of things to come was clear. Laws enacted by previous governments were reinforced with vicious amendments and were vigorously enforced by officials who, for sheer brutality, seemed to have been specially recruited from some prehistoric bush where cruelty was a highly prized virtue. Soon the expression, 'The devil has been let loose on this country', became current among Africans.

Responding to this new challenge, the ANC adopted in

1949 a Programme of Action that stipulated that boycotts, strikes, non-collaboration, and 'civil disobedience' would now be used as methods and forms of action in the political struggle. The Programme contemplated participation by the masses of the people. It did not raise the question of violence versus non-violence. The appearance of the word 'non-violence' in the political vocabulary of the ANC was a product of the objective conditions under which the Programme was being put into action. The use of the expression 'civil disobedience' in the Programme was, however, of significance. The ANC was an ordinary political organization that had always used methods of political pressure recognized in a democratic country. These methods had been non-violent, but there had been no specific declaration of policy excluding violence or positively proclaiming non-violence. In the course of normal demonstration or other forms of political action, the people could conceivably have been provoked into conduct that amounted to civil disobedience, and this could have happened without a policy decision authorizing such conduct. Why then did the 1949 ANC conference go out of its way to provide for 'civil disobedience'?

The force with which apartheid struck at the African masses called for action, and the conference decided to commit the organization to specified drastic forms of action. But the Programme of Action did not define 'civil disobedience'. Did it mean civil disorder? Mob violence? Rioting? It most certainly did not mean any of these types of conduct. The keynote of the disobedience was to be discipline. The expression 'civil disobedience' referred to the deliberate breach, or defiance, of Government laws, regulations, and orders. The conference, in interpreting civil disobedience in terms of disciplined and purposeful mass action, emphasized non-violence. It called for self-control on the part of the people and urged them to withstand acts of provocation by the police, who were obviously anxious for a show-down. Failure to emphasize the need for discipline would have been a fatal political blunder. Non-violence was thus a political tactic that could be changed according to the demands of the political situation.

On 1 May 1950, 18 Africans were killed by the police during a one-day strike staged as the climax to a provincial campaign for universal adult suffrage. On 26 June 1950, the Africans' first national protest strike was called. The strike was the culmination of a country-wide campaign of protest against the Unlawful Organizations Bill introduced by the Government and aimed at stamping out all opposition to its racial and oppressive policies. It was also intended as an act of mourning for the Africans killed on 1 May and earlier in the liberation struggle. The strike was a great success and demonstrated the readiness of the oppressed people for determined political action. The Unlawful Organizations Bill was withdrawn as a result of the protest agitation. (It was later introduced and enacted, with slight textual amendments, as the Suppression of Communism Act.)

The policy of uncompromising apartheid was carried out with vigour, violence, hate, and haste. This has remained the pattern of Nationalist Party rule in South Africa to the present day. The country has been in a state of perpetual political crisis now since 1948. It has been the blackest period in the past 60 years and, for the Africans, the bloodiest since the Boer invasions of the eighteenth and nineteenth centuries. In 15 short years, hundreds of innocent Africans have been shot dead by the police; many more have been wounded by police gunfire during raids, while under arrest, and while in prison; and many have been beaten to death on white-owned farms. In addition, millions of Africans have been convicted of petty offences, and the average number sentenced to death annually, for what are essentially political offences, has been higher than in any corresponding period since Jan van Riebeeck landed in the country in 1652.

When this gruesome phase in the history of the country began to assume a regular pattern in 1950, numerous protests and demonstrations against Government policy were staged by many organizations from every racial group. In one way or another, the various groups and movements representing the vast majority of the population voiced their protest. These groups saw the clear advantage in co-ordinating the anti-apartheid forces and encouraging joint action against the common enemy. Furthermore, since it was the express aim of the Government to enforce sharp racial divisions among the population and to set up separate and possibly hostile racial camps, the very act of co-operation and unity among all opponents of racial discrimination and white domination was in itself an attack on Government policy. It was, therefore, of great political and strategic importance for the African National Congress to rally, and to welcome, the support of other oppressed groups and of democratic whites. The South African Indian Congress and the Coloured people's leaders readily accepted a basis for conducting joint campaigns.

At its conference in December 1951 the ANC decided to launch the Defiance Campaign. The story of this dignified, disciplined, and peaceful campaign is well known. It won many friends for the African cause in South Africa and abroad, and served to focus the attention of influential sectors of world opinion on the South African political scene. Within South Africa, the Defiance Campaign strengthened the liberation movement and set the tone for future action. Although toward the end of the campaign the Africans were provoked into some violence, they had amply demonstrated their capacity for self-discipline and their readiness for militant struggle. This meant that it was possible, without resorting to violence, to force the Government into a position in which its policy became unworkable.

In the years following 1952 hundreds of leaders were banned from taking part in political activities or attending gatherings. Many were restricted to defined areas while others were banished from their homes. Scores were imprisoned, and meetings and processions were prohibited in many parts of the country. Despite all this, however, and despite the fact that the most influential leaders were cut off from the people, the pressures of mass political action throughout the country continued to rise, compelling the Government to fall back on an ever-increasing list of repressive and restrictive laws. It made greater use of the police force, equipping it with a growing pile of arms, ranging from locally produced pistols to tanks supplied by Great Britain.

When these measures failed, the Government resorted to banning political organizations and placing the whole or parts of the country under a State of Emergency. The reaction of the ANC to its banning in 1960 was to announce that it would conduct the liberation struggle underground. The March 1961 (All-in African) conference of 1,500 delegates representing 145 organizations, at which Nelson Mandela was the main speaker, was organized largely under illegal conditions. It demonstrated the power of the underground organization and the unity of the people. Following this conference, preparations started for a three-day national strike to commence on 29 May 1961. The strike drew unprecedented support from the mass of the African population and was fully backed by the Indian and Coloured communities. Faced with this tremendous political demonstration — which was a triumphant breakthrough for a liberation movement operating under a cloud of repressive legislative prohibitions and restrictions — the Verwoerd Government abandoned the political fight and took to arms. The unarmed demonstrators and would-be strikers were confronted with practically the entire South African Army, fully equipped and ready for war.

. . . An intensive policy of soliciting and mobilizing world condemnation of apartheid started shortly after the launching of the Defiance Campaign. Visitors to South Africa — numerous journalists, distinguished authors, leading world personalities, and representatives and members of overseas organizations — were briefed in detail on the tyranny of apartheid. By means of annual memoranda sent by the ANC and the SAIC to the United Nations and by South African delegations attending international conferences, the word 'apartheid' spread to many parts of the world. The arrest of African leaders on charges of high treason followed by an appeal by Africans for an international boycott of South African goods further increased world support, and offered people and organizations in different countries an opportunity to give tangible expression to their sympathies for our cause. By 1960 the degree of world interest in South Africa was such that the Sharpeville massacres provoked an explosive and universal barrage of indignant protests. This cold-blooded carnage brought the whole of mankind face to face with the essentially inhuman and barbarous nature of apartheid.

Many people and organizations in different countries, notably in Britain, Scandinavia, and the United States, took up the issue, and, since 1960, campaigns have been organized to rally support for the boycott of South African goods and for other economic sanctions. Several governments, particularly the newly independent African states, Asian nations, and the socialist countries, have supported United Nations resolutions calling for economic sanctions against South Africa. The United States and Great Britain, which, of all the UN member-states, have the biggest stake in the South African economy, have, however, consistently and strenuously resisted the move to impose sanctions on South Africa. This has so far made it impossible for the UN to employ the only form of peaceful and effective intervention open to it, and has consequently enabled the South African Government to pursue its policies with only limited interference from the outside world. Hence the emergence of violent methods of struggle in South Africa.

It would be wrong to conclude that it is now too late to influence the trend of events in South Africa by way of external pressures. On the contrary, the challenge of the present situation is the greater not only to those who abhor racialism and all that goes by the name of apartheid and white minority rule, but also to those who disapprove of all violence. The sooner South Africa is isolated economically, politically, and culturally, the shorter will be the duration of this, the last and bitterest phase of the struggle for human rights and freedom in Africa.

1.2 FIGHT TO BE FREE
(Report of the National Executive Committee to the ANC annual conference, 17-18 December 1955)

We of the African National Congress meet once again to review South African and world events; our Congress policy of rights and progress for all the people of our country; our desire for world peace and friendship among the peoples of the world.

Apartheid is enslaving the people of South Africa today but in the great world outside, race discrimination and colonialism are being replaced by human brotherhood and the independence of nations. Countries which less than one decade ago were the subjects of colonial powers have thrown off their bonds and asserted their right to take part in international affairs as complete equals. In the last ten years the maps have had to be re-drawn, the face of the world has changed, the people of great parts of Asia have risen to their feet, and now the freedom struggle is spreading to our own continent, Africa. Centuries of colonial oppression have been ended for many millions and for millions more the struggle for liberation is reaching new heights. *We do not doubt that within our lifetimes the millions still oppressed throughout the world will govern themselves freely.*

The road to freedom is no easy one. Savage wars have been unleashed against the peoples of Kenya, Malaya and Vietnam, savage campaigns of annihilation against the peoples of French Africa, by those seeking to stamp out the people's freedom movements. The colonialists strive to prevent the floodlight of world enquiry being focussed on what happens in their colonies; they seek to deny the United Nations the right to discuss their policies and to actively safeguard those liberties enshrined in the UN Charter and Declaration of Human Rights.

The deprivation of human liberties; policies of genocide or mass extermination against a subject people; the denial of rights to a people because of their colour; these evils are not the domestic concern of ruling nations: they are the affair of

A portrait of Oliver Tambo taken at the time of the Treason Trial.
(Eli Weinberg, IDAF)

all peoples. Even from those colonies in Africa where the people have been kept in the most dire subjection, denied rights of assembly and organization and cut off from contact with the outside world, the demands for self-government, for independence and for freedom are ringing out.

Colonialism will be overthrown. It will take longer in some countries than others. Nowhere will freedom come about independently of the people's struggles, and everywhere the colonial and master powers will fight bitterly to retain their possessions. But everywhere the people's movements are growing, developing, maturing; new militant forms of struggle are adopted; a new determination is growing among the people; a brotherhood and a confidence for freedom are being forged and the day to liberation draws nearer.

This was the great significance of the Bandung Conference held in Indonesia in April of this year. The conference of 29 Asian and African powers represented the new era of colonial liberation and was therefore one of the most important events of our time. *There entered into the world arena a great new force for freedom and for peace.* The resurgent peoples of Asia and Africa who for centuries experienced the bitterness of colonial oppression will not rest until all are liberated from this evil. So the conference at Bandung pledged to fight until the last remains of colonialism have been wiped from the face of the earth. The conference deplored the policies of racial segregation and discrimination which form the basis of government and human relations in large regions of the still exploited world — including our own country, South Africa. It proposed economic and cultural co-operation between the Asian and African people, and demanded increased representation for the people of these two continents in the United Nations.

With the greatest enthusiasm, we greet the achievements of the Bandung Conference which will inspire colonial people everywhere to redouble their efforts for freedom.

We greet with enthusiasm the decision to convene yet another Afro-Asian conference next year in Cairo.

The coming together of the Asian and African powers is a

great force in the world not only for freedom but also for peace, and none should feel the need for peace more deeply than the colonial people who have seen so many wars fought against them in their own lands to rob them of their country's natural wealth and of their liberty. *National rights and independence are not secure in a world at war; and peace is needed for the people to advance and prosper.* All mankind needs the ending of the cold war that divides the world into two hostile armed camps and prevents the development of trade, of economic and cultural exchange.

The pessimism of those who once used to say that war is inevitable has been confounded by the great victories for peace won recently by the peace-loving people of the world. Concrete steps towards peace and the easing of world tension were taken at top level meetings of the big powers. The pressure of the people brought to a stop the colonial wars in Korea and Vietnam.

The people see the choice clearly as one of *co-existence*: all nations, governments and systems learning to live in one world — or of *no existence*: a war of atomic horror weapons which threatens to wipe out mankind. The people made their pressure felt and forced their governments to negotiate around the conference table. Great steps have been taken to preserve the peace but the dangers of war can only be averted while the people remain vigilant and organize and fight for peace. War is an opportunity and the means to colonial powers to invade new territories, to swell their profits from the armaments industry and the pillage of subject countries.

The colonial peoples need liberation, freedom, independence. But *we who fight for freedom fight also for peace that our children may grow up in a world of prosperity and international friendship.*

At Bandung where Africa and Asia took their stand so firmly for world peace and freedom were present Moses Kotane and Maulvi Cachalia. In the great Bandung Assembly our voice was heard, and Kotane spoke there for the real aspirations of the South African people, as he had done for many years at home.

At the United Nations, by contrast, the South African Government representatives have withdrawn from this session of UNO rather than face the criticism and denunciation of the world. But running away from criticism does not defeat the critics and serves only to condemn the South African Government and isolate it from world opinion. South Africa cannot evade the judgement of the world: the judgement is against apartheid and discrimination and for equality and human rights

The suggestion in the latest United Nations report on South Africa, while still condemning the apartheid practices of our Government, is that the application of apartheid is 'slowing down', that the operation of this policy is characterized by 'gradualism' and 'flexibility'. The events of the past year alone do not bear out this theory, nor do the experiences of those who are the chief victims of the apartheid policy: the Non-White people.

Above all, this approach misses so sadly the real purpose of the apartheid policy of the Nationalists. Under cover of the airy talk of complete territorial apartheid, of the endless discussions by the Dutch Reformed Church ministers and the SABRA professors, one bout after another of oppressive, discriminatory legislation is being inflicted on the people. While its long term aims are theorized about in the press and the debating chambers, the people are already experiencing the disasters of apartheid. The repression of the state has never been so severe, both the attacks on the political movements and on the rights of the individual and the family; and these attacks have never been directed against such large numbers of the people as they are today. What are these if not the results of apartheid? The talk may be of 'separate homes for the Africans in the Reserves', of 'their own cities', rights in 'their own areas' and 'separate development'; but these plans are an apartheid pipe dream, an illusion, and the *actuality of apartheid today is the denial of all rights to those millions living and working in the towns and poverty-stricken rural areas.*

This is exactly the purpose of the apartheid theory: to inflict discriminatory laws on the Non-White people under the guise of letting them develop one day in their own areas. It may well be recognized that the facts of history work against this illusion of apartheid and that it is a political and economic impossibility, but meanwhile none should fail to see that the Nationalists are *today* whittling away our rights, sacrificing us on the altar of apartheid, and reducing the people to a state of semi-slavery.

If ever there was a year when apartheid played havoc with the rights of the people, it is the period under review.

The forcible removal by army and police of the people of Johannesburg's Western Areas to Meadowlands; the plans of the Minister of Native Affairs, Dr Verwoerd, to move the entire African population of the Western Cape Province; the enforcement of the Bantu Education system; the packing of the Senate by Nats in preparation for the removal of Coloured voters from the common roll; the implementation of the Population Registration Act; the reclassification of Coloureds; the alteration of the judiciary to suit the interests of the Nats; the enforcement of the Bantu Authorities Act; the continuation of exiles and bannings of leaders; the ruthless raids on people's meetings, private offices and private homes and even religious institutions; the introduction of ethnic grouping; and the creation of slums under the site-and-service scheme; the application of the Group Areas Act with the sole purpose of economically ruining the Non-Europeans — the Indians in particular; the shameless pass laws and beer raids, persecution of people under the pass laws and finally the threat of the extension of pass laws to women by January next year.

Here in South Africa none can be in doubt as to the growing ruthlessness of the Nationalists and their determination, to use the words of the Prime Minister, to pursue their policies 'relentlessly'.

The relentless pursuance of Nationalist policies, instead of serving to stiffen the opposition of the United Party has helped to dismember it. Instead of presenting to the electorate an alternative to the Nationalist Party policies, the United Party offers a copy of these policies, a slightly milder version. 'To get into power again the United Party must get more votes, and these votes can only come from the moderate Afrikaners', said Sir De Villiers Graaff, the chairman of the Cape United Party, in November. 'The moderate Nationalists must be made to feel that there is a place for them in the United Party.' Here is a simple telling admission of the policies of capitulation followed by the United Party, policies which have led many former United Party supporters to abandon the faint-hearted policies of the official opposition and to seek more principled opposition to the Nationalists in such protest movements as the Covenant Movement and the campaigns of the Black Sash women. The will to fight the Senate Act and other dictatorial measures is stirring many European voters who have turned to mass protest movements in an attempt to revive and revitalize the opposition. *But so long as it is not recognized that the only real bulwark, the only firm defence against dictatorship and fascism is the will of the Non-White people for democracy, all opposition politics of White voters alone will continue to be shadow play, unreal and ineffective.*

More votes, yes, that is the issue. Not winning Nationalist votes to the side of the United Party, but extending the vote to all the people.

'No government can justly claim authority unless it is based on the will of the people', says the Freedom Charter:

> Every man and woman shall have the right to vote for and to stand as candidate for all bodies which make laws. All people shall be entitled to take part in the administration of the country.

This is the only way to defeat the police state, this is the only way forward.

The great road forward is lit by the Freedom Charter, adopted at the Congress of the People at Kliptown on June 25 and 26. Which of us who head the idea of the Congress of the People first proposed at our Queenstown Conference by Professor Matthews foresaw that it would be such a brilliant success? History was made at Kliptown in June of this year.

The Freedom Charter was not just another political document, the Congress of the People just another conference. *The Freedom Charter is the sum total of our aspirations, but more: it is the road to new life.* It is the uniting creed of all the people struggling for democracy and for their rights; the mirror of the future South Africa. The defeat of the Nationalists and the course of the Congress movement depends on every fighter for freedom grasping fully the meaning and significance, and the purpose of the Freedom Charter.

The Charter is no patchwork collection of demands, no jumble of reforms. The ten clauses of the Charter cover all aspects of the lives of the people. The Charter exposes the fraud of racialism and of minority government. It demands equal rights before the law, work and security for all, the opening of the doors of learning and culture for all. It demands that our brothers in the Protectorates shall be free to decide for themselves their own future; it proclaims the oneness of our aims for peace and friendship with our brothers in Africa and elsewhere in the world.

This is the pattern of the new South Africa which must make a complete break with the present unjust system.

The Freedom Charter has opened up a new chapter in the struggle of our people. Hitherto we have struggled sometimes together, sometimes separately against pass laws, and Group Areas, against low wages, against Bantu Education and removal schemes. With the adoption of the Charter all struggles become part of one: the struggle for the aims of the Charter.

. . .We would . . . be failing in our duty if we did not express our high appreciation of the efforts made in the carrying out of our major campaigns during this period.

In the Anti-removal campaign in the Western Areas, the Anti-Bantu Education campaign, the campaign for the Congress of the People, there are regions and branches which distinguished themselves as a result of which they have emerged strong.

In conclusion, friends, we thank all those who made it their duty to put personal business aside in order to serve the nation during the period under review. We further call upon them in the coming year and upon all true patriots, all democrats, all lovers of freedom to resolve once more that South Africa shall become a free land, free from Nationalist tyranny and become a happy place for all to live in, during our life time.

Mayibuye i Afrika!

1.3 REPORTS FROM THE PROGRESSIVE PRESS

New Body Formed to Fight Racialism
200 Europeans Meet With Defiance Leaders

Walter Sisulu, Yusuf Cachalia and Oliver Tambo, on behalf of the Defiance Campaign, the African National Congress and the South African Indian Congresses, emphasized that the campaign was not directed against any racial group. Its basic purpose is to achieve the recognition of Non-Europeans as human beings by the peaceful method of passive resistance. Mr Tambo said that a clause in the constitutions of both Congresses pledges them to work for the ideal of full democratic rights for all South Africans. The silence of European democrats to the challenge of the issues involved in the Defiance Campaign is being construed by Non-Europeans as acquiescence in and approval of the Government's policies. This is rapidly creating the belief among large numbers of Non-Europeans that all whites are hostile to them and their aspirations and that the situation is being transformed into a white versus non-white struggle.

(*Advance*, *27 November 1952*)

Amendment to the Suppression of Communism Act to Evade the Appellate Division's Judgement

'The highest court in the land has affirmed the simple and universally-acknowledged principle that a man should not be condemned unheard. It is deeply disturbing that the Minister's immediate response should be to repudiate that principle and seek to arm himself with new powers to

override it. I protest, and I think all democrats should protest too.'
(Advance, 10 December 1952)

The Congress of the People

Referring to allegations in a press statement by Brigadier Rademeyer following last week's ejection of the CID from the Transvaal preparatory conference for the Congress of the People, Mr Tambo, a member of the National Action Council organizing the Congress, told a press conference that the Acting Police Commissioner's statements were uncalled for, misleading and possibly irregular from a legal viewpoint.

'Brigadier Rademeyer's statement implies that this organization is planning a revolution and to overthrow the state by force. Such statements are utterly misleading as to the purpose and objects of the sponsoring organizations. The composition and objects of these organization were made known to the country and to the world . . . The Congress of the People has been created for an altogether lawful purpose.'

Mr Tambo declined to comment further on Brigadier Rademeyer's statements in so far as they related to a *sub judice* matter. 'Our attorneys' attention has been drawn to them and they will take the necessary steps.'

He did, however, draw attention sharply to the 'increasing tendency of the police authorities to issue statements on political movements and on meetings of lawful organization. This tendency was unprecedented in South Africa, caused considerable unrest and indicated the approach of a police state.'
(Advance, 5 August 1954)

The Bantu Education Act

'When Verwoerd says that children who boycott Bantu Education schools will lose their places, which will be filled by others, he forgets to ask himself: Who will these others be? Does he perhaps imagine African parents will be eager to send their offspring to schools for apartheid, where the doctrine of African inferiority will be imprinted on their impressionable minds? The ANC is preparing instructions of all its branches on the implementation of the resolution condemning Bantu Education.

'The African people are not going to be intimidated by Dr Verwoerd's statement. He comments so early after the passing of the resolution because he is worried at the determined opposition to his schemes. To warn the parents about their children being replaced by other children when withdrawn is to miss the point that we are going to stop both those who are attending school, as well as those who are not yet attending school from doing so. We trust that most of the churches will continue to support us on this issue, as they have done on past issues, since it is clear that this education is incompatible with Christian precepts.'

(New Age, 6 January 1955)

Persecution Under the Pass Laws

'The large-scale pass arrests, the periodic swoops on Africans for passes, are coming to be accepted by far too many white South Africans as the 'normal' thing. Not a day passes but raiding parties scour Johannesburg and other large cities to make arrests, and although the pass laws have always been one of the most hated and arduous forms of oppression imposed on Africans, the drag-net for victims has never been cast so wide, the laws so unsympathetically administered, and the victims of these inhuman laws so numerous.

'Issued just as the Government has announced a Bill to amend the Abolition of Passes and Co-ordination of Documents Act (the amendment tightens up loopholes in the Act and stipulates that 'foreign natives', including those from the Protectorates, carry a separate type of reference book) this statement recalls that at the time of the introduction of the law in 1952 it challenged the bluff of the Nationalists that this law was really to 'abolish' passes. Its warning that the new Act was a more vicious application of the pass restrictions than ever before has been borne out by events in the last three years.

'In the period that the provisions of the new law have been

applied, countless people in many parts of the country have been ruthlessly persecuted and harried; men and women removed from their homes in urban areas; workers refused permission to enter urban areas from rural areas; and countless more subjected to arrest, enquiry and detention. Young men leaving school and anxious to enter jobs in industry are refused permission to do so and are endorsed out of the urban areas. In the towns they are forced to live the life of the hunted, continually trying to avoid the roving pick-up van.

'Living in the cities has become a nightmare for all Africans of pass-bearing age, as night and day police in plain clothes are stationed on street corners, near pass offices, outside stations; are constantly searching in locations and suburbs, and busy trapping passing Africans. A never-ending manhunt for pass offenders is being conducted in South Africa. Among the thousands detained every day for pass offences or investigation are many Africans in employment, who subsequently lose their jobs after being kept in prison cells pending investigation or trial on some petty pass infringement. No worker may accept employment unless he has the permission of the Labour Bureau and the working of the bureaux ensure that Africans have to accept work earmarked for them, even if they can independently find work at higher pay or work of a more skilled nature. A man once registered at the bureaux in some labouring category is pegged in that category for a lifetime. Officials at the pass offices are 'little Hitlers' and authorities unto themselves, with the power to make snap decisions which will determine the future of individuals and whole families. In only very rare cases is there any appeal from the decisions of the officials.

'The pass laws are now openly being used as a form of political persecution and intimidation.

'During the school boycott the Minister of Native Affairs threatened all school boys over the age of 16, who did not return to school by his appointed date, with compulsory registration as work-seekers and deportation to labour colonies if they did not find employment.

'Local authorities are also using the pass laws to persecute active ANC members. When it is found impossible to arrest them on any more serious charge, they are apprehended for non-payment of poll-tax, of a contravention of permit regulations or some minor offence.

'Only last week the Secretary for Native Affairs informed the Cape Town City Council that under the Urban Areas Act children were forbidden to enter and remain in urban areas beyond the 72 hour limit, and that African children from country areas should therefore not be admitted to schools in the towns.

'The courts are clogged with pass cases. "Crime figures" in the Union have shot up alarmingly, the monthly figures of convictions having trebled since 1936. But an examination of these figures shows that convictions for serious crime, theft, drunkenness and assault have not risen startlingly, and that the increase is in the number of convictions under the pass and permit laws.

'Investigations under section 10 and 14 of the Urban Areas Act, which might result in banishment from urban areas, impose the utmost hardship on Africans. The ANC demands the total abolition of the pass laws. It also calls on its branches to protest at the constant raids; to be vigilant for the people's rights; to fight every endorsement out of the urban areas; to support the Cape campaign against the expulsion of African women; to link all campaigning, and in particular preparations for the forthcoming Congress of the People with the pass laws; and to increasingly fight against these laws which are a cornerstone of apartheid oppression.'
(New Age, 12 May 1955)

Every African Against Apartheid
'The slogan of the conference might well be "Every African Against Apartheid". These are days of grave crisis for the African people. The Verwoerd bills of the last session of Parliament — the amendment to the Urban Areas Act and the Native Administration Act and the Prohibition of Interdicts Act — are new Acts of tyranny which climax painful years in which this Government has piled one injustice after

another upon our people.

'The anti-apartheid conference initiated by the Federation of Interdenominational Ministers is most timely and should be welcomed throughout the land. I fully support the idea of this conference.

'Many things still divide us but the threat to our existence and our rights must now bring us together. Petty differences among the African people and their organizations where they exist must be submerged in the interests of a firm unity in the face of attack by the Nationalists. Every African must clearly understand that apartheid means permanent inferiority and acceptance of any apartheid scheme, whether it goes by the name of 'separate development' or any other label means the abdication of our human rights.

'Conference must not be a mere talking shop. From its sessions must grow a new understanding and determination to fight for the basic civil liberties that are the birthright of all peoples — against the threats to the independence of the churches from state control and Government interference; against arbitrary deportations and exilings; against the slamming of the doors of the courts of law in our faces; against the never-ending uprooting and removals of our people and the pin-pricks and humiliations which are our daily experience under the system of apartheid.

'From this conference should emerge a united people attempting not to form themselves into a single body, but to forge ways and means for all the varied organizations and representative groups of our people to act together for the common interest, against attacks on us and for our rights.'
(New Age, 19 July 1956)

Not Aimed at Whites or Afrikaners

Mr Tambo: The economic boycott is not aimed at whites or Afrikaners as such. Anti-Nationalist Afrikaners and other Europeans are called on to join the boycott.

New Age: Is a further list of products to be boycotted likely to be released?

Mr Tambo: We have announced the first list. After full

investigation, additions will be made and released at suitable stages of the campaign.

New Age: Is this a national boycott?

Mr Tambo: Yes, it offers an opportunity to the millions of people in all parts of the country to participate by an act of self-denial in a nation-wide protest against the arrogance of the Nationalists and their utter contempt for the rights of individuals.

New Age: What must shopkeepers who presently sell these goods on the boycott list do?

Mr Tambo: The boycott commences on 10 June. This gives shopkeepers reasonable notice to dispose of and to make no further orders for the affected goods. There is certainly no intention to involve them in losses. On the other hand we do not believe that they will be acting in their interests if they attempt to oppose, ignore or in any way to undermine the campaign.

New Age: Is the boycott appeal directed only to members of the ANC?

Mr Tambo: The campaign is being conducted jointly by the ANC together with anti-Nationalist organizations of Europeans, Indians, coloured people and trade unions. An appeal is made to all members of the public, including those who do not support the full aims of the Congress Alliance, to observe the boycott as a token of protest against Government policy.

New Age: Is this boycott anti-white or anti-Afrikaner? At whom is the boycott aimed?

Mr Tambo: The boycott is not aimed at whites or Afrikaners as such. The Nationalist Party has gone out of its way to set up financial and business ventures as a part of its political plan. It is only such enterprises that will be affected by the boycott. The Congress boycott sub-committee includes European representatives and calls upon anti-Nationalist Afrikaners and other Europeans to join the boycott. The Congress movement is strongly opposed, on principle, to any form of racialism.

New Age: Critics of the campaign have suggested that there are many other ways of protest open to the people and that a boycott of some Nationalist goods is an ineffective method of protest. Any comment?

Mr Tambo: There are, of course, many other ways to protest, and our organizations have been and will continue to be most active in advocating and pursuing such methods. The boycott does not clash with other kinds of political activity. In the course of conducting the campaign our organizations will endeavour to persuade the people of the reasons for not buying the listed products. This is valuable educational and political work.

I do not think the economic boycott could be described as 'ineffective'. Although one does not expect the Government to fall overnight as a result, hitting Nationalists in the sensitive region of the pocket may bring them to their senses more effectively than many more conventional protests which they have ignored.

(New Age, 6 June 1957)

Evidence to Commission on the Dube Riots

Tribalism has failed throughout history and it is bound to fail here as well. To introduce tribalism in the urban areas is to act against the natural course of the forces of social change.

A memorandum submitted by the ANC stated that the causes of the Dube riots were ethnic grouping and the general policy of racialism; the sense of dissatisfaction, discontent and frustration under which Africans live as a result of numerous discriminatory and repressive laws operating against them; the miserable wages paid to African workers; the fact that Africans are constantly being hunted and hounded by the police in connection with petty offences, viz., pass laws and poll tax, a practice which does not allow the Africans to live the lives of normal human beings; and the migratory labour policy, which makes the African workers temporary sojourners in the urban areas with no permanent homes.

Asked to suggest what should be done, Mr Tambo said that the evils brought by the migratory labour system could be reduced to a minimum by the encouragement of a settled community in which the worker lived with his family in the area of his employment. The employment could be provided either by the employer or by the employee, if he was paid adequate wages.

Q — Would you say that the tribal fights that have been going on in the Transkei are due to the operation of discriminatory laws?

A — We are not saying that there can be no fights between tribal groups except as a result of oppressive laws. But what we say is that in this instance tribal fights between ethnic groups are likely to occur frequently because of the effects on the people of these laws.

Mr Tambo was closely questioned in connection with the Congress statement that the African people are mishandled by the police, insulted and beaten up and that they finally land in gaol for no fault of their own, or for the most trivial reasons. The partial attitude of the police is a major contributory cause to the tension and resultant violence now under enquiry.

Q — Why do you say the police are partial. It is one thing to attack the police for being incompetent but quite another to say that they are partial. Just what do you mean?

A — That is the feeling of the people.

Q — Yes, people who are misguided and misinformed can say that, but what do you yourself say? Do you agree with that statement?

A — I cannot disassociate myself from the statement.

Q — Can you tell us why?

A — The position is this. Firstly, the police should have expected that there would be trouble at Mofolo North, which is a Zulu area, and they should not have taken the procession through Mofolo North. They could have taken a different route. For instance, the route they took on their return from the cemetery. When the police reached Mofolo North there was no necessity for the police to shoot.

Q — But we have it on record that the Zulus adopted a threatening attitude.

A — That is precisely our point. The police fired at the people because they showed an attitude.

Q — When the police officer spoke to the leader of the Zulus asking him to disperse his people, the leader of the Zulus raised the weapon he was carrying and was about to strike when the police officer fired at him.

A — If that evidence is correct, there was no necessity for the other police to shoot.

Q — The evidence is that the Zulus threw stones at the police.

A — Yes, that is the mystery. According to the evidence not a single policeman, not a single Mosotho was struck by a stone, and our point is that in these circumstances the shooting by the police was absolutely uncalled for if they were being impartial peace-makers.

Q — How does your organization arrive at the conclusion that the discriminatory laws have resulted in a clash between the Zulus and the Basutos.

A — Take for instance the pass laws have been a subject of protest by Africans ever since they were introduced. And far from being abolished, they have been intensified and made applicable even to women. Hundreds of thousands of Africans have been arrested under the pass laws and their protests have yielded no results whatsoever. They have been placed in a position where they feel they have no redress for their grievances. The only redress is that they get arrested. Therefore their life now is not a life in which grievances are redressed by discussion and negotiation.

(New Age, 27 February 1958)

Verwoerd Cannot Kill the Spirit of the People

'The position of the masses in South Africa is akin to slavery. There is no such thing as a home for our people. Jobs are being reserved for whites and Africans are being forced on to farms as cheap labour.

TREASON TRIAL

The ACCUSED

DECEMBER 1956

'The Accused' at the Treason Trial in 1956. Oliver Tambo is on the extreme left, 6th row from bottom; Nelson Mandela towers above his comrades in the centre of the 3rd row from the bottom; Lilian Ngoyi is seated, 4th from left, 5th row from the bottom; Chief Luthuli is 4th from the right in the 4th row from top.

'But every discriminatory law passed, every hardship imposed on the people has not been able to kill their spirit to continue with the just struggle to make South Africa a democracy where every section of the population will enjoy freedom.

'Speaking about the future of South Africa to the Provincial Conference of the Natal ANC, Mr Tambo said that Verwoerd would deal with the country and its people as he had done with Zeerust. The murders, the killings, the mass arrests of people and the banishing of chiefs and leaders . . . those were the consequences of Verwoerd's policies. His record in dealing with the people of Zeerust and Sekhukhuneland had earned him the leadership of the Nationalist Party and the Premiership. The Nats say 'South Africa must be made safe for the Whites'. Their position as masters over the Non-Europeans must be secured at all costs. To achieve this end we have the Bantu Education Act, passes for women, Bantu Authorities, the Group Areas Act and a host of other oppressive laws.

'Our people's opposition to oppression, discrimination and slavery had given rise to mass arrests and mass trials such as the Treason Trial. Thousands of people were being sent to gaol for their opposition to tyranny . . . These are good people made into criminals by Government policy. Mr Tambo condemned the informers and spies who were trying to destroy the people's movement. These people were trying to sow discord at a time when the people's leaders were facing a capital charge of treason.

'The Government's policy affects us all and we should therefore face the enemy together. A united struggle is our best answer to apartheid, which threatens to destroy South Africa. We have the task of bringing peace and happiness to all the people of this land.'

(*New Age, 10 October 1958*)

ANC Stands by the Alliance With Congress of Democrats

'It would be surprising and unnatural if the policy of the ANC provoked no criticism from any source whatsoever. Indeed, recognizing that the ANC is anything but infallible, its leaders have not infrequently gone out of their way to invite criticism and comment on matters appertaining to the struggle and have as often urged free and frank discussion at all levels of the organizational structure.

'Mistaking this attitude on the part of the ANC leadership for an invitation to them to indulge in puerile pranks, the editor, reporters and 'Africanist' correspondents of the *World* have been pouring out cheap abuse about the ANC being controlled by the Congress of Democrats.

'Others, employing the columns of *Contact,* the Liberal Party organ, and *Indian Opinion* have joined the chorus, though they failed to stop at the level of the *World.*

'In isolated cases public speakers have attacked the alliance of the ANC with the Congress of Democrats not on the ground of control of the one by the other, but because COD is "an extreme leftist organ" and "does not honour Western civilization or Christian values".

1949 PROGRAMME

'The adoption by the ANC of the 1949 Programme of Action was in large measure an answer to the vicious pace at which the Nationalist Government was attacking the democratic rights, particularly of the African people. The 1948 general election ushered in a new political era in which the ANC, if it was to fulfil is historic task, was called upon to go into action on a militant programme.

'It says much to the credit of the ANC that it has honoured the 1949 decision to embark upon mass action, and in the political conflict that mark the period from early 1950, its leaders have been banned, banished, deported, arrested and persecuted, it has been declared illegal in certain areas and in others the right of assembly has been severely curtailed. In spite of all this the ANC has not abandoned the fight, nor have its leaders retreated to take shelter behind ideological platitudes.

'The Nationalist attack was not concentrated on the African

people. The Suppression of Communism Act affected every democrat and served as a barrage to keep off the forces of democracy whilst anti-democratic legislation was being passed and enforced.

'The Defiance Campaign uncovered and produced a large body of people of all races, in all parts of the world, who were sympathetic to the cause of the Non-European people and of democracy. There was at the time a plan for co-operation between the main Non-European political organizations only. Following the lessons of the Defiance Campaign, the need was felt for an organization through which the ANC and other Non-European bodies could make contact with those whites who were prepared to join the non-European in their fight for freedom and democracy.

'In the absence of an organized body of European opinion openly and publicly proclaiming its opposition to the Government's racialist policies and supporting the Non-European cause, the political conflict was developing a dangerously black versus white complexion. Such a situation no doubt suited the present Government, but it did not suit the ANC nor the movement for liberation, and had to be avoided.

'It was to a packed meeting of Europeans in 1952 that leaders of the ANC and the SAIC appealed for an organization that would take its stand alongside the three main Non-European organizations in their resistance to Nationalist tyranny, which was preparing to arm itself during the 1953 session of Parliament with the Criminal Law Amendment Act and the Public Safety Act, in addition to the Suppression of Communism Act. In response to the appeal, those Europeans who saw the approaching danger to South Africa and to democracy, admitted the justice of our cause and had the courage to identify themselves with that cause, came forward to found the South African Congress of Democrats (SACOD). Whether they were Communists or anti-Communists was immaterial. In any event, in terms of the Suppression of Communism Act everybody was a "Communist" who disliked the Nationalist Government's policies and said so.

'Whether the men and women who came together as the COD did, or did not, honour Western civilization or Christian values would have been difficult to say, assuming the question was relevant. The Nationalist Government has already claimed that it is protecting Western civilization and is acting in the name of Christianity. The present leader of the Nationalist Party, Dr Verwoerd, claims that God chose him as Prime Minister and God is supposed to have done this in spite of the sordid tale of misery and disaster which forms part of the record of Dr Verwoerd's administration and the Department of Native Affairs.

One might well ask, what would have been the fate of "Western" civilization if England had withdrawn from the last war when Russia joined the Allies against Germany? Or if America had stayed out of the war because Communist Russia was in it?

WHO CONTROLS WHOM?

'Let us examine the other objection to the alliance of the Congresses, namely that the Congress of Democrats controls the ANC. Can it be said that there is anything which, but for its association or alliance with the COD, the ANC would have done or refrained from doing? It surely cannot be suggested that the ANC would not have conducted a militant struggle against oppression. The main feature of the 1949 annual conference of the ANC was its adoption of a Programme of Action, not a programme of inaction, and in taking this decision, the ANC was not influenced or directed by any other organization, although, as indicated earlier, it was largely influenced by the politics of the Nationalist Party Government. And what the ANC has done since 1949, both before and after the formation of COD, has been to carry out its decisions to embark on militant action.

'It is true that other aspects of the 1949 Programme have not been carried out. These are certainly less hazardous than 'mass action' and are no doubt more attractive to those who cannot but have regard to considerations of risk and safety. In fact, it is significant that a large percentage of the brave and courageous men who are busy carrying out a programmed of action against COD have had little contact with the campaigns conducted by the ANC since 1949, their source of information about such campaigns being what they read in newspapers and books. Once cannot help feeling that had they accorded the 1949 Programme a status in any degree higher than a suitable topic for discussion at academic meetings of political clubs or literary and debating societies, they would know that in the field of political strife the COD has stood, not with the Nationalists, but with the ANC as a friend and ally, and not a dictator and controller, and that it hardly merits being placed in the position of an enemy of the oppressed people.

'It is safe to give the assurance that the present leaders of the ANC will leave it to the Nationalist Government and those who sympathize with it, either to attack and victimize any of the Congresses or take steps in form of propaganda or otherwise, to weaken and undermine the liberatory front.

INFERIORITY COMPLEX

'If, as has been alleged *ad nauseam,* the COD has been dominating or controlling the ANC by virtue of the mere fact that it is a "white" organization, then the COD cannot be blamed for their being "superior". In that event the "inferior" ANC, to save itself from this inevitable control or domination, must either run away from the COD and, necessarily, from the anti-apartheid struggle in which COD is involved, or alternatively, the ANC must join hands with the Nationalist Party and fight the COD. The ANC will do neither.

'Those Africans who believe, or have been influenced by the belief, that they are inferior or cannot hold their own against other groups, are advised to keep out of any alliance with such groups and, prevention being better than cure, to refrain from joining the people in their active struggle for basic human rights, for in such a struggle many races are to be found.

'The ANC is not led by "inferiors". It does not suffer from any nightmares about being controlled or dominated by any organization; it is not subject to any such control or domination, and will not run away from the political struggle, or from any group or organization. On the contrary it will continue to lead the movement for liberation against injustice and tyranny to freedom and democracy.'

*(**New Age,** 13 November 1958)*

2

EXTERNAL MISSION

Introduction

When Tambo went into exile in 1960, the process of decolonization had only recently begun in Africa. Newly independent African states condemned apartheid and began an international drive towards isolating South Africa diplomatically and economically. Resentment against white colonialism was fuelled when on 5 October 1960 white South Africans voted, by the narrowest of margins, to become a Republic, duly declared on 31 May 1961. In March of that year South Africa was forced out of the Commonwealth. The white minority regime withdrew into a *laager,* protected to the north by a cordon of states in which white supremacy held sway. Its other neighbours, Lesotho, Botswana and Swaziland, were nominally independent but actually dominated by South Africa because of migrant labour and economic dependence.

Reacting to the banning of the ANC, the wholesale arrests of leaders and activists, and the clamp-down on all public protest, the ANC resolved that the non-violent path could not be sustained. It created a military wing to prepare for a new mode of struggle initially based on sabotage. On 16 December 1961 Umkhonto we Sizwe, with Mandela as Commander-in-Chief, announced its existence with a manifesto and attacks on Government buildings in Johannesburg, Port Elizabeth and Durban. Umkhonto disavowed all types of terrorism and stated that its targets were installations not persons. There followed a year and a half of underground organization and actions, until in July 1963 most of the top Umkhonto leaders were arrested at Rivonia, near Johannesburg, and sentenced to life imprisonment.

With the gathering storm of state oppression inside South Africa, it was Tambo's initial task was to establish a foreign mission. He devoted himself to fundraising and diplomatic

Oliver Tambo with Julius Nyerere, shortly after Tambo went into exile in 1960. *(IDAF)*

representations in world forums. In June 1960 Tambo was instrumental in establishing a South African United Front with the SAIC, the PAC and SWANU. It lasted until early 1962 when it broke up as a result of PAC hostility to co-operation with the ANC.

By this time the sabotage campaign had begun inside South Africa, while the external mission arranged training facilities and funds for Umkhonto recruits. After the Pan-African Freedom Movement for East, Central and Southern Africa meeting in Addis Ababa in February 1962 — to which Mandela made a surprise visit — funds were promised by a number of countries and training facilities made available in Algeria. Over the following two decades substantial military assistance came from the socialist countries of Europe, from Cuba and from several African countries. Close links were also established with the Conferencia das Organizaçoes Naçionalistas das Colonias Portuguesas, an alliance of Frelimo, MPLA and the Guinean PAIGC.

Over the same period representations were made to the United Nations on the evils of apartheid. Tambo appeared as a petitioner before the Special Political Committee and in 1963 tangible diplomatic success was achieved when the United Nations Security Council appointed a group to examine the crisis in South Africa. In June 1964 the Security Council passed a resolution condemning the conduct of the Rivonia Trial two days before sentence was handed down. Soon after, a Special Committee Against Apartheid was set up and from early 1967 was serviced by its own Unit on Apartheid within the Section for African Questions in the Security Council. However, the South African Government retained formal representation at the United Nations

Between 1963 and 1965 thousands of suspected ANC members were arrested in the Eastern Cape, Transvaal and Natal, severely damaging the internal movement. In early 1963 Tambo was joined in the external mission by Moses Kotane, Treasurer-General of the ANC and general secretary of the South African Communist Party (SACP), Duma Nokwe, the ANC Secretary-General, and J.B.Marks, a veteran of the ANC and trade union movement. From this point on the most important Congress Alliance leaders were either in gaol or in exile and the internal movement severely battered.

In 1963 the Organization of African Unity was established and the Pan-African Freedom Movement was incorporated as the African Liberation Committee, presided over by the Tanzanian Foreign Minister, Oscar Kambona. Tanzania now became the most important supporter of the ANC and Dar es Salaam the centre of its external organization. Over the next few years four guerrilla training camps were set up and at one of them, Morogoro, the ANC headquarters were based. It was from these bases that Umkhonto recruits were later moved to Zambia. Early in 1967 they undertook their first joint military campaign into Rhodesia and continued to infiltrate thereafter. In the same year Chief Luthuli died and Tambo became Acting President-General.

2.1 THE RIVONIA TRIAL
(Address to the Special Political Committee of the United Nations General Assembly on 8 October 1963, the day the 'Rivonia Trial' began)

I wish to express my deep gratitude for the privilege accorded to me in addressing this important body . . . This is consistent with the declared desire of the nations and peoples of the world to see the end of apartheid and white domination, and the emergence of a South Africa loyal to the United Nations and to the high principles set forth in the Charter — a South Africa governed by its people as fellow citizens of equal worth whatever the colour, race or creed of any one of them. This kind of South Africa is the precise goal of our political struggle.

In thanking you and your Committee, therefore, Mr Chairman, I wish to emphasize that I do so not only on my own behalf, but also on behalf of my organization, the African National Congress, and its sister organizations in

South Africa, on behalf of the African people and all the other victims of racial discrimination, together with that courageous handful of white South Africans who have fully identified themselves with the struggle for the liberation of the oppressed people of South Africa.

I should also like to take this opportunity to place on record the deep appreciation of my people for the steps which have been taken by various governments against South Africa. On the other hand, I cannot exaggerate the sense of grievance — to put it mildly — which we feel towards those countries which have done, and are even now doing, so much to make apartheid the monstrous and ghastly reality which it is, and which have thereby created in our country the conditions which, if nothing else happens, will ensure an unparalleled bloodbath. Assured of the support of these countries the South African rulers, who boast openly of this support, are not only showing open defiance of the United Nations and treating its resolutions with calculated contempt, but they are liquidating the opponents of their policies, confident that the big powers will not act against them.

This brings me to the special matter which, with your permission, Mr Chairman, I beg leave to submit to the distinguished members of this Committee for their urgent consideration, and which arises out of news of the latest developments in the South African situation.

By a significant coincidence, the first day of this Committee's discussion of the policy of apartheid happens also to be the first day of a trial in South Africa, which constitutes yet another challenge to the authority of the United Nations and which has as its primary aim the punishment by death of people who are among South Africa's most outstanding opponents of the very policies which the General Assembly and the Security Council have in numerous resolutions called upon the South African Government to abandon.

Today some 30 persons are appearing before a Supreme Court judge in South Africa in a trial which will be conducted in circumstances that have no parallel in South African history, and which, if the Government has its way, will seal the doom of that country and entrench the feelings of bitterness which years of sustained persecution have already engendered among the African people. The persons standing trial include Nelson Mandela and Walter Sisulu, who are household names throughout South Africa, Nelson Mandela being known personally to a number of African Heads of State; Govan Mbeki, a top-ranking African political leader and an accomplished economist, who has borne the burdens of his oppressed fellow men ever since he left university; Ahmed Kathrada, a South African of Indian extraction, who started politics as a passive resister in 1946 at the age of 17, since when he has been consistently a leading participant in the struggle of the Indian and other Asian South Africans against the Group Areas Act and other forms of racial discrimination, and has, with other Indian leaders, joined the Africans in the liberation struggle; Dennis Goldberg, a white South African, whose home in Western Cape was the scene of a bomb explosion in 1962, when Government supporters sought to demonstrate their disapproval of his identifying himself with the African cause; Ruth Slovo (*née* Ruth First), a white South African and mother of three children, author of a recently published book on South West Africa, and one of South Africa's leading journalists. I could enumerate several others, and as I have shown, they consist of outstanding African Nationalist leaders, as well as others who have for long been associated with every conceivable form of protest against injustices perpetrated in the name of Christian civilization and white supremacy. Trials against well over 100 others are due to start at other centres in different parts of the country.

The charge against the accused is said to be 'sabotage'. This means, in fact, that they have contravened a law, or a group of laws, which have been enacted for the express purpose of forcibly suppressing the aspirations of the victims of apartheid laws, which no active opponent of the policies of South African Government can evade. A study of the statutory definition of 'sabotage' — which distinguished delegates will find in official documents circulated to you — will show that a person accused of sabotage can be sentenced to death for one of the least effective and most peaceful forms of protest against apartheid.

The relations between the Government and those it rules by force in South Africa have never been worse. The law of the country has, since the 1956 Treason Trial, been altered so as to make it practically impossible for an accused person to escape conviction. Lawyers who accept briefs in political trials have been subjected to increasing intimidation and it has now become difficult to find counsel to appear in such trials. This has been particularly true in the case of the accused who are now facing trial. The law of procedure has also been altered so that the State allows itself any amount of time to prepare its case against accused persons, while the defendants, held in solitary confinement, are kept ignorant of the charge against them until they appear in court. The time allowed them to prepare their defence is subject to the discretion of the court, and in the majority of cases the State insists on proceeding with the trial with as little delay as possible. Preparing a defence from a prison cell hardly enables an accused person to make any proper preparation.

An atmosphere of crisis has been whipped up and its effects have been reflected in the severity of sentences passed by the judges, and, not infrequently, in the statements they make in the course of pronouncing sentence. Of special significance in this regard is the judgement passed last week by a Pretoria judge on seven Africans, whom he found guilty of allegedly receiving training in the use of firearms in a country outside South Africa. In sentencing each of the accused to 20 years imprisonment, the judge stated that he had seriously considered passing the death sentence, but had decided not to do so because he felt that the accused had been misled. This judgement and these remarks are a sufficient — and deliberate — hint as to what sentences the South African public and the world are to expect in the new trials, where leaders of the political struggle against the apartheid policies of the South African Government are the accused. It is known that the State will demand the death sentence.

Already more than 5,000 political prisoners are languishing

in South Africa's gaols. Even as recently as the month of September of this year, and after the Security Council in its resolution of 7 August had called for the release of 'all persons imprisoned, interned, or subjected to other restrictions for having opposed the policy of apartheid', three detainees have died in gaol in circumstances strongly suggesting deliberate killing. All these are the direct victims of a situation which would never have arisen had the South African Goverhment taken heed of the many appeals which have been addressed to it by the world public and expressed in resolution of the General Assembly and the Security Council.

I cannot believe that the United Nations can stand by, calmly watching what I submit is genocide masquerading under the guise of a civilized dispensation of justice. The African and other South Africans who are being dragged to the slaughterhouse face death, or life imprisonment, because they fearlessly resisted South Africa's violations of the United Nations Charter and Universal Declaration of Human Rights, because they fought against a government armed to the teeth and relying on armed force, to end inhumanity, to secure the liberation of the African people, to end racial discrimination, and to replace racial intolerance and tyranny with democracy and equality, irrespective of colour, race or creed.

Every single day spent in gaol by any of our people, every drop of blood drawn from any of them, and every life taken — each of these represents a unit of human worth lost to us. This loss we can no longer afford. It is surely not in the interests of South Africa or even of the South African Government that this loss should be increased any further.

2.2 ACCOMPLICES OF APARTHEID
(Address to the Special Committee Against Apartheid, 12 March 1964)

. . . In response to the appeals we made in the name of our people, when our delegation appeared before your Committee last year, we are grateful, Mr Chairman, to note that both the Security Council and the General Assembly have adopted resolutions imposing an embargo on the supply of arms to South Africa and calling for the release of all persons detained or otherwise restricted because of their opposition to the policies of apartheid. It is common knowledge, however, that the South African Government has completely, and openly, ignored these resolutions. The behaviour of this member state of the United Nations in persistently flouting well-considered decisions of this world body calls for immediate investigation.

In conformity with its disregard of world opinion, the South African Government has continued to press on with the enforcement of its apartheid policies, which are invariably aimed at the black people of South Africa — I would include all who are not considered white — and pursued for the sole benefit of the white population. Giving added encouragement and strength to this sustained persecution of our people, foreign investment has continued to pour into South Africa in an unbroken stream.

Last year, we proposed that those countries which have involved themselves economically on the side of our oppressors 'be called upon to withdraw forthwith from the arena of conflict in our country and that they should be specifically indicted in the forums of this Organization'. We went on:

As a first step in the process of censuring those bodies and organizations which deliberately flout the decisions of this Organization by giving support and aid the the white racists in South Africa, we propose that a blacklist of companies such as De Beers Limited, African Explosives and Chemical Industries and others which collaborate with the South African Government in the manufacture of ammunition in the country should be compiled. Members of this Organization should be called upon to sever relations with these companies.

We are pleased to note that at its recent meeting in Lagos, the Council of Ministers of the Organization of African Unity has decided to establish a Committee charged with the task of compiling a comprehensive report on the nature and extent of trade conducted by certain countries and companies with South Africa, on the one hand, and with member states of the Organization of African Unity, on the other hand. This report, we learn, will be submitted to the Conference of African Heads of State for decision and necessary action. It is our hope that such a report will be made available to member states of the United Nations sympathetic to the cause of the African people in South Africa and wishing to join the African states in taking measures against the South African Government and all its active supporters.

White immigrants, mainly from Great Britain, have recently been entering South Africa in large batches, no doubt to share in the all-white looting of African labour, to render numerical support to the South African Government and to give political expression to the solidarity which the home countries of these immigrants have with white domination in South Africa. Member states of the United Nations, who have joined in the condemnation of racial discrimination in South Africa and who have either connived at or encouraged emigration to South Africa, are helping to extend the area of racialism and racial conflict in the world to their own countries. We would urge this Committee to take steps to bring this practice to the notice of the United Nations.

Repeated reports indicate that South Africa is enjoying an economic boom. This is no doubt encouraged by a sense of security induced by the belief that with arms supplied by its friends, the South African Government is able to ensure stability in South Africa. In explanation of this stability, gleeful fingers are pointed at the leaders of the liberation movement and other opponents of apartheid, who are either languishing in gaol, subject to various restrictions, being tortured or facing trial on charges carrying penalties which range from long terms of imprisonment to death by hanging.

While we do not feel the need to argue with those who regard this form of stability as real, we consider it pertinent to ask who, as between the white supremacist in South Africa and the profit-seeking foreign investor, is the happier to see the Africans and other opponents of racial discrimination hounded, harassed and herded into gaols, tortured, sentenced and hanged? Who is the greater racialist as between those who formulate and enforce theories and policies of racial superiority and those who furnish the capital, technical knowledge and manpower for the execution and maintenance of those policies?

In the past we have stated, and we repeat now, that the oppressed people in South Africa must and will settle accounts with their oppressors by any methods and means open to them, the determining consideration being whether they want to achieve their freedom at all costs or to live in bondage forever. But insofar as the South African situation is the immediate concern of the United Nations, then those outside South Africa who are accomplices in the perpetration of an acknowledged vice must account for their conduct to world opinion.

We would strongly recommend that this Committee in its search for modes of action against apartheid should give a substantial share of its time and energies to a consideration of the means by which such accomplices can be made to reconcile their public protestations with their deeds. For it would be dangerous, even if it were possible, to continue pretending that the joint condemnation of apartheid by its opponents and ardent supporters is sufficient to dislodge a system, which draws strength from a combination of economic power, military strength and an unbridled zeal for the use of brute force.

It is important to be clear as to what makes apartheid possible and what guarantees its continuance.Reputed leaders of our people — men of unquestionable integrity and uncompromising enemies of any evil system practised by man on man — are today standing in danger of losing their lives, precisely because they are the men they are. It is true that for many years the whole world has warned the South African Government of the unavoidable consequences of its conduct of affairs in South Africa. But it is equally true that for many more years the South African Government has received all the financial and material encouragement it needed for continuing and persisting in its policies and practices. We cannot over-emphasize the urgency of identifying all those forces and influences which should be held answerable for any past, present or future loss of life in South Africa.

Mr Chairman, following a long list of political trials in various parts of South Africa, 19 political leaders, including a girl of 17 years, have recently been sentenced in Pietermaritzburg, Natal, to terms of imprisonment of from 5 to 20 years. Twenty-five other leaders are on trial in Ladysmith, Natal, and in Cape Town the case against 11 leaders and trade unionists — among them there are four women — has been proceeding now for five months, the charge against the accused being incitement to acts of sabotage.

There are many other similar trials, but mention must be made once again of the Pretoria case against Nelson Mandela and others, which is now approaching its closing stages, the State having given all its evidence against the leaders. This case will be resumed on 7 April, when evidence on behalf of the leaders will be tendered. This is the case which was the subject of a resolution adopted by the General Assembly in October last year. The fact that this trial continued uninterrupted, despite that resolution, presents the United Nations with one of its crucial tests. It is a case which is capable of giving rise to serious complications in South Africa and beyond its border, and one which should be kept under the closest observation by the Committee.

We would urge the Committee in its reports to underline the importance of individual member states of the United Nations taking active steps to prevent the South African Government from embarking on acts and carrying on a policy so inescapably subversive of peace. It is our feeling that not enough is being done at the international level to challenge the right of the South African Government to hold as criminals, to persecute and even kill men, women and young people, whose basic and sole offence is their opposition to inhuman practices.

If there was any doubt in the mind of anyone that what the

South African Government is asking for is trouble, the Bantu Laws Amendment Bill, now before the all-white South African Parliament, should remove that doubt. In one of its key clauses the Bill establishes a network of what are euphemistically termed 'Aid Centres'. These are in fact slave labour detention camps, which are intended to entrap all Africans out of the Bantustan area. It will be recalled that the Bantustan scheme seeks to confine some four million Africans in poverty-stricken, cheap labour reservoirs, presently known as reserves. Africans forced by hunger and starvation out of these reserves or Bantustans will be caught in this network. Those at present living outside the reserves will similarly be regimented into the scheme. The Africans ensnared in these 'Aid Centres' will be distributed as black labour to white masters and farmers throughout the country. The end result will be a homeless, migrant, slave population of 11 million Africans. Even the practice of catching Africans in the streets and selling them to white farmers, which was stamped out by the courts a few years ago, is now being re-introduced and legalized in the Bill.

Thus, straight from listening to years of condemnation of the ruthless system by which whites maintain themselves in power over Africans, and after hearing warnings that such a system endangers peace and security as much in South Africa as everywhere else in the world, this arrogant collection of power-drunk, race maniacs have now produced an apartheid measure which deals with the African on the basis that he is purely and simply a thing — a chattel in the control and service of the white man. He is a labour unit, not a living human being with personal and civil rights; not a man entitled to freedom and the right to plan and run his own life, and determine his own destiny. To these men who boast of the strongest bonds of friendship between them and the British and Americans, the African is at best a slave in all but name. They own and possess him, and have now evolved a scheme for selling him.

No one can doubt any longer now that life for the African in South Africa is not life. If it is, it is worth nothing. But we promise in that event that no other life in South Africa is worth anything — white or non-white. Let the United Nations and the world, therefore, save what it can — what it cannot, will either be destroyed or destroy itself.

2.3 THE BEGINNING OF THE ARMED STRUGGLE
*(Mr Tambo speaks to **Sechaba**, April 1968)*

Sechaba: Mr Tambo, you have just completed a tour of some African countries. What was the aim of this tour and what are its results?

Mr Tambo: Our delegation has been to Algeria and Tunisia. Other ANC delegations have visited other states. The need for the delegations to undertake these mission arises directly from the unfolding crisis in southern Africa. After all, we are not fighting an individual cause. Africa has committed herself to the total liberation of the continent before any individual independent state can consider itself truly independent. At the moment the greatest problem facing Africa in terms of liberation is in southern Africa. And within southern Africa itself, the hardest core of reaction is the South African regime. It has always been clear to us that an armed struggle against South Africa poses immediate dangers and threats to the entire continent of Africa, if it supports that struggle. We have always warned that South Africa's annual military budget, which now stands at £128 million, is intended not only for the ruthless suppression of the liberation movement in South Africa, but also for the support of reaction in the rest of southern Africa and for the invasion of the African continent itself. We think it dangerous to minimize the threat to the independence of the African states, and as it is part of our plan to intensify the revolution, we feel it incumbent on us as leaders to discuss the implications of the revolution with African leaders . . .

Sechaba: You were Nelson Mandela's legal partner in Johannesburg. Is there hope for the victims of the Rivonia Trial?

Mr Tambo: It is true that I was a legal partner of Nelson Mandela, but I was, even more importantly, his partner in the struggle for liberation. His imprisonment and that of other leaders and members has, of course, deprived the struggle of the important contribution of a powerful body of leaders. Nevertheless, all reports we get from our colleagues on Robben Island, in Pretoria Gaol and other South African prisons, are consistent in affirming the high morale of these leaders and their great expectation for the success of the struggle which has resulted in their incarceration . . .

Sechaba: At what stage is the ANC? What are its real perspectives and prospects?

Mr Tambo: For a long time the ANC conducted a militant struggle by non-violent methods. This became particularly intense during the 1950s and gradually led to a stage at which the movement switched over from non-violence to the phase of armed struggle. During 1967 the first armed clashes occurred between, on the one hand, the combined forces of the Smith and Vorster regimes and, on the other hand, the united guerrillas of the ANC and ZAPU. It can be said that for the ANC this is the beginning of the armed struggle for which we have been preparing since the early 1960s.

It is a phase in which we can rightly claim to have scored victories by virtue of the superiority which our fighters demonstrated over the racist forces, sending a wave of panic throughout the area dominated by the racist regimes and arousing the masses to a new revolutionary mood. This is, however, only a small beginning in terms of the bitterness and magnitude of the revolution which is unfolding and which embraces the whole of southern Africa. But it is an impressive and effective beginning, providing what I consider a guarantee for the success of the armed struggle.

Although the armed conflicts to which I have referred took place in Rhodesia, they involved South Africa because South African troops, personnel and finance are already involved in maintaining and sustaining the Smith regime.

And the problems of the oppressed peoples of Zimbabwe and South Africa are becoming progressively identical. An armed struggle in Rhodesia is an armed struggle against part of the racist combine which is the Rhodesia-South Africa axis. This explains why the South African regime was rocked by the striking power of the guerrillas in Rhodesia, as violently as if these battles had taken place within the borders of South Africa. And this explains why we regard the clash between the people's guerrillas and the racists as the beginning of the armed struggle for which the masses of our people have been preparing.

Sechaba: Which countries support your movement?

Mr Tambo: As a liberation movement, we endeavour to secure the support of all countries, organizations and peoples throughout the world. We have been successful, I think, in focusing international attention on the evils of the South African racist regime; and there are many countries, governments and organizations which support not only the struggle of our people against racism and oppression generally, but support the ANC as the movement leading the liberation struggle in South Africa. The degree of support of course varies from country to country. In the African continent all the members of the OAU support the ANC, although some are supporters in addition of smaller parties in South Africa. We have the support of all the socialist countries with a few exceptions. Practically the whole of anti-imperialist Asia supports the ANC. And in Europe, America and Canada we enjoy the support of all important organizations. We are supported by leading movements in Latin America and the revolutionary Government of Cuba.

Sechaba: What is your programme of action?

Mr Tambo: Our programme of struggle is geared to what is known as the Freedom Charter, which is a statement of the objectives of our political struggle. It sets out the kind of South Africa we shall establish upon taking over power. In terms of that programme, we fight for a South Africa in which there will be no racial discrimination, no inequalities based on colour, creed or race — a non-racial democracy which recognizes the essential equality between man and man. We shall abolish all the machinery whereby a few live and thrive on the exploitation of the many. The wealth of our country, which is abundant, will accrue to the equal benefit of all the people of South Africa. The power of government will rest in the hands of the majority of the people, regardless of considerations of race. But our first and immediate task is to win over the power to rule our country as it should be ruled, that is, to replace the regime which consists of a white minority with a people's government enjoying a mandate from all the people. It is the people who will decide on the methods and the techniques for putting into effect the principles set out in the Freedom Charter.

Sechaba: What are the liberation movements that support the ANC? Is there co-ordination between the ANC and these movements, especially regarding the armed struggle?

Mr Tambo: It has been a cardinal feature of the policy of the ANC from its very inception, to work for the unity of the people engaged in the common struggle for attainment of common objectives. In pursuance of this policy, within South Africa the ANC has rallied within the liberation movement all organizations and parties opposed to the South African racist regime and prepared to struggle for its total overthrow. Thus it is that the ANC embraces within itself a number of progressive and militant organizations, who accept its leadership and programme of action. Outside South Africa it has sought to pursue the same policy of unity and co-ordination of activities among liberation movements and has established very close working relationships with the fighting movements of southern Africa, and with the majority parties in other parts of Africa . . .

Sechaba: Is there no gap between the leaders outside the country and the people inside?

Mr Tambo: The fact some leaders of the liberation movement are outside their respective countries means that in varying degrees there is a break between them and the leaders involved in the struggle within these countries. It is a gap forced upon the liberation movement by adverse circumstances and constitutes one of the problems which the liberation movement must solve. But it does not represent a total break. There is communication between leaders outside and those within the country and it is one of the tasks of the liberation movement as a whole to strengthen and consolidate these communications. At a certain stage of every liberation struggle, the need arises for the movement conducting the revolution to be in firm contact with the forces outside its country. This involves placing some of the leaders outside the country and the effectiveness of the arrangement always depends on the strength and durability of the lines of communication between the leaders inside and outside the country. It is to be expected that these lines of communication constitute one of the main targets of attack by the enemy.

Sechaba: In what form do the United Nations decisions help you, especially those concerning economic sanctions?

Mr Tambo: It was at the instance of the ANC that sanctions against the South African regime came to be considered at the United Nations. Thanks to the vigilance and consistent support of the African states as well as Asian and socialist countries, the United Nations has taken a correct position in adopting resolutions supporting sanctions against South Africa. To the extent that these sanctions have so far not been applied with any appreciable effect on South Africa, the resolutions have not helped us. But they have failed to take effect precisely because South Africa's major trading partners have persisted in their policy of economic support for apartheid, despite these resolutions, and have as a result sabotaged their effective execution.

There are many countries, however, in Africa and elsewhere, who have honoured these resolutions, and in doing so have helped us not only to weaken the South African regime, but also to maintain the type of international pressure which is of considerable assistance to our cause. The decision to apply sanctions against South Africa was vigorously opposed by Britain and is still being opposed. But its correctness as a method of international attack on an evil regime was demonstrated by Britain herself, when at her own instance the United Nations invoked sanctions against Smith. But these sanctions also failed precisely because to succeed they would have had to be applied against South Africa as well. This would be to the detriment of apartheid, in the enforcement of which Britain and other powers would play a vital role . . .

Sechaba: How do you conceive the struggle against the arms race of the South African racist regime and the supply of weapons by the big powers?

Mr Tambo: As a liberation movement we are part of an international movement against racism, colonialism and imperialism. We enjoy the support of peoples the world over, including the USA, Britain, West Germany, France and Japan, the main suppliers of the South African regime. The struggle is one struggle waged by all right-thinking and freedom-loving peoples of the world against the South African regime, as being part of and an instrument of the forces that are hostile to the interests of mankind. Our share of this common battle is to fight and destroy the enemy within South Africa with the assistance and support of all our friends; but our international friends have also their own special share of this burden, that is, to get their governments to disengage from South Africa. What is even more important, they should not permit their governments to send arms, which are expressly intended for the liquidation of the people. They must not give their labour to the manufacture of weapons, helicopters, armoured cars and submarines for export to South Africa. To participate in these ventures against the workers whose cause we fight is to commit an act of betrayal against us. At this time in particular, we expect anti-racists, anti-colonialists and anti-imperialists everywhere to play parts in the armed struggle.

2.4 THE LIBERATION MOVEMENTS OF SOUTHERN AFRICA

(Joint statement of the Liberation Movements to the Fifth Assembly of Heads of State of the Organization of African Unity, held in Algiers from 13—16 September 1968, read by Oliver Tambo)

Mr President, Your Imperial Majesty, Your Royal Majesty, Your Excellencies and distinguished guests, allow me on behalf of the liberation movements, the revolutionary fighters and oppressed peoples of our countries to express our profound thanks to the Organization of African Unity for the opportunity afforded us to address this august assembly at this critical moment in the history of our continent . . . The liberation movements and over 30 million oppressed Africans they represent are at war. On the one side are the armies of white supremacy united in the unholy alliance of Portugal, Rhodesia and South Africa. On the other are the liberation movements with their guerrilla forces, bravely challenging the military machine of white supremacy, which has the direct and indirect support of imperialist powers such as Britain, the United States, France, West Germany, Japan and Belgium.

The struggle for freedom in Mozambique, Angola, Namibia, Zimbabwe, South Africa and Guinea-Bissau is being intensified. In each case the struggle involves the training and building of liberation armies, providing them with weapons of war, medicines, food and equipment necessary to survive harsh conditions such as deserts, floods and cold. We have to build propaganda organizations, both inside and outside our countries, capable of maintaining the support of the population, inspiring them with the noble aims and tasks of the struggle. We have to develop highly efficient underground movements capable of functioning under the noses of our enemies in conditions where the simple distribution of a leaflet carries the death penalty, as in South Africa, under the Sabotage Act.

The efforts of the liberation movements have been impressive, despite great difficulties. They have built armies

Oliver Tambo arriving with Amilcar Cabral for the Fifth Assembly of the OAU Heads of States, Algiers, 1960. *(IDAF)*

which are holding down thousands of men serving the states of white supremacy. Vast resources are being expended by our enemies in their efforts to frustrate the liberation movements . . .

. . . The struggle is going to be a grim and bitter one. The states of white supremacy in southern Africa control the wealthiest and most highly developed part of our continent. They will fight to the last to retain their ill-gotten gains. Therefore, the liberation movements and Africa as a whole must be geared for a ruthless struggle, in which no quarter can be asked or given.

. . . These days it has become fashionable for some African countries to flout or circumvent the obligations of the OAU Charter by referring to their problems and the necessity to have relations in one form or another with our enemies in Portugal, Rhodesia and South Africa. This is an issue so vital to the future of our people that we must be forgiven if our frankness takes precedence over etiquette.

Let us say at once that we are not unmindful of the problems and difficulties that beset our fellow Africans in many states as a result of the neglect and exploitation by former imperialist powers. Nor should we be thought of as dreamers living in a fairy-cloud cuckooland. We understand the realities of the situation faced by some countries, but we feel that there should be a scrupulous avoidance of any words or actions aimed at dealing with that situation which may in the circumstances amount to a betrayal of our peoples. It is inconceivable that some Africans should achieve happiness on the basis of the tears and grief of other Africans. In any event, the states of white supremacy, which appear impregnable today, are headed for inevitable defeat at the hands of aroused peoples and we must make it clear that no agreements or arrangements with our enemies, entered into at the expense of our people, will have much hope of survival.

There exist circumstances that require that we should express ourselves strongly on this matter, particularly in the light of what is clearly a well-planned offensive by South Africa and its allies against the liberation movements and

African states. Because of the tendency to underplay the role of Portugal in the unholy alliance of Salazar, Smith and Vorster, the following facts need to be emphasized. First, Portugal is encouraging foreign investment in the colonies. The Portuguese Government has declared that 'if we encourage the Western powers in the exploitation of the resources in our territories, these powers will be more convinced of the need to assume their military defence'. Secondly, their trade links with Rhodesia have been used by the imperialist countries to undermine and defeat the sanctions resolutions against the Smith regime. Thirdly, the Portuguese Government has launched a diplomatic offensive aimed at winning support for its African forces.

The nature of apartheid as a system of oppression and exploitation of the African people of South Africa is notorious enough. But recently it has become clear that the Republic of South Africa has embarked on a complex and many-sided offensive against the liberation movements and the independent African states. The policy of South Africa has been a carrot and stick policy. On the one hand, South Africa has presented itself as an altruistic state interested only in developing friendship with African independent states with the intention of promoting trade and technical aid. Despite the inherent absurdities of a policy of oppressing Africans at home while making friends with them across the borders and abroad, white South Africa is pursuing its aim skillfully and relentlessly. The strategic object of this aspect of the South African Government's policy is to create a series of client states, which will provide a base directed against the liberation movements and the independent states of Africa, so that, in fact, the aid and trade ultimately have military and strategic aims in view.

In case the carrot of aid and trade does not achieve its aims, South Africa has other weapons in her armoury. In various parts of the continent there is evidence of subversion supported by South Africa and its allies in Rhodesia and Portugal. Intelligence groups have been set up in many countries: assassins, saboteurs and mercenaries are to be found

wherever they can fish in troubled waters. Bribery and cor-
ruption are used unhesitatingly. We feel that more attention
should be paid to this aspect of South African aggression. A
powerful propaganda campaign has been mounted by Radio
South Africa and other agencies with the aim of denigrating
the OAU and supporters of the liberation movements, while
praising to the skies those who are prepared to sell their souls
for a mess of potage. And standing as a grim support for
direct aggression against independent states — whether in
the form of threats or action — is the formidable military
machine which now costs hundreds of millions of pounds
(sterling) to maintain and develop. Already this machine is
active in Zimbabwe, Namibia, Angola and Mozambique. In
South Africa itself the military manoeuvres, code-named
'Operation Sibasa', were obviously intended for sinister
purposes.

The white supremacists in southern Africa are bold and
aggressive to the point of madness. This is perfectly illust-
rated by their attitude on the question of Zimbabwe. South
African military forces were requested by Ian Smith to help in
the fight against the ZAPU-ANC forces in August 1967. Since
then the South African forces have been greatly expanded
and the intervention has been more blatant. A few days ago
Vorster, the fascist Prime Minister of South Africa, reported
that in his talks with Mr Thompson, the British
Commonwealth Secretary, he had made it clear that South
African military forces will go wherever there are 'terrorists'.
He also made it clear that the forces sent to intervene in
Zimbabwe will not be withdrawn . . .

In our struggle the aid and support of the OAU play a considerable role. It is, in our humble opinion, vital that such
support must be given to movements that are effective and
have the support of the masses. This issue need not be surrounded by a host of technicalities and complicated reasoning. As the fighting spreads and develops, this issue will be
resolved on the basis of concrete evidence. We welcome the
practice of sending OAU missions to the fighting zones to see
for themselves what is actually taking place. There are also

other methods, which do not depend on press reports or even the claims of organizations, that should enable realistic assessments to be made regarding these movements . . .

. . . The aid and assistance needed in the war are considerable. It is not just a question of the volume, which must be commensurate with the demands of the struggle, but more and more we are now confronted by the need for haste. The situation in the fighting zones is constantly changing. Africa must therefore find means to ensure that there are swift responses to requests for help and in the facilities provided. Delays and red-tape should not stand in the way of victory in the battles we are fighting.

Over 30 million Africans are not represented as states in the Assembly of the OAU. Our faith in the OAU rests in the justified belief that nothing, not even national or state interests, will ever make Africa forget those oppressed Africans. If we did not believe this, we would not be here.

On our part, in the name of our people, we are determined to fight and make the kind of sacrifices which made revolutionary Algeria free and independent in a struggle against one of the world's greatest powers. We shall carry on the fight, no matter how long or difficult it may be. We shall win because Africa must be freed.

2.5 SOUTH AFRICA AND IMPERIALISM
(Statement to the Preparatory Meeting of the Non-Aligned States, May 1970)

Your Excellencies, the purpose of this brief statement is to draw attention to the flagrant violation by the white minority South African regime of those fundamental principles to which all member states here are committed: the right to self-determination and national independence; the equality of all peoples, irrespective of race, colour or creed; the defence of all persons, groups and nations from oppression and exploitation; the raising of the standard of living and culture of all, without discrimination; and the promotion of international co-operation and world peace.

The stubborn persistence of the white minority regime in pursuing its racialist and fascist policies is certainly no accident. It is a carefully planned and systematically prosecuted criminal conspiracy, to consolidate and extend their ideology of racialism and fascism whose basic economic objective is the ruthless exploitation of the African people, whose military and political aim is the defence of imperialism, fascism and the subversion of national independence in Africa and Asia.

The South African white minority regime has over the past few years matured to become a fully fledged member of the imperialist conspiracy both financially and militarily. The South African racists' allies, the imperialist powers, Britain, the US, France, Portugal, West Germany, Japan and others, have been building the white regime into a dangerous, aggressive and expansionist state. It is this imperialist conspiracy which today is guilty of the crimes and atrocities against the people of South Africa, southern Africa, Africa, Asia, and Latin America for which Hitler's Nazi bandits were arraigned and convicted by the world at the Nuremberg trials.

Just as in the case of Hitler's Nazi Germany this criminal conspiracy is aimed at regaining lost colonial territories and countries, the plunder and exploitation of the peoples and the resources of their country, and the perpetuation of a system of amassing fabulous profits for industrial and armaments monopolies. It is a desperate plot for the imperialist second Reich in an era when socialist and national revolutions have made empires shrink.

South Africa clearly demonstrates the wolfish nature of this conspiracy. The natural wealth of South Africa is, to say the least, fabulous. It is the source of 75 per cent of the gold in the capitalist world. Minerals like copper, iron ore, coal, manganese, diamonds, chromium, nickel, thorium, vanadium, uranium and numerous others are mined there. It is a treasure chest for foreign capital and investment. Foreign investment is estimated at £3,000 million of which Britain accounts for about 60 per cent and the US 13 per cent. Through the ruthless exploitation of African labour the rates of profits in South Africa are higher than anywhere else in the world. The British monopolies are guaranteed 12.5 per cent as against 8.5 per cent in the rest of the world; the US, 20.6 per cent as against 8.5 per cent in the rest of the world. Japan, West Germany and other western countries have made South Africa the hunting ground for super-profits.

South African companies, like the Anglo-American Company under Harry Oppenheimer and many others, have all got interlocking interests and directorships with British and US companies. Economically therefore, the South African racists who cling to apartheid are an integral and key part of the sinister plot of exploitation by the imperialists on an international scale. The merger of white South African capital with international finance has been a specific feature of South African penetration in the economies in many countries in Africa and elsewhere.

There is no other country in the world in which the imperialists have been prepared to relegate their differences to the background and unite their efforts economically, technically and militarily as they have done in South Africa. The beneficiaries of Nazi Germany and the paymasters of Hitler were I. G. Farben, Siemens, Krupp, Deutsche Bank and others. It is hardly surprising that these companies have joined their South African, British, French and US counterparts in supporting the colonialist and racialist regimes of southern Africa. The Cabora-Bassa project exposes once more the dangerous alliance of South African and international finance in the consolidation of the bulwark of reaction in southern Africa.

Financially, South Africa is the spearhead in Africa for imperialist capital penetration and the subversion of the achievement of genuine national and economic independence in Africa, Latin America and South-east Asia. The aggressive, offensive and expansionist policies of the South African racist Government have been expressed in different ways at different times by spokesmen of the racialist Government itself. Sometimes these were blatant threats of armed aggression against Zambia and Tanzania. At other times they were couched in terms of extending the 'hand of friendship' to independent African states.

Spokesmen for the racist regime have stated over and over again that they were an integral part of the western system and boasted that the western imperialist powers were dependent on the racist state for the defence of the western way of life in Africa. Vorster's Government even claims that it has the same role to play in Africa as the US has in the world — the policeman against 'communism'. Vorster arrogantly claims the right of the South African Government to intervene in the affairs of African states, as the US has done in so many instances in the world and brutally in Vietnam now.

The watchdog for the imperialists in southern Africa against the achievement and consolidation of national independence in southern Africa is the racist minority regime of South Africa, and her allies Smith and Caetano. The white minority regime does not act merely as an agent but also as a partner. Recently the racists' spokesmen have made this abundantly clear. In October 1969 the Minister of Defence, P. Botha, stated that whatever the situation might be with other western countries, South Africa was already involved in a Third World War, militarily, economically and diplomatically. On 25 October, Hildgard Muller stated in Britain that South Africa is no longer on the defensive, her priority was Africa. He also deplored Britain's compliance with the arms embargo.

The 'hand of friendship' which Vorster constantly extends to African independent states is an octopus tentacle for the domination of Africa, politically and economically, by South African and imperialist powers. The 'outward or northward policy' is a neo-colonialist device to expand and spread the ideological and financial interests of South African and international finance, to subvert political and economic independence and support for the national liberation struggle.

Militarily, too, South Africa is part of the aggressive imperialist bloc. It is an important detachment in the imperialist global military strategy. The role of imperialist powers in giving massive all-round assistance in building that monstrous fascist army in South Africa is systematic and deliberate. When the army was reorganized in 1969, the then Minister of Defence, Erasmus, justified the arms build-up as 'a measure to ward off a threat from loud-mouthed Afro/Asians in the North'.

The purpose of the reorganization of the South African armed forces, and the swelling of the military machine was in fact, firstly, to suppress the national liberation movement not only in South Africa, but in the whole of southern Africa, secondly, to threaten African independent states and where necessary in pursuance of expansionist policies to invade them, and finally to give support to the imperialists in the event of a global war. The imperialists gave and still give assistance for the building of the armed forces of South Africa to fulfil the above aims. France openly defies the UN embargo on arms and is today the biggest single supplier of arms to South Africa The US, despite its avowed claim that it is abiding by the arms embargo, last year sold 10 million dollars worth of arms to South Africa.

South Africa does not merely confine her military role to Africa. With the closure of the Suez Canal and the withdrawal of Britain from the Far East, the imperialists and the South African fascists regard the South African military force as the most important alternative in filling the vacuum in the southern hemisphere. Hence the continued overt and clandestine military support. The proposals to find a place for the fascists in NATO and the plans for a South Atlantic Treaty Organization in which the racists will play a major role are part of the sinister plot against the national liberation struggle and national independence in Africa, Asia and Latin America. Apartheid has been extended and entrenched in Rhodesia by Smith with the full support of South Africa and the imperialist powers. Both Britain and the US have systematically sabotaged all effective international action.

South African fascists and their imperialist allies have set themselves the task to suppress the national liberation movement and to subvert national independence. The struggle for

ANC leaders at the 46th National Congress in 1958. (right to left) Moses Mabhida, Albert Luthuli, G.S.D.Nyembe, Oliver Tambo, ANC Chaplain, Diza Putui, Alfred Nzo. *(IDAF)*

national liberation and the consolidation of national independence are inextricably interlinked and bound together, because the greatest enemies of national freedom, the oppressors and exploiters allied internationally, remain the greatest enemies of national independence throughout the world.

The achievement of national independence and the consolidation of independence are themselves a great contribution to the whole anti-imperialist struggle. This has been clearly demonstrated by the change in the balance of forces in the international forums and particularly the massive onslaught on racialism and colonialism in the UN and its agencies, the OAU and other international and continental agencies. This is a great achievement. The joint strength of the progressive movements and states has a great potential.

Imperialists have through their armed repression in southern Africa compelled the oppressed and exploited peoples to meet this repression with armed revolt. The whole area has become the theatre of what will be one of the most fierce armed confrontations between the racialists and fascists on the one hand, and the people's forces on the other. In this struggle the imperialists' involvement on the side of reaction is complete and irrevocable. The involvement of the democratic and progressive forces on the side of the armed national liberation struggle should be equally complete.

. . . Your Excellencies, the armed struggle in South Africa will be protracted and costly in terms of human life. This is not the choice of the people. However protracted it might be, whatever the cost may be, its victory is assured. We are confident that this meeting will draw the attention of the summit meeting to the urgency and gravity of the armed struggle in South Africa, and the need to give it massive and all-round assistance.

3
REBUILDING FROM MOROGORO

Introduction

In the mid-1960s the external mission had assumed the task of representing and leading the movement as a whole, including the internal units. Due to reverses at home, it had to carry out the process of reconstruction from outside. There were no structures left inside to receive the armed cadres who returned to the country. The strains on the external movement were considerable. In late April 1969 an important National Consultative Conference was held in Morogoro. It lasted a week and was attended by 70 delegates from the ANC and allied organizations. The Morogoro meeting was held to make a thorough review of the state of the movement and its role in the struggle. The leadership was subjected to severe criticism — the executive resigned *en bloc* to make way for new people, though many were re-elected. A central issue was the relationship between the external movement and the struggle in the country, since it was accepted that the ANC's internal organization had been severely disrupted. A Revolutionary Council was established under the National Executive to oversee the day-to-day direction of Umkhonto.

The Morogoro Conference also introduced two important policy changes. The first concerned the role of whites, Indians and coloureds who worked with the external mission. The other Congress bodies (SAIC, the Coloured People's Congress [formerly SACPO], SACOD) did not have exile organizations. Although a practice was made of including non-Africans in diplomatic delegations, there was a strong desire for a more formal association. This was an issue that had been debated over some years. It was decided at the conference to allow non-Africans to join the external ANC as individuals, although the National Executive remained an all-African body reflecting a concern that the national movement should not move too far ahead of mass consciousness at home. Secondly, a 'Revolutionary Programme' was adopted which was an annotated version of the Freedom Charter. It provided an explanation of the key clauses of the Charter, such as, 'The people shall govern', 'The people shall share in the country's wealth' and 'The land shall be shared among those who work it'.

In the five years following the Morogoro conference the political balance shifted significantly against the South African Government. The process began with the reawakening of black working-class militancy beginning with the 1972-3 strikes in Natal, Transvaal and Cape, and the impending success of Frelimo in Mozambique and MPLA in Angola. The independence of both countries from Portugal in 1975 had an enormous psychological impact inside South Africa, inspiring strikes by students in black schools and universities. It also created the opportunity for effectively infiltrating armed and other cadres through these countries into South Africa.

The ANC also chalked up major successes in mobilizing international opinion against apartheid. Its secretariat was moved from Morogoro to Lusaka, where it was not so isolated, and offices and representatives were established in numerous countries throughout the world. This expanding network gave the ANC a higher international profile than ever before. The demand for comprehensive economic sanctions gained more support throughout the world, but was not made mandatory by the United Nations owing to Security Council vetoes by the United States, Britain and France. However, in 1974 the General Assembly refused to accept the credentials of the South African Government, marking the changing political tide.

3.1 CROSSROADS AT MOROGORO
(Extracts from the political report of the National Executive Committee to the Morogoro Consultative Conference, 25 April-1 May 1969)

The vital and central tasks of the African National Congress today is the intensification of the armed struggle for the overthrow of the white fascist regime and the liberation of our motherland. Today armed struggle together with other forms of struggle constitute the weapons of the oppressed in our country against the oppressor. How can we intensify the revolution? What forms of organization can ensure the maximum mobilization of all the resources at our disposal? What are the motive forces of our struggle and their potential? What strategy and tactics are to be employed?

These are some of the problems and questions that require our consideration and solution. Our struggle is being waged in a complex and difficult national and international situation. The correct solution of the problems of our revolution requires a proper understanding of the international as well as the national situation. This involves a correct assessment of the strength and weaknesses of the enemy and its imperialist allies, as well as our own strength and weaknesses, our potential and that of the whole anti-imperialist forces.

Our immediate enemies, the white fascist regime in South Africa, are an important and integral part of the imperialist camp. Internationally the imperialists' main preoccupation today is a desperate attempt to stem the anti-colonialist movement, and to regain their former positions of political, economic and military dominance over the peoples of the world. To achieve their objective they have embarked upon a global strategy of reactionary and brutal counter-attack against progressive governments and revolutionary liberation movements. The imperialists resort to numerous methods, for instance:

— The creation of hotbeds of war all over the world including acts of provocation, direct and indirect military intervention as in Vietnam and South East Asia, the Middle East, Korea, Cuba, West Berlin and Czechoslovakia.

— The establishment of military bases at strategic points and the selection of springboards in all continents from which they launch their acts of aggression and subversion. In the Middle East, Israel acts as catspaw of imperialism; in Asia, Japan. In Africa fascist South Africa is the main bulwark and fortress of reaction and imperialism. It is of vital economic and strategic value in the whole global strategy of imperialism.

— The subversion of anti-imperialist governments. Military coups in Latin America and Africa have been engineered systematically in the last three years.

— The hindering of progress towards economic independence in developing countries through neo-colonialistic machination, carefully manipulated 'aid' and loans, the fixing of prices of commodities to the disadvantage of developing countries, the unequal trade agreements, the export of both private and state capital. All these are designed to keep independent and developing countries economically dependent on the colonialists. South African fascism itself has reached a stage where it is offering state financial 'aid' to African independent states. It is already implementing the scheme in Swaziland, Lesotho, Malawi, and Botswana . . .

— Increased support and reinforcement of reactionary regimes militarily, economically and technically against the liberation movements and revolution. The concerted support by the imperialists of the racist minority regimes of Vorster, Caetano, and Smith . . . is now a public and well-known fact. In Latin America and Asia, too, the United States in particular, supports its puppet regimes against revolutionary movements.

— Assassination and the murder of leading members of progressive and revolutionary movements have now become part of the stock-in-trade of world reactionary forces. In Kenya a few years back it was Pio Pinto. Then

Comrade Sigauke of Frelimo, now recently Comrade Eduardo Mondlane of Frelimo. There are no limits to the cowardly and dastardly crimes of the imperialists and their agents.

— Imperialist agents are busy trying to foment division, conflict and desertions in the ranks of the liberation movements and progressive organizations. The agents of reaction use all methods ranging from the exploitation of genuine grievances and differences to naked slander, distortions, lies and bribery.

— Efforts to discredit and denigrate the liberation movements and their leadership, both among the people and internationally, are one of the main objects of the psychological warfare conducted through the radio, press and whispering campaigns. The work of Radio RSA, Radio Bantu and Msakazo is notorious in this respect . . .

— Spies, informers, and traitors are lavishly bribed to inform on the liberation movements, to enable the oppressors to wreck the revolutionary struggles for freedom.

The objective of the imperialists in their global strategy is to isolate, undermine, subvert and wreck everything whether it be a state or organization which is progressive and anti-imperialist and to consolidate and reconstruct all pro-imperialist, and reactionary institutions in the world.

Opposed to this frantic counter-offensive is the mighty anti-imperialist force and movement. It is the united force of popular, progressive and revolutionary states and organizations. The apparent strength of the imperialists is in their massive military and economic potential. Politically they are weak and getting weaker by the day. They are incapable of complete unity even among themselves because of the constant rivalry to re-divide markets. In addition the rise of anti-imperialist revolution is constantly undermining the false image of their superiority. Even militarily their 'invincibility' is being exposed by the humiliating defeats they are suffering from smaller and relatively weaker nations which are economically less developed. The dilemma of the US in

Vietnam caused by the shattering and humiliating blows from the heroic people of Vietnam exposed the basic weakness of the leading and most aggressive imperialist powers.

In addition, the developing countries no longer wish to associate themselves openly with the capitalist system which to the vast masses of the people spells ignorance, disease and poverty. The impact of socialism on the masses of the people is steering states of the Third World to pronounce their objectives as socialist in one form or the other.

Mass support and even submission is shrinking in the direction of resistance and revolt both in the former colonial countries and amongst vast sections of the populations in the imperialist countries themselves. The anti-communist bogey through which the imperialists try to justify all their reckless and brutal interference is wearing thin as a veil to hide their fiendish plots of plunder, greed, exploitation, aggression and atrocities, which they perpetrate against the peoples of the world.

As the capitalist world begins to shrink, the rivalry between the imperialists for markets and dominance increases and so do their differences and conflicts. Military and economic organizations like NATO, CENTO, SEATO, the OAS and the Common Market, which were set up to protect shaky imperialists economically and militarily, become insecure and are in a constant state of crisis. The domination of her partners by the US is being challenged. The prestige of the imperialists and especially that of their leader, the United States, is dwindling. Throughout the world criticism of their complete disregard for human rights and their support for fascist and racialist states like South Africa, Portugal, and West Germany is mounting and becoming more caustic. Economic crisis is seriously aggravating their position at home and abroad. The imperialists appear strong, formidable and sometimes even invincible but in fact they are growing weaker and weaker as the socialist community grows stronger and liberation movements in Africa, Asia and Latin America struggle more fiercely for independence; and the masses in the imperialist countries themselves challenge the policies of the rulers.

THE ANTI-IMPERIALIST MOVEMENT

Apart from inherent causes leading to division amongst the imperialists, one major factor which has contributed to the crisis in which imperialism has found itself is the growing might of the anti-imperialist movement. The anti-imperialist movement is the united struggle and effort of all anti-imperialist states, organizations and individuals throughout the world. It is a broad movement composed of people with different political beliefs, of different races and colours, from different walks of life but who are united by their hatred of the evils of imperialism and racialism and their firm belief in national independence, genuine democracy, race harmony and peace.

The pillars of the anti-imperialist movement are the Soviet Union, the socialist states in alliance with the progressive states of Africa, Asia and Latin America, the revolutionary liberation movements in countries which are still under colonial or white minority rule, and the democratic forces in the imperialist countries themselves. The anti-imperialist movement is based on the fact that the destinies of all peoples struggling against imperialism are interlinked and inextricably interwoven. The joint and concerted action of all progressive forces against imperialism and the mobilization of the vast masses of the people into a united anti-imperialist front constitute a mighty and invincible force for the destruction of the imperialists. Unity and action are therefore cardinal in the fulfilment of this objective.

The African National Congress and the oppressed and exploited peoples of South Africa together with all genuine democrats are an integral part of the anti-imperialist movement of the world. We share with all other anti-imperialist peoples of the world common aims and objectives and common enemies. There are numerous international organizations whose basic object is the mobilization of the people against imperialism, like OAU, WFTU, WIDF, WFDY, IUS, the World Peace Council, the Afro-Asian Solidarity Organization, the Afro/Asian/Latin American Solidarity Organization, the

Democratic Jurists Association, the Afro-Asian Writers Association, AATUF, the Pan/African Youth Movement, the African Women's Conference, and others. The African National Congress has and still participates as fully as it can in the activities of these bodies and in many instances serves on their executive bodies. This apart from the bitter struggle of the people in South Africa against the fascists and imperialists has been a significant contribution to the global anti-imperialist struggle.

It is impossible, if not fatal, to divorce the struggle of our people in South Africa from the struggle of the peoples of the world. Is the participation of the African National Congress in these international bodies useless and wasteful? Certainly not. Not only do we join the powerful mass of mankind fighting precisely what we are fighting for against the same enemies, but we are able to disseminate information about our struggle, thereby strengthening ourselves and our allies and obtaining both moral and material support for our struggle. The international support for our struggle against the South African fascists has been mounting. But misconceptions and even ignorance of the conditions in our country and the struggle are still there in the most unexpected quarters. This is sometimes due to the fact that the enemy and its allies are busy through a well-organized internationally pro-apartheid lobby. distorting and lying about the situation in the country. It is of course correct that action inside our country is a more positive and dynamic contribution towards the struggle against imperialism. But the action itself and constant international explanation and agitation must go hand in hand. It is not necessary to go into details of how the so-called 'Mau-Mau' struggle was slandered and isolated by the British to the extent that it was not understood and not effectively supported by the international progressive world for lack of proper publicity. Much harm resulted from this circumstance. Karl Marx's call, 'Workers of the World Unite', is equally applicable to the anti-imperialists at this grave and critical time: 'Anti-imperialists of the World Unite!'

The past decade has been an era of national revolution and

upsurge of anti-imperialism which has resulted in the most rapid and unprecedented disintegration of colonialism in its old form. The frontiers of imperialism have shrunk under the pounding blows of the offensive launched by the liberation movements throughout the world.

Within a period of less than ten years the number of independent African states has reached 41. The phenomenal victory by the national liberation movements over the imperialists was made possible by a number of factors. First, the fundamental change in the world situation which has been brought about by the steadily growing strength of socialist countries which are selflessly dedicated towards the struggle for the destruction of colonialism. Secondly, militant and determined liberation movements have been growing in the colonial countries. Thirdly, systematic and conscientious efforts have been made by all anti-imperialist forces throughout the world to force unity and to pool their resources against colonialism. Fourthly. the inherent greed of the imperialists has produced conflict within their own ranks which has resulted in manoeuvres and counter-manoeuvres against each other. Finally each imperialist country has been weakened by crisis and internal problems within its own state, and the vigorous onslaught of working class and other democratic movements.

The victories of the liberation movements particularly in Africa whether they were achieved by peaceful or violent means have been a source of great inspiration to millions of oppressed people and have given impetus and momentum to their dream which almost immediately became a reality. The growth of regional, continental and international anti-imperialist organizations and the numerous acts of solidarity amongst the anti-imperialist people have become a life belt to those who are still battling in the storm against the racialists, colonialists and fascists. One of the great achievements of this era has been that colonialism as an ideology has been outlawed internationally and the people have discovered their immense strength to assault it successfully. The myth and facade of the invincibility of the racialists, colonialists and imperialists have been disproved forever. The victories of the national liberation movements were in most cases not easy, smooth and complete, nor was the retreat of the imperialists always unplanned or a complete defeat. Imperialism resorted to many political, military, economic and other stratagems to extend its lease of life and to save as much as it could in its erstwhile colonies.

In parts of the world like southern Africa and Guinea-Bissau, the imperialists are continuing to resist the legitimate demands of the people through ruthless repressions and terrorism. This is no accident but a deliberate design by the imperialists to maintain these areas as their last frontiers, as bastions of colonialism and as a springboard for re-colonization. Imperialists have never approved the abolition of colonialism and of the oppression and exploitation of the people. They were forced out of their former colonies by the strength of the people. They tried to cover their retreat by making loud announcements that they were 'granting the people their independence'. This was a despicable lie. It is only through the courageous struggles and sacrifices of the people that they have won their freedom. The disintegration and collapse of colonialism and the growth and unity of the anti-imperialist forces have driven the imperialists to desperation which has led them to launch a sinister and vigorous counter-offensive against the newly independent states, the national liberation movements and the anti-imperialist organizations.

This counter-offensive is yielding spectacular victories for the imperialists and temporary and serious reverses for the African revolution as well as dangerous cracks in the unity of the anti-imperialist forces of the world. The initiative which had been so firmly held by the anti-imperialist forces of the world is in grave danger due to this counter-offensive of the imperialists.

It is true that the initiative has not been lost yet. But within the space of two years the imperialists have done sufficient damage to independent states, liberation movements and anti-imperialist organizations to shake us out of our complacency and to call for greater vigilance and a closer study of the methods of the imperialists. The victories of the imperialists and the reverses of the revolutionary anti-imperialist forces are undoubtedly a temporary phenomenon. That is a fundamental fact derived from an understanding of the character of the epoch in which we live. However, comforting as this fact may be in the long run, it is no solution to the grave problems which now face us. Nor is it an effective answer to the grim counter-offensive which is causing so much suffering to millions of people.

The real solution can only be found by an exhaustive and candid examination of the strength and weaknesses, mistakes and faults, the potential of the anti-imperialist forces on the one hand and, on the other, the strategy and tactics of the imperialists which have enabled them to exploit these weaknesses and mistakes to score the victories they have recently scored.

. . . Imperialist military intervention and aggression in Vietnam, the Dominican Republic, and the Congo, the numerous counter-revolutionary coups and all forms of subversion to restore the domination of the colonialists have succeeded particularly because of the discord which exists in the anti-imperialist forces. The forums of the anti-imperialist organizations are not platforms for ideological and interstate disputes but are an anvil where all anti-imperialists should try to forge their common weapon to fight imperialism. Difficulties there might well be between members of the anti-imperialist movement but these must never be made to appear more important than the historic and common duty of destroying the monster of colonialism in all its forms.

The anti-imperialist forces have scored numerous victories and their potential in unity and concerted action is boundless. It is therefore the solemn duty of all genuine anti-imperialists to strengthen the unity of this mighty force, and to make it as invincible as it should be. Those who continue to sow discord and confusion are consciously and unconsciously trying to divert the movement from its objectives and are assisting the imperialists and undermining the revolutionary struggle.

For reasons which we will show later the African National Congress is deeply interested in the unity of the anti-imperialist movement. The success of the struggle in South Africa, its duration and cost in human life depends to a great extent upon the solidarity, strength and unity of the anti-imperialist forces of the world.. . . As we have stated before imperialism and fascism are using South Africa as their base and springboard for launching a counter-revolutionary offensive in Africa. The aggressive nature of these forces constitutes a direct threat to peace and independence not only in Africa but also in the rest of the world. In this situation, and as an internationalist duty, it is crucial that all progressive forces the world over should realize that they constitute one of the main motive forces in wiping out imperialism and fascism in South Africa. That realization must be translated into action in support of the national liberation movement in South Africa as led by the ANC.

The duty of the anti-imperialist forces that stand against Vorster fascism is no less today than the duty that faced the progressive forces against Hitler Nazism during the Second World War. From the progressive point of view there must be a fundamental change of outlook and attitude towards the struggle against fascism in SA. The anti-imperialist movement has tremendous potential. The urgent and immediate need is to cement unity. There is need to work out and implement the global strategy to counter the imperialists, to examine the activities of the numerous components, to ensure greater co-ordination and an avoidance of duplication. Above all, aggressive imperialist counter-attack requires a bolder assault by the anti-imperialist forces along every front.

THE AFRICAN REVOLUTION

. . . The African Revolution has had a tremendous impact on the world. It has swept aside the hollow myth of white rule based on alleged superiority of the white over the black. In the world forums the rapid appearance of African states has tilted the balance against the former imperialist states.

In the independent states themselves massive funds have been allocated for the first time to secure proper education and health facilities for the people. Africanization of the civil services is proceeding apace. The beginnings of economic development have been laid. The power of the African states is being steadily built up in all spheres of human endeavour. Yet it should be remembered that the states of Africa start their independent existence with a terrible legacy of colonial rule which deliberately kept the people ignorant, disease-ridden and poor. Furthermore the imperialists never intended to abandon their interests. Therefore through their agents they continue to do everything to place difficulties in the way of African unity and advancement.

The Organization of African Unity is one of the most hopeful symbols of African aspirations and determination to carve a proper place for our continent in the world. As far as we of the African National Congress are concerned the achievements of the Organization both in terms of its contribution to the solution of interstate problems and its support of the anti-imperialist struggle have been great.

This is not to say that there are no weaknesses in the OAU or in some of the states composing this great organization. But on the whole it can be said that our struggle in common with that of many other countries has received solid support from the OAU. It would perhaps be regarded as invidious to single out the states that have given us help and would be tedious to list them all. Yet we cannot but place on record our appreciation of Zambia, Tanzania, UAR and Algeria who have been our mainstay through many a difficulty.

It is not realistic for us to expect that every country in Africa must do the same or give equally to the struggle against the bastion of reaction in southern Africa. The states of white supremacy are strong and are backed by powerful international forces. But in the long run the anti-imperialist and anti-racist forces in Africa will rally to our support.

. . . The situation in southern Africa is a menace to African security and an imminent and serious threat to world peace. This has sometimes been expressed but it has perhaps never been so vital as now, to make the point again and again and to examine its full implications and the consequences which flow from it. The white minority and fascist regimes in southern Africa have maintained through military force and police terrorism systems which have been condemned the world over as a crime against humanity. Nevertheless, in flagrant violation of world condemnation, these racialist regimes have intensified their ruthless oppression and exploitation of the people.

There are many reasons why these white regimes have been able to sustain and maintain systems which are against the general trend of the African revolution and world development. One of them is that Smith, Vorster and Caetano have systematically built and consolidated what is now known to be the Unholy Alliance. It is an alliance based on common ideology — the maintenance of colonialism, racism and fascism. It has a common economic objective — the exploitation of the peoples of southern Africa and their resources. It also has a common political and military objective — to stem the spread of the African revolution and to subvert it where it has already been successful. The South African forces are conducting military action jointly with the Portuguese against MPLA in Angola. Last year it was established that South African helicopters were operating against MPLA militants in their Eastern front. For purposes of working out joint strategy the Portuguese Commander-in-Chief and the South African Commandant-General meet at least once a month. Military support and contingents of South African troops in Mozambique have been the subject of frequent reports. The question of South African troops in Zimbabwe is notorious enough.

THE ROLE OF SOUTH AFRICA

South Africa is the main pillar of this alliance. With its tremendous economic resources, its military might which is out of all proportion to its needs, it stands out as the senior partner and gives technical, financial and military aid to the

Smith regime, Caetano in Mozambique, and Angola. Smith openly declared to the Congress of his party last year that, but for the assurance of South African support, he would not have declared UDI.

The South African regime has acquired all the aggressive features of an imperialist state. It is only necessary to mention the brazen annexation of South West Africa against decisions of the United Nations; the constant threats of military attacks on Zambia and Tanzania; the acts of subversion, sabotage and spying carried on in African states; the export of mercenaries — these are all signs of her expansionist policy. Behind this Unholy Alliance is an even more dangerous alliance of the imperialists — the US, Britain, France, West Germany, Japan etc. They have deliberately tried to build southern Africa, and South Africa in particular, into a fortress of racialism and colonialism, the last outpost of imperialism in Africa and a ready spring-board to endanger the sovereignty of African states and threaten world peace. South Africa is the treasure house of the imperialists, but more than that, it is one of their most important strategic military bases and ally in their global strategy directed against the forces of national liberation, democracy and peace.

The enormous military might of South Africa has been built with the direct assistance of the imperialist powers. They supplied the technical know-how, the materials and the manpower to accelerate the growth of that monstrous arsenal in South Africa. This was part of a well considered strategy. The Minister of Defence of the white minority regime in South Africa has stated openly that the role of South Africa in Africa is the same as the role of the US in the world and that was to fight what he called communism. The commitment and involvement of South Africa in the global strategy of the imperialists is no new phenomenon. In the historic patriotic war of the People's Republic of Korea, South Africa did not hesitate to send its military personnel there to fight against the people of Korea. Only recently in the Middle East war, so-called South African volunteers were mobilized to render aid to Israel. Financial support was also given. The South African

Government boasts that it is the most 'stable' ally of the imperialist powers and offers them ready passage via the Cape to prosecute their nefarious plots and war in South East Asia.

. . . Britain is involved in one of the most despicable acts of treachery against the African people of Zimbabwe. The British Labour government has permitted and encouraged the white minority to seize and monopolize political power despite British assurances that there will be no independence before African majority rule (NIBMAR). Smith has now introduced a fascist constitution which is intended to relegate the majority to the dust-bin. Despite world-wide popular demand and in spite of the fact that Wilson himself declared UDI an act of rebellion by Smith and his racialist henchmen, the British Government has consistently refused to use force to restore order in Rhodesia. Britain has deliberately resorted to all forms of ineffectual methods, numerous and worthless talks, cunningly manipulated sanctions which allow the Smith regime to get its wants through the backdoor, South Africa.

Both the South African regime and Britain are vitally interested in retaining Rhodesia as a buffer state forming part of a reactionary iron belt barrier with South West Africa in the west, Angola in the north-west and Mozambique on the east to protect the imperialist treasure house, South Africa, from any outside attack. When the guerrilla activities started in Zimbabwe, South Africa without hesitation sent thousands of troops and a vast quantity of military equipment to the rescue of Smith's weaker forces. The basic purpose was to protect the buffer from collapsing and to keep guerrilla onslaught as far as possible from the borders of South Africa. Everything is being done to make sure that South Africa itself did not become a theatre of war. The imperialists are aware of the hatred of the people of South Africa towards imperialism and guerrilla war there might spell the end sooner than bargained for. If Rhodesia fell to the liberation forces the people of South Africa would have a friendly border on their side and this would qualitatively change the situation in favour of the liberation movement in South Africa.

In pouring their forces into Rhodesia the Vorster regime

was trying to solve one problem, but it has in fact created numerous others. One of them was what is, and will be for a long time, the bane of South African military strategists. This is the fact that by undertaking the defence of southern Africa the fascist regime is giving its military force an impossible task; drawing them out of their base; creating a long line of defence over a wide area. But on the other hand to fail to do this will be to allow the liberation forces in the neighbouring countries to achieve victory. The heavy casualties inflicted by our forces came as a shock and had an adverse effect both on the morale of the so-called 'superior' white forces and on the white population in South Africa. This is part of the reason why Vorster is urging a settlement between Britain and Rhodesia at all costs. The burden of defending Rhodesia is creating problems and difficulties for the South African regime.

For us the main strategic question is to see that the guerrilla struggle spreads to South Africa itself. When that happens the dispersal of the enemy will in strategic terms be complete. This is not to say that the enemy will in fact be tactically dispersed. This depends on how widespread and effective guerrilla war is throughout southern Africa. But clearly we need to disperse the forces of white supremacy throughout the region both in territorial terms and in numbers of engagements. For this we need to launch the struggle at home . . .

Oliver Tambo with Robert Mugabe, Prime Minister of Zimbabwe, September 1987. (*Pieter Boersma GKf*)

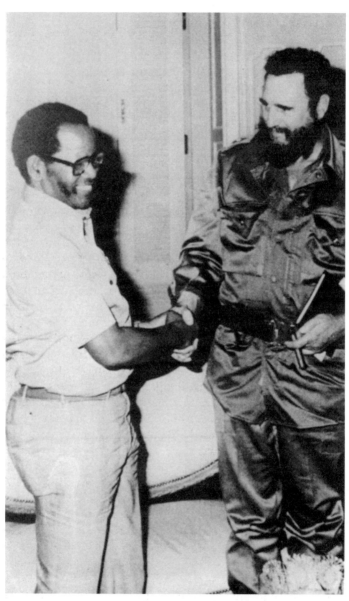

With Fidel Castro in the 1970s. *(IDAF)*

3.2 AFRO-ASIAN SOLIDARITY
(Message to the Afro-Asian People's Solidarity Organization, January 1971)

Twelve years ago the people of Africa and Asia met in the revolutionary capital of the UAR to map out a strategy for the eviction of the colonialists from Africa and Asia, and for the liquidation of world imperialism. They formed the Afro-Asian People's Organization, which soon grew into a great collective — a movement of the peoples not only of Asia and Africa, but of the whole progressive world.

Today, the Afro-Asian People's Organization meeting in council in the new revolutionary capital of Libya can proudly cast its eyes to the east of Tripoli, to the west, to the African land mass in the south, and even to the north across the waters of the Mediterranean, and see great young independent nations growing from the ruins of colonial domination. All those who participated in the historic meeting of 1958 share the sense of achievement we all feel today, as we enter the dynamic and highly explosive decade of the 1970s.

Even as we survey the world scene from this northern city of Africa, we see not only the new flags of freedom flying where once colonialism ruled supreme, but we also see the banners of revolutionary anti-imperialist detachments as they engage the enemy in fierce and bitter conflict in different parts of the world. Indeed, this Council meets at a time when, as never before, the strongholds of imperialism, colonialism, neo-colonialism and racism are being challenged, harassed and attacked in a global anti-imperialist offensive which, even in the short space of time since the last meeting of the Council, has assumed a new intensity and a new ferocity, precisely because of the resolute determination of the peace-loving peoples of the world to seize, and retain, their dignity and independence — a determination which is matched by the equal resolution of the imperialists not only to retain what remains of their shrunken empires, but also to re-conquer and nullify the hard-won gains of the national liberation movement, the world socialist system and the toiling workers and peasants of the world. Thus, the struggle of the great and heroic people of Vietnam against US imperialism continues unabated; US intervention in the internal affairs of the people of Indo-China falls into line with Washington's global strategy for domination; the intransigence of Israel in its continued occupation of Arab lands and its denial of the just demands of the Palestinian people has turned the Middle East into an explosive battle ground seriously endangering world peace and security; the courageous people of Guinea-Bissau are pushing the NATO-supported Portuguese colonialists out of Africa in the course of bitter armed confrontation; the black masses and youth of America wage a militant struggle against racial discrimination, exploitation and US imperialism; the revolutionary people of Cuba and Latin America continue to resist the same imperialism; and in embattled southern Africa, the peoples of Angola, Namibia, South Africa, Mozambique and Zimbabwe are fighting wars of liberation against an imperialist-backed alliance of Portuguese colonialists, Rhodesian racists and South African fascists.

There is clear evidence that imperialism is losing ground, but it is also clear that the bitterest battles have yet to be fought for the complete defeat of imperialism.

It follows from what I have said that the Afro-Asian revolution, which AAPSO was formed to accelerate, remains — and will yet remain — an unfinished revolution, especially if the mighty anti-imperialist forces continue in their present state of disunity, and if 'massive' or 'increased' material assistance to fighting peoples ends, where it begins, in speeches and resolutions.

If, therefore, I have any message for this Council meeting, comprising militants and revolutionaries from the battlefronts of armed conflict, it is a simple one. First, with the object of launching a decisive offensive to crush all resistance to the force for peace and progress, let AAPSO initiate a new and powerful campaign to sink all differences and forge a solid united front of all anti-imperialist forces. Secondly, let this Council adopt a resolution in which it deplores the fact that the hundreds of millions of the people of the world who support the national liberation movement cannot provide enough firearms, trucks, food, medicine and funds for even the handful of liberation movements fighting against colonialism and racism in Africa.

In conclusion, I wish to salute this Council meeting in the name of the fighting people of South Africa and to acknowledge the valuable assistance and support given by our independent brothers and sisters in Africa and AAPSO countries, and by our brothers in the socialist countries in Europe. In particular, I salute the leaders of the new, dynamic and revolutionary Republic of Libya, which joined the vanguard of the anti-imperialist forces at a crucial moment in the history of the Middle East, and which has already played a historic role in its massive assistance to the struggle of the Palestinian people against Israeli domination. And here it is appropriate to recall the tragic and ill-timed death of one of Africa's political giants — an unequalled leader of his people — the late President, Gamal Abdel Nasser. He fell like the great soldier he was, in the forefront of the fierce struggle for the rights of man, for justice, for freedom, for peace. It is our historic task as the Afro-Asian People's Solidarity Organization to continue that struggle with added vigour until final victory is won.

3.3 'WE WHO ARE FREE TO EAT AND SLEEP AT WILL'
(New Year's address to the ANC External Mission, 1971)

. . . The opening of a new year is the occasion for an exchange of greetings. We send our sincere and brotherly greetings and best wishes to you all and to your families. Through you we greet all our supporters and fellow-workers for freedom and peace in southern Africa.

Today, it is ever more important that we continue to hold in our hands the weapon of unity we have, in the past, wielded with such dramatic results in our external work. It is the weapon with which we have built up a volume of international support for our struggle, and a mountain of international pressure against the racists, such as cannot but give great satisfaction to our colleagues who languish in South African gaols. With that weapon of unity we have stood firm in the face of sustained and powerful enemy attacks — attacks mounted from different points, at different angles and with different methods. With that weapon in our hands, we have gone to war and it inspired the gallants of Umkhonto we Sizwe in the historic battles of Wankie and Sipolilo. They fought and fell, they punished and routed the imperialist agents under the banners of the ANC in the name of a united and suffering people. With that weapon we shall fight and fall, we shall conquer and be free.

It is a weapon the enemy has sought to take from the oppressed people. The colour bars and job reservations, the Bantustans, the Coloured and Indian Councils, the Group Areas and ethnic groupings, the Fort Hares and Turfloops, — all these attack the weapon of unity. 'Hold fast on it,' Chief Luthuli cries from the grave. 'Hold it fast.' It is not yours, it belongs to the suffering people, to posterity; it is the key to posterity. 'Hold it!' That is the call from Mini, Saloojee, Florence, Solwandle and others; from Mercy Tshabala, Paul Petersen and Patrick Molaoa; from Nelson, Walter, Goldberg, Mlangeni, Billy, Govan, Motsoaledi, Dorothy, Bram, Ramotse and millions of our people. And we shall hold it.

We who are free to eat and sleep at will, to write, to speak, to travel as we please; we who are free to make or break a revolution, let us use our comparative freedom, not to perpetuate the misery of those who suffer, nor to give indirect aid to the enemy they fight by withholding our own contribution.

We have an unequalled capacity for rallying to the banners of the ANC and consolidating our ranks when danger threatens. And danger does threaten. The campaign to break Africa's resistance to apartheid and her support for the liberation struggle in southern Africa has scored significant successes. Vorster, Suzman and lesser agents of colonialism have turned Africa into a veritable hunting ground for stooges and indigenous agents of racism. Mrs Suzman deserves special mention. This sweet bird from the blood-stained south flew into Zambia and sung a singularly sweet song:

I am opposed to apartheid;
I am opposed to the isolation of South Africa;
I am opposed to violence;
I am opposed to guerrillas;
I am opposed to the Lusaka Manifesto;
I am opposed to the decision of the World Council of
Churches;
I know the Africans can do nothing to cause political
change in South Africa;
I am in favour of change;
I am clearly in favour of change,
But determined to prevent change.

Some African leaders have been offering their services as Bantu Commissioners in the political power structure of the racist regime. Encouraged by France, they see themselves sitting at a table with the racists, talking about the 'Bantu', after the fashion of all Bantu Commissioners — the 'Bantu' who are not credited with the ability to talk for themselves.

A dialogue over the heads of the South African oppressed and over their leaders will never take place, unless it is a dialogue where a black chief sells his people into slavery as some black chiefs did centuries ago. But we refused to be sold then, and we refuse to be sold now. 'No sale in the south!' we say to our brothers. 'No more Bantu Commissioners either — we have enough and to spare!'

What Vorster's African campaign amounts to is a counter-offensive to isolate our people and our movement from the solidarity forces we have built, and which have placed South Africa in relative isolation. A recognition of this danger among others welds us into a united force.

Our militants are active both in and outside South Africa. The progress of our underground activities confirms the irrevocable commitment of our members to the cause of freedom, and to the armed struggle as an essential pre-condition for the achievement of that cause. In their work, our organizers are inspired by the fighting mood of the oppressed masses themselves.

The enemy's own creations — the so-called Transkei Parliament, the Coloured Legislative Council, the Zulu Bantustan, the Urban Bantu Councils — these have become battle-grounds of freedom, where the true representatives of the people are fighting the racists and rejecting their regime. What we see and hear is but the tip an iceberg of revolutionary resentment against white rule. But although our people are fighting courageously, our own history of political struggle has taught us that they fight without arms. Hence the people's faith in the prospects of an armed struggle, which we launched in Zimbabwe, and for which white children and white women in South Africa are being prepared. Let them prepare hard and fast — they do not have long to wait.

In the mean time the black people of racist South Africa must recognize that freedom for South Africa will come only when they rise as a solid black mass, rising from under the heel of the oppressor and storming across colour barriers to the citadels of political and economic power. Then only shall the noble principles enshrined in the Freedom Charter see the light of day and turn South Africa into a happy home not only for black people at last, but for all people.

Let us, therefore, be explicit. Power to the people means, in fact, power to the black people — the gagged millions who cannot set foot in the Cape Town Parliament where Bantustans and Coloured Councils are made; the most ruthlessly exploited, the tortured victims of racial hatred and humiliation. Let the blacks seize by force what is theirs by right of birth, and use it for the benefit of all, including those from whom it has been taken. And who are the blacks in South Africa? They are the people known, and treated, as 'kaffirs', 'coolies' and 'hotnots', together with those South Africans whose total political identity with the oppressed Africans makes them black in all but the accident of skin colour. Where this identity is not merely reformist but is revolutionary, there you have, in my view, a black man. This type of black man in South Africa is rare today. But he will grow in numerical strength, as we drive our point deeper and deeper with the Spear of Nation.

There may be some controversy over the views I have expressed. Any such controversy will be welcome, if it springs from differences of honest opinion on how best to exploit the revolutionary potential of the masses of the people and employ it in the destruction of a monster that has been terrorizing them for centuries. What seems clear in my own mind is that the black man is a vital and decisive factor in the survival or demise of fascist South Africa — indeed as vital and decisive as his cheap labour is to the economic might of the fascist state.

What does all this mean for those of us who for the time being operate outside South Africa? As I see it, it means we must work together, hand in hand, to build and consolidate power at the mass base, which in the South African context is black. As members of the ANC external mission — by which I understand the political militants and activists who are together outside South Africa under the leadership of the ANC — as mature members of this external mission of our movement, let us go out to the world, and back to the urban and rural areas of our common homeland, as one man, with one voice and one cause, which is power to the black people of fascist South Africa! Maatla! Mayihlome.

3.4 INCREASE OUR STRIKING POWER
(Statement to the 9th Extraordinary Session of the Council of Foreign Ministers of the Organization of African Unity, Dar Es Salaam, May 1975)

On behalf of the African National Congress, we express our gratitude to the Party, Government and people of Tanzania, who have made excellent arrangements to facilitate our participation at this meeting. This is in character, for Tanzania, under the unsurpassed leadership of President Julius Nyerere and TANU, was born through struggle, into a struggle. It has lived and grown high in revolutionary stature. Tanzania has

Oliver Tambo chatting with President Kaunda of Zambia and President Nyerere of Tanzania as the leaders depart from the Dar es Salaam Summit. (*Narendra Gajjar, Camera Press*)

been, and continues to be, a secure and reliable rear base for the national liberation struggle in southern Africa, a staunch defender of African unity. It is appropriate that this country should host this historic meeting.

In the name of all the men, women and children brutalized for decades by successive all-white regimes in South Africa, we commend the Ministerial Council of the Organization of African Unity on convening this Extraordinary Session. It is the first time, since its establishment 12 years ago, that the Organization of African Unity has convened a special Ministerial Council Meeting for the purpose of discussing the South African situation. Twelve years is a long time in our rapidly changing political situation. But it is a short time in the life of an inter-State organization like the Organization of African Unity. Yet in this short space of time, through its record of support for total liberation of Africa, the Organization of African Unity has developed such power and prestige that its decision to hold this meeting on South Africa, in the wake of the collapse of the unholy alliance, has attracted intense international attention. This is particularly so in South Africa, among both the oppressor and the oppressed, including the national leaders of our people who are languishing in enemy prisons. John Vorster, the white minority regime's Prime Minister, confirmed the crucial nature of this conference, when, making his first-ever reference to an OAU decision, he stated: 'The forthcoming OAU conference in Dar es Salaam could influence the course of events in Africa for a long time to come.'

We agree with his assessment but not with the veiled threat it carries. In convening this meeting, the OAU correctly focussed attention on South Africa as the most urgent issue facing Africa today. For the continued existence of the apartheid regime constitutes the principal obstacle to the complete and rapid emancipation of all the peoples of southern Africa. It delays the process of decolonization in that region and postpones the total liberation of Africa. In addition it constitutes a threat to the security of free African nations and world peace.

At the outset of our discussion on South Africa let us endeavour to establish a common understanding of what the true nature of apartheid is and hence what the real issues before this meeting are. Apartheid has often been equated with racialism. We need, however, to understand that racialism cannot be separated from the political oppression and economic exploitation of the black people. It serves both, and is in turn sustained by both. It is an integral part of a socio-economic system peculiar to South Africa, but one which has all except the geographic features of colonialism. The difference between South Africa and other systems of colonialism is, therefore, that in South Africa, colonizer and colonized live side by side within the same country. Colour and race are used as a dividing line between the resident white army of occupation and their subject population — the black people. The extreme exploitation of labour is the *raison d'être* of this system. A vast apparatus of restrictive laws and practices, coupled with the dispossession of Africans from their land, ensures the availability of cheap and forced labour. Above all, as a fundamental condition of its survival, the apartheid regime maintains a complete monopoly of State power and seeks by terrorist methods to make the people acquiesce in their own servitude.

African nations, Mr. Chairman, are not unfamiliar with this colonialist pattern, for in their own countries there have been played many variations of the exploitation of the African peoples under colonial rule. In South Africa the methods have been more intensely applied and the repression more severe because of the relatively large concentration of the oppressor within the country, aided and abetted by powerful international financial interests.

Therefore the problem that Africa has to face in South Africa is essentially a colonial problem, and like colonialism elsewhere it has to be removed root and branch. Attempts to bring about reform within the existing system can never provide a satisfactory solution and can never be a substitute for resolute anti-colonialist struggle for national liberation.

Let us consider then the context in which we have to work

for the removal of this colonialist system from our continent. The issue before us, Mr.Chairman, is not how to reform apartheid. The changes we seek in South Africa are not encompassed by being able to share a park bench with a white man, or to be allowed to enter an all-white theatre. We demand a fundamental transformation whereby, in our country, we shall have the same right of self-determination which free Africa has won for itself, which peoples fighting colonialism have won elsewhere in the world. That right is not negotiable.

Yet this is the one fundamental change that the system can never voluntarily concede, for upon the continued denial of any access to State power depends the very structure of apartheid. The objective of our struggle must therefore be the seizure of that power. As Comrade Samora Machel, President of Frelimo, stated in his historic and stirring message on the occasion of the Investiture of the Transitional Government of Mozambique:

> To decolonize the State means essentially to dismantle the political, administrative, cultural, financial, economic, educational, juridical and other systems which, as an integral part of the colonial State, were solely designed to impose foreign domination and the will of the exploiters on the masses.

It is only when political power has been won by the masses in South Africa that we will be able to begin the immense task of completely dismantling the structures and institutions of apartheid. In the context of the apartheid system, such a change can only come about through armed struggle by the revolutionary forces in our country.

OUR ARMED STRUGGLE

This is why the legitimacy of our armed struggle has been endorsed at successive meetings of the OAU and by the international community as a whole. It was reaffirmed by the East and Central African Heads of States in the Mogadishu

Declaration. Earlier, as part of the struggle for the transfer of power to the majority in South Africa, independent Africa had adopted the demand of the African people for the complete international isolation of South Africa in all spheres — diplomatic, political, military, economic and cultural. The implementation of this policy, which was spearheaded by the OAU and enforced by many countries and organizations throughout the world, led to an increasing weakening of the regime's international ties and aggravated its economic problems by isolating it from extended markets required for its expanding economy.

Vorster was therefore compelled to try and break out of the isolation into which he was being forced and to extend South Africa's sphere of influence from its immediate environment in southern Africa into the heart of independent Africa. Overtures were made to free African States with a view to establishing a dialogue. The dialogue proposed by Vorster specifically excluded dialogue about apartheid and the ways in which this inhuman system might be eliminated. What was demanded of Africa was that it call off its boycott of the apartheid regime and open its doors to the superior economic power of South Africa. This would have the effect of inhibiting support for the liberation struggle. We now know that this policy coincided with the long-term planning of southern Africa's future in foreign policy-making circles in the United States, as subsequently revealed in Kissinger's National Security Memorandum N.39. However, events in Africa have not followed the pattern envisaged by Vorster and international imperialism.

The heroic peoples of Guinea-Bissau, Mozambique, Angola, Sao Tome and Principe, and Cape Verde Islands advanced rapidly to victory; and substantial gains have been made by the revolutionary movements leading the masses in Zimbabwe and Namibia. Inside South Africa there is a revolutionary ferment manifested by a series of mass strikes by black workers, the growing militancy of the youth and an ever greater rejection of all aspects of apartheid policy — all these are continuing features of the present situation.

These developments have radically shifted the balance of forces in our sub-continent towards the fulfilment of the objectives of the liberation movement and confirm the correctness of the stand taken by ourselves and the OAU. In an attempt to contain the internal upsurge, and undermine the growing strength of the liberation struggle, Vorster intensified his brutal repression, and at the same time embarked upon an accelerated implementation of his Bantustan programme. The latter was an attempt to retribalize and divide the African population and thereby to strike a deadly blow at the very foundations of the national liberation struggle. There is no forum in the world today more aware of the dangers of retribalization of Africa than this. No member of the Organization of African Unity will accept the principle or practice of Balkanization.

The Bantustan programme is also intended to divert the attention of the people from the struggle to seize power where it resides in Pretoria by creating the illusion of an unreal independence in an uncertain future. To give credibility to this illusion, it was necessary for the minority regime to install a number of tribal functionaries who would be the instruments for the implementation of Pretoria's apartheid policy. Dignified by the title of 'homeland leaders', they were also to be used as itinerant salesmen for the Bantustan illusion in the outside world. They were to be the bridgehead of a new dialogue offensive — this time called 'detente'.

Once again Africa's response can only be an unequivocal rejection of dialogue. For, while playing for time Vorster is simultaneously preparing for the final confrontation. He has escalated his armament programme and is strengthening South Africa's ties with his traditional allies — Britain, the United States and France. This year, the military budget has been doubled to a total almost R1,000 million (£600 million), a sum greater than the annual national income of most African countries. The NATO powers continue to supply South Africa with arms in defiance of UN resolutions. Furthermore, in pursuance of their self-imposed task of protecting the world, the NATO powers have appointed Vorster to a leading role in policing the Indian Ocean without reference to the countries of Africa and Asia, thus underlining the role of the apartheid regime in South Africa as the main threat to the security and peace of Africa.

Despite this, however, the victories being scored against colonialism and imperialism throughout the world, the international and continental conditions, have created a situation most favourable for the success of armed struggle in southern Africa. The armed liberation movements and peoples of Vietnam and Cambodia are on the verge of final victory. In the Middle East progress is being made towards a just settlement that will vindicate the armed struggle of the Palestinian people for their legitimate rights supported by the Arab and African States, and the whole of democratic mankind. The Lisbon coup which destroyed the fascist regime in Portugal showed that the victorious struggle of the peoples of Guinea-Bissau and Cape Verde, Mozambique, Angola, Sao Tome and Principe, under the leadership of their heroic liberation movements, has furthered the process of revolutionary change not only in Africa but in Europe too.

The Lisbon *coup* deprived South Africa of its colonial ally while the victories of the peoples of Mozambique and Angola destroyed at a blow South Africa's strategy of surrounding itself with a ring of buffer States. In assessing the various political, economic and military manoeuvres of Vorster it is important to appreciate that they emanate from a position of weakness and not of strength. The time has clearly come to pursue the retreating enemy, not succumb to his blandishments.

The role of the Vorster regime in South Africa, Zimbabwe and Namibia no longer permits of a tight compartmentalization of the struggle in these three areas. The solution of the Zimbabwe question today, whether by negotiation or armed struggle, involves the Vorster regime. As Vorster stated brutally when addressing his electorate in November last year: 'The South African troops in Rhodesia are there to protect South Africa's interests and not anyone else's.'

President Nyerere, in opening this Conference, presented a

characteristically lucid analysis of the issues in southern Africa, and stated: 'Whether, therefore, we are talking about Rhodesia, Namibia or South Africa, itself, the effective authority is South Africa.' The OAU, in our opinion, must adopt a strategy, which recognizes not only the indivisibility of the enemy, but also the dominant role of the South African regime in the area. In Zimbabwe, Namibia and South Africa, which share common borders, there are liberation movements and revolutionary forces committed to revolutionary struggle, and capable of confronting the common enemy on the three fronts simultaneously.

The mobilization of African and world support for this three-fronted offensive is the urgent task to which this conference must address itself. We therefore call upon this august assembly to reaffirm the correct stand of the OAU and the UN of recognizing the liberation movement as the authentic representative of the struggling people in our country and spokesman of the South African people as a whole. The OAU should reaffirm its condemnation and total rejection of the Bantustan policy and puppet figureheads imposed upon the people by the Pretoria regime. In particular, the OAU should refuse to recognize the projected pseudo-independence of the Bantustans.

Africa must reaffirm its adherence to the diplomatic, political, military, economic and cultural isolation of white South Africa and call upon all member States to refrain from establishing any such contacts. In particular, Africa must continue to work for the immediate expulsion of the Pretoria regime from the United Nations Organization.

Finally, and above all, the OAU must call upon all the member States and the world to spare no effort in helping increase the striking power of our liberation movement in the struggle for the seizure of power not only in South Africa, but also the striking power of the ANC and the people of Zimbabwe in the struggle against the illegal settler regime of Ian Smith, as well as the striking power of SWAPO and the people of Namibia in the struggle against domination by the fascist regime in South Africa.

Although we have so far devoted our comments to what Africa and the world can do for us, we know that in the final analysis the liberation of our country is primarily the task of our liberation movement and our united people. The African National Congress, conscious of its historic duty to the people of our country, to Africa and to the whole of mankind, is determined to pursue this historic mission to final victory.

In this struggle our organization is aware of the forces of evil and oppression that are arraigned against it. Events have fully borne out the fact that international imperialism is committed to defend and buttress the regime of terror in our country. We are also aware of the fact that with trickery and duplicity our enemy is frantically attempting to seduce the so-called uncommitted forces all over the world. Time and the irreversible course of events are, however, working in our favour. The revolutionary mood of the oppressed masses of our country is surging forward. The whole of democratic mankind is on our side.

3.5 MOROGORO REMEMBERED
(Extract from the Political Report of the National Executive Committee to the second National Consultative Conference, Lusaka, June 1985)

The apartheid regime has survived for 37 years now. Born three years after the destruction of its fascist and Nazi progenitor, this regime was an historical anachronism from the very first day of its existence, a remnant of an epoch that was passing away. That it continues to exist to this day is a measure of the tenacity of the forces of imperialism and reaction which, in the last four decades, have sought to reverse the results of the Second World War and to stop the process of the democratic transformation of our planet to which the defeat of Nazism gave a new and added impetus.

It was because of this global offensive of imperialism that, as we met in Morogoro in 1969, a war of liberation was raging in Vietnam and the rest of Indo-China. The Arab peoples were rebuilding their forces in preparation of a renewed offensive to annul the gains that Zionist Israel had made during the six-day war of 1967. At the same time, we were still experiencing the influx into our country of a new wave of European immigrants. These were the so-called freedom fighters from Czechoslovakia who fled to apartheid South Africa, there to be received by the Pretoria fascist regime with what it considered well-deserved accolades.

Portugal and Spain still suffered under the yoke of fascist dictatorships. For two years, the Greek people had been living under the tyranny of a military junta that had been sponsored by US imperialism. At the same time, the United States was engaged in feverish efforts to stop Salvador Allende's election as President of Chile the following year, a campaign that led to his assassination in 1973 and the victory of the counter-revolution.

As we met in Morogoro to confer about our own struggle, the peoples of Guinea-Bissau, Angola, Mozambique and Sao Tome and Principe, as well as those in East Timor, still suffered under the yoke of Portuguese colonial domination. Zimbabwe was ruled by the white minority Smith regime whose illegal unilateral declaration of independence was a scant four years old.

Indeed, so confident was the counter-revolution of its strength in southern Africa that the US government of the day could adopt, in 1969, the so-called National Security Study memorandum 39. Among other things, this official document said: 'For the foreseeable future South Africa will be able to maintain internal stability and effectively counter insurgent activity.' This infamous document went on:

The whites are here to stay and the only way that constructive change can come about is through them. There is no hope for the blacks to gain the political rights they seek through violence, which will only lead to chaos and increased opportunities for the communists . . . We can, through selective relaxation of our stance towards the white regimes, encourage some modification of their current racial and colonial policies. . . At the same time, we would take diplomatic steps to convince the black states of the area that their current liberation and majority rule aspirations in the south are not attainable by violence and that their only hope for a peaceful and prosperous future lies in closer relations with the white-dominated states.

The memorandum dismissed the liberation movements of southern Africa as ineffectual and not 'realistic or supportable' alternatives to continued colonial rule. It ruled out any possibility of victory by these movements and questioned 'the depth and permanence of black resolve'.

Within our country, the Vorster regime was at the pinnacle of its power. It felt that the period of extreme reaction which the racists had unleashed when it banned the ANC, with Vorster as the general officer commanding the campaign of repression, had succeeded in smashing the revolutionary movement. The Pretoria regime also thought that it had further secured itself by helping to suppress the armed liberation struggle in Zimbabwe, in which units and cadres of the Luthuli Detachment of Umkhonto we Sizwe had participated with outstanding heroism and skill. Despite the fact that the UN General Assembly had terminated South Africa's mandate over Namibia — a decision which Vorster dismissed as 'ridiculous and impracticable' — the apartheid regime felt that it could continue its domination of Namibia for as long as it wished.

In opinion polls, white South Africa hailed Vorster as an 'excellent' Prime Minister and helped him in 1970 to defeat the Herstigte Nasionale Party in the white general elections held that year. It was in this situation that the Morogoro Consultative Conference was convened in 1969. Yet when it met it was not in a mood of pessimism. Rather, it was characterized by high revolutionary enthusiasm to confront our problems frankly and squarely and find solutions so that we could further intensify the struggle and, in practice, demolish the misguided confidence of the apartheid regime and its allies.

Many who participated to ensure that the Morogoro Conference was the success that it was are no longer with us. I refer to such outstanding leaders, stalwarts and activists of our movement as Moses Malume Kotane, Uncle J.B.Marks, Yusuf Mota Dadoo, Mick Harmel, Duma Nokwe, Robbie Resha, Kate Molale, Flag Mokgomane Boshielo, M.P.Naicker, Ngcapepe Ntunja and others. They left us a heritage of unwavering commitment to the people's cause, a spirit of self-sacrifice for the victory of our struggle and a revolutionary morality and practice which did not allow for personal ambition, factional conspiracies or cowardice and timidity in the face of an enemy counter-offensive. As we observe a minute's silence in their honour, let them serve as our example of the kind of cadre we must produce to carry their work forward to its successful conclusion.

Out of Morogoro came significant results, the most important being the reorientation of our movement towards the prosecution and intensification of our struggle inside South Africa, the restoration and reinforcement of unity within our own ranks and the integration of all revolutionaries within the ranks of the external mission of the ANC.

It is important to observe that, at Morogoro, our movement did not seek to underestimate the importance of or downgrade our international work. Indeed it could not, as the work that our movement had done, up to that point in our history, provided exactly the rear base from which we would carry out our internal work. The Morogoro Conference sought to ensure that we achieved the proper balance between our internal and our international struggle, with the internal being primary.

Once more, this Conference will have to address itself to this question, taking into account the altered circumstances of our struggle, the changed balance of forces at home and abroad and our immediate tactical, operational and strategic tasks. We shall come back to this issue later.

With regard to the issue of unity within our own ranks, the Morogoro Conference drew attention among other things to the importance of strengthening the links between the leadership and the membership, the necessity for the leadership to be accountable to the movement as a whole and the need to have clear strategic and tactical perspectives and a programme of work around which the membership would unite in pursuit of common objectives.

These questions remain important still. Conference will therefore need to make the necessary assessment to ensure that, at all times, we enjoy maximum political and organizational unity within our own ranks and that all members are actually involved in activity which contributes to the advance of our struggle.

The question of open membership, as it has come to be called, is also on our agenda. In the period since the Morogoro Conference dealt with this issue, the National Executive Committee has raised it with the membership, at home and abroad, with a view to determine whether as a movement we still felt it was justified to keep the restrictions that were decided upon at Morogoro. There has been extensive discussion of this question. It should not be difficult for us to reach agreement and, building on what was decided at Morogoro, to take decisions that will take our movement and struggle further forward.

The decision of the Morogoro Conference helped us to overcome many shortcomings and to gear our organization to make a more effective contribution to the mounting struggle inside our country and the anti-imperialist offensive of the peoples internationally. For, indeed, as the world forces of reaction basked in a passing glow of superior strength in 1969, the revolutionary and democratic movement was engaged in ever mounting struggles to wrest victory from the oppressors and the exploiters. Five years after our Conference, the situation in our country, in our region and in other parts of the world was very different.

Already by 1969 the masses of our people had begun to stir, in the process of overcoming the reverses and relative lull imposed on us by the brutal counter-offensive that the enemy had unleashed and which had resulted not only in the banning of the ANC, but also in the Rivonia and other arrests, the assassination and execution of patriots and the systematic use of torture as an instrument of state power.

In particular, the youth and the workers were once more taking up the cudgels, engaging in boycott and strike actions during 1972 and 1973. Student organizations and trade unions were formed which served as the means to arouse the people and mobilize them to attain the level of mass activity which we had last seen with the general strike of 1961 organized to oppose the establishment of a racist republic and to demand one that was representative of all the people of our country. Black Consciousness became a fact of our political life during this period.

In part, the resumed mass activity in our country was inspired by the stirring battles that our combatants had fought in Zimbabwe. Our successes in sending cadres of Umkhonto we Sizwe into the country, through the machineries of the Revolutionary Council which had been established at the Morogoro Conference, raised the confidence of the masses of our people in their own ability to confront the apartheid regime successfully.

At the same time, our organized contact with the people had improved. The voice of our movement was also reaching our people through increased propaganda, both written and through radio. In short, both politically and militarily, our people were once more beginning to feel the organized presence of our movement among them and drew courage from this, to break out of the state of dormancy that the enemy had sought to impose on us through a policy of terror.

Outside our country, on the eve of our conference at Morogoro, the international democratic struggle had erupted with particular intensity especially in Western Europe and North America. In 1968, millions of people in these regions joined in mass struggles for the democratization of their societies and in favour of a just world order. But as we have said, the counter-revolution succeeded in Chile; in 1973. Salvador Allende was murdered, with hundreds of others. Thousands of others were imprisoned, tortured and driven into exile. With the coming to power of the Pinochet junta, the Vorster regime found an ally in South America. However, these events did not and could not change the fact that the progressive forces were advancing. In 1972, the Soviet Union and the United States had concluded a treaty limiting strategic nuclear weapons. This was an important victory of the world peace forces which had been engaged in struggle for decades to save humanity from a nuclear holocaust.

In 1973, the Arab armies succeeded in inflicting a major defeat on Zionist Israel for the first time in a quarter of a century, forcing US imperialism to seek new measures to protect its client state in the Middle East. At the same time, the prestige of the African liberation movements had grown to such an extent that for the first time, in 1973, the OAU Summit voted to seat the liberation movements at all OAU meetings as observers. That advance within the OAU was also accompanied by the further improvement of our relations with the independent states of our region. In the years 1973-74, the ANC normalized its relations with the Governments of Botswana and Lesotho. This underlined the importance of the countries of our region in terms of their support for the cause of the liberation of our country.

In this respect, we should note and pay tribute to the sterling role that the independent states of our region have played in the furtherance of our struggle. Today, we meet in one of these, among people who assisted us even before their independence and who are today hosting this important gathering. All of these countries have, each according to its ability, including the latest among them to achieve independence, made it possible for us to survive outside the borders of our country and to advance our cause at home and abroad. We have to ensure that, at all times, we guard the fraternal relations that exist between them and ourselves, whatever strains these relations may come under now and again.

Other countries in our continent and Africa as a whole have also played an important role in the struggle against the apartheid regime, confirming the primary importance of our continent as our first rear base.

During 1973, in an outstanding victory for the world forces

of progress, US imperialism was compelled to enter into agreements with the genuine representatives of the people of Vietnam, as a result of which US forces withdrew from Vietnam. The puppet regimes of Thieu and Lon Nol were left to fend for themselves. This victory, in particular, symbolized the end of a chapter in world history which had been characterized by a determined drive by world imperialism, led by the USA, to impose its will on the peoples of the world. The collapse of this policy in the battlefields of Indo-China, and in the streets of the USA itself, created increased possibilities for an accelerated progressive transformation of the world, including our region of southern Africa.

It was in this situation that Portuguese fascism collapsed, thanks to the heroic struggles waged by the peoples in the African Portuguese colonies and the democratic forces in Portugal itself. That was in 1974, five years after the Morogoro Conference and five years after the US Government had reached its conclusion that 'the white (regimes) are here to stay'.

It was also during the same year that the leaders of the Zimbabwe liberation movement were released from Smith's dungeons in preparation for a negotiated settlement of the Zimbabwe question. Some of them had spent more than a decade in detention. Further afield, in Europe, again in 1974, the fascist military junta in Greece was defeated and democracy restored to that country.

Thus we can say that in the five year period after the Morogoro Conference the balance of forces had shifted radically in our favour, both regionally and globally. If in 1969 the apartheid leaders were revelling in the permanence and invulnerability of their power, by 1974 they had to sing a different tune.

In that year, Pik Botha made the hollow promise that 'we shall do everything in our power to move away from discrimination based on race or colour'. Vorster followed him a few days later pleading: 'Give South Africa a six-months chance by not making our road harder than it is already'. But, of course, the apartheid regime had no intention of addressing itself to the fundamental question of majority rule in South Africa. Rather, it was involved in a determined effort during 1974 to break out of its international isolation and to legitimate itself, particularly in Africa. Through this offensive, originally carried out in secret, which it described as detente, the racist regime sought to isolate the ANC from independent Africa, to defeat the strategy of armed struggle for the liberation of South Africa and drag Africa into a dialogue that would help to perpetuate the apartheid system.

In this offensive, the apartheid regime and its allies sought, among other things, to utilize a faction which had emerged within our ranks and which posed as the true defender of the policy of our movement. This is the group which ultimately emerged in public under the name 'ANC (African Nationalist)'. This faction resorted to the well-tried counter-revolutionary positions of anti-communism and racist chauvinism, in an effort to change the strategic orientation of our movement, undermine the unity of the democratic forces of our country and win recognition for itself by the most backward forces in world politics. By a policy of vilification and outright lies, it tried to discredit the leadership of our movement and to foment a rebellion from within the ANC in the hope that it would regain the positions it had lost at the Morogoro Conference. For its activities this faction won the public recognition of the Pretoria regime which showered praises on it as the genuine leadership of the ANC and of our people.

True to the traditions of the ANC and in the interest of the maximum unity of our movement and people, our leadership worked hard to show these people the error of their ways and to reintegrate them within the structures of our movement. Many of them had made important contributions to the advance of our struggle and were leading cadres of our organization. As part of this process, we held a Conference of the ANC in 1971 where the differences that had emerged within the ANC were discussed. That Conference reaffirmed the decisions taken by the Morogoro Conference as well as the general strategy and tactics of our movement. It also agreed that members of this faction should still be given specific tasks within the movement, taking into account their seniority. In the end, our efforts came to nothing as this group continued its factional activities.

Nevertheless, such was the level of consciousness and the commitment of the membership to the basic positions of the ANC, that this faction could not and did not succeed in its purposes. This important victory had important implications in the decisive struggle for the unity of our people and the broad movement for national liberation . . .

4
THE SOWETO UPRISING

Introduction

In October 1976, having been accorded the status of official observer at the United Nations, Tambo addressed the General Assembly as the legitimate representative of the South African people. He spoke against the background of the Soweto uprising which had begun on the 16 June and reached its pinnacle in the countrywide stay-at-home in September. The June events initiated popular protest that has kept the regime off balance ever since. What began as a student demonstration against the use of Afrikaans as a medium of instruction in black schools, became an uprising against the apartheid system. The scale of revolt was unprecedented and, although by the end of 1977 the popular rebellion had subsided, the political struggle for liberation was transformed.

During the Soweto uprising Black Consciousness was the dominant ideological current in the townships amongst militant youth. They rejected the paternalism of white liberalism and eschewed all organizational ties with whites in affirming a cultural identity as blacks. The state responded by banning most Black Consciousness organizations in 1977 and murdering one talented leader, Steve Biko.

But the fact that the popular rebellion did not become an insurrection pointed up limitations in Black Consciousness ideology. There had been a lack of political direction to guide the outbreak of collective anger in the townships and, although there was some solidarity between the youth and workers, the gulf had not been bridged. Among the youth there arose an awareness that revolution required organization and comprehensive policies capable of guiding struggle through different phases. Whatever the strengths of the upsurge of 1976 they lacked a strategy and tactics which could only be found in the leadership of the ANC. Many

[handwritten margin note: BC, lacked strategy + tactics of ANC. Showing ANC were better @ some things.]

Soweto youth underwent a re-evaluation of Black Consciousness and some leading Black Consciousness thinkers like Biko came to accept the policies and leadership of the ANC. There was an exodus of thousands of young militants from South Africa who found their way to the ANC. Umkhonto was boosted by the new intake of highly motivated recruits and guerrilla activity inside South Africa in the late 1970s reached a new peak. At the end of the decade the changed balance of forces tilted even further towards liberation as the struggle for independence in Zimbabwe reached its climax.

The Soweto uprising evoked a strong wave of sympathy around the world. The ANC was called upon to respond and explain the significance of the mood of rebellion seen on television screens. It was also required to explain its own relevance to the new situation, especially as the militants at home often seemed to be acting independently. ANC representatives at international meetings spelled out the character of the movement, its perspectives for struggle and the requirements of the impending revolution. It was soon apparent that the long years of patient work externally had brought recognition for the ANC as the leading force in the overthrow of apartheid.

4.1 BLACK CONSCIOUSNESS AND THE SOWETO UPRISING

(Extract from the Political Report of the National Executive Committee to the second National Consultative Conference, Lusaka, 16-23 June 1985)

. . . As we have said, it was during this period that the Black Consciousness Movement emerged as a distinct political and organizational force within our country. Naturally, the ANC had to define its attitude towards this force. In a statement issued after its second session in 1973, the NEC said:

In the last few years . . . there has come into being a number of black organizations whose programmes, by espousing the democratic, anti-racist positions that the ANC fights for, identify them as part of the genuine forces of the revolution.

The NEC went on to elaborate the following important positions:

> The assertion of the national identity of the oppressed black peoples is . . . not an end in itself. It can be a vital force of the revolutionary action involving the masses of the people. For it is in struggle, in the actual physical confrontation with the enemy, that the people gain a lasting confidence in their own strength and in the inevitability of final victory — it is through action that the people acquire true psychological emancipation.

sees BC as a phase toward emancipation

Proceeding from these positions, the ANC sought to establish relations with the forces represented in the BCM and to impart to them the collective revolutionary experience of our people contained in and carried forward by our organization. Our aim was to establish close fraternal relations with this movement and encourage it to grow, but as an instrument for the mass mobilization of our people into struggle.

The process I am describing was by no means easy and straightforward. Already, the idea was beginning to emerge among some circles, particularly outside our country, that the BCM could consolidate itself as, at worst, a political formation to replace the ANC and, at least, a parallel movement enjoying the same legitimacy as the ANC.

It was of primary importance that we should deny our opponents any and both of these possibilities. Despite the severe setbacks we had suffered during the sixties, the enemy had failed to remove the ideas and prestige of the ANC from among our people. This, together with the activities that we undertook within the country, meant that the youth whom the BCM was organizing were at least conscious of the ANC, despite the fact that many had grown up without any direct contact with us. This served as a basis for us to score significant achievements in terms of building our relations with

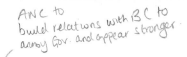
ANC to build relations with BC to annoy Gov. and appear stronger.

activists of the BCM and frustrating the scheme to build up a so-called Third Force.

It is also important at this stage to recall that, during this period, our movement was confronted with strong pressure from within the OAU to unite with the PAC. The leadership and the membership jointly resisted this pressure because we were convinced that such unity must grow in struggle among forces that are actually confronting the enemy. We were, further, not prepared to lend credibility to a group which, even then, had discredited itself as a divisive factor within our broad movement, whose complete collapse would help to limit the possibilities of the counter-revolution to plant its agents among the masses of our people.

In our discussions, we should take all these historical experiences into account because, as we shall show later, the idea of a Third Force did not disappear and is still with us today. Its creation will remain a strategic objective of the forces of counter-revolution.

In this regard, it is important to confront the matter objectively that within it, our broad movement for national liberation contains both a nationalist and a socialist tendency. Our national democratic revolution has both class and national tasks which influence one another. This is natural given the nature of our society and oppression and our historical experience. One of the outstanding features of the ANC is that it has been able to encompass both these tendencies within its ranks, on the basis of the common acceptance of the Freedom Charter as a programme that encapsulates the aspirations of our people, however varied their ideological positions might otherwise be.

The forces of counter-revolution continuously seek to separate these tendencies both politically and organizationally, set them at loggerheads and thus divide the national liberation movement. That is why the enemy always speculates about divisions between 'Marxists' and 'nationalists' within our ranks. It is on this basis that the PAC was formed, as well as the group we have spoken of which called itself ANC (African Nationalist). Our enemies had entertained hopes that the

BCM would emerge, survive and grow as the organized representative of the 'nationalist tendency' within the national democratic revolution, independent of the ANC.

These issues are of relevance to this day particularly because certain elements within the country, which describe themselves as belonging to the Black Consciousness movement, have set themselves against the democratic movement. At the same time, significant numbers of democratic activists, particularly from among the youth, see the ANC as a socialist party and project it as such. Though it came into being later than the period up to 1974 that we have been talking about, it might be appropriate at this stage to refer also to the formation within the ANC of a 'left' faction which dubbed itself the 'Marxist Tendency' within the ANC. This faction came out in opposition to our ally, the South African Communist Party and sought to shift both SACTU and the ANC in a so-called left direction. Members of this group are no longer within our ranks. It is, however, true that some of their ideas have penetrated sections of the democratic movement inside our country. These need to be combated, once more, to ensure that this movement does not splinter into left and right factions.

We cannot over-emphasize the strategic importance of ensuring the unity of the ANC, the broad democratic movement and the masses of our struggling people on the basis of our programme, our strategy and tactics. In the five year period immediately following the Morogoro Conference, we can report that our movement achieved these objectives in the face of actual attempts to divide us.

We have already referred to the contribution that the BCM made to the activization of our people into struggle. This is a positive contribution that we must recognize and to which we must pay tribute. We should also recognize the significant input that the BCM made towards further uniting the black oppressed masses of our country, by emphasizing the commonness of their oppression and their shared destiny. These views were built on political positions that our movement had long canvassed and fought for. Nevertheless, we must still express our appreciation of the contribution that the BCM made in this regard while recognizing the limitations of this *ANC* movement which saw our struggle as racial, describing the entire white population of our country as 'part of the problem'. → *creating Apartheid*.

Taking into account the collective experience of our people, our principled positions and the tasks of our revolutionary movement, our Conference will also have to address itself to the question of the unity of the motive forces of our revolution and the need, at all times, to take correct positions on the national question.

We should also draw attention to the fact, whose organizational and operational implications will be spelt out in the NEC report as presented by the Secretary-General, that the Morogoro Conference viewed our struggle as politico-military. The Revolutionary Council was mandated to conduct such a struggle. The document on strategy and tactics adopted at the Morogoro Conference discussed at length the issue of the relationship between the political and military struggles, emphasizing the primacy of the former. In the actual conduct of our struggle in the period up to 1974, we concentrated on political work, especially on the task of establishing contact with our people at home and rebuilding our organized presence inside the country. On the military side, we also emphasized organizational work, namely, the building up of Umkhonto we Sizwe inside the country in terms of both men and materials.

We raise this question because we shall have to discuss it once again but in the light of our experience, the current situation and our perspectives. This issue bears not only on the conduct of our struggle inside the country, but also on such questions as our structure, the training and deployment of cadres and the exercise of the function of leadership. Thus we need maximum clarity on this issue so that we can proceed towards the seizure of power in the most effective and efficient manner possible.

When we entered the second five year period after the Morogoro Conference, we were better prepared to face the challenges that this period posed. With the benefit of hindsight, we could possibly describe the years 1969-74 as, for us, the Period of Regrouping and Recovery.

It was during this period that we fully took into account the fact that our reverses at home, particularly during the years 1963-65, compounded by the death of our late President, Chief A.J Luthuli in 1967, had imposed on our External Mission the task of representing and leading our movement as a whole, including its internal units. We had to carry out the process of reconstruction from outside. There were no structures inside the country to receive the units of the Luthuli Detachment that had trained outside. It was the response to this reality, the fact that this External Mission took on those internal tasks in a serious and determined manner, that gave the period 1969-74 its distinctive character and enabled us to recover the possibility to move further forward, confidently, to exploit the greater possibilities that emerged in the next five year period.

We could perhaps characterize this latter phase as a Period of Consolidation and Further Advance. It was a period during which our movement worked to defend the gains we had made and to use those gains further to step up the struggle, finally to liquidate the achievements that the enemy had scored when it launched its campaign of extreme reaction in the early sixties.

When the NEC considered the implications of the accession to power of Frelimo and the MPLA in their respective countries, it concluded that there has emerged in southern Africa a new kind of state power. Fundamentally new types of property were being established and consequently new social relations were emerging. For the peoples of southern Africa, Mozambique and Angola were the latest examples demonstrating that exploitative relations are a transitional phase in the development of human society.

We were convinced that the option made by Angola and Mozambique for a socialist orientation of development was viewed by the imperialists as a declaration of war on their economic and ideological positions in a region that has

Oliver Tambo with pupils and teachers at the Solomon Mahlangu Freedom College in Morogoro, Tanzania. *(IDAF)*

traditionally been one of their preserves on the continent. Imperialism was therefore bound to use all means and methods at its disposal to seek to destroy the popular power that had come into being in our sub-continent.

We also concluded that the white minority regimes of Salisbury and Pretoria, together with their imperialist allies, saw in SWAPO, the Patriotic Front and the ANC, liberation movements that were determined to dismantle the colonial economic structures and install a new socio-economic order in the region. We were certain that the imperialists knew that such a victory would put an end to the continued plunder of our region by international capital and reinforce the advances made in Angola and Mozambique towards complete national and social emancipation.

As Conference will recall, Mozambique attained its independence on 25 June 1975. In this regard, we might consider sending a message from this Conference to the people of Mozambique on the occasion of the 10th anniversary of their independence. Angola became independent on November 11 of the same year. Between these dates and the time of the revolution in Portugal, a complicated situation obtained both in Mozambique and in Angola, with the forces of counter-revolution involved in a series of desperate assaults aimed at destroying Frelimo and the MPLA and preserving Mozambique and Angola as objects of imperialist plunder. The most determined counter-revolutionary offensive took place in Angola, spearheaded by an open invasion of that country by the racist army of the Pretoria regime and supported by US imperialism and puppet forces within Angola. At the same time, the progressive forces in Africa and the world were forced to wage an intense struggle for the recognition of the People's Republic of Angola.

Our National Executive Committee kept this situation under review continuously. We took the positions that we must defend the MPLA as the proven representative of the people of Angola, assert the legitimacy of the People's Republic of Angola, as well as support the right of the people of this country to determine their own path of development and to establish their own system of international relations. In this way, supporting the positions of the MPLA, we came out against the notion of a government of national unity that would have legitimized the puppet UNITA and FNLA. We stood for the immediate expulsion of the Pretoria invasion force from Angola and fought against all imperialist intervention.

We were convinced that the counter-revolution had to be defeated. Failure to achieve this victory would have constituted a severe setback not only for the people of Angola, but also for the liberation struggle in our region and the process of the progressive renewal of our continent. Accordingly, we battled within the OAU in particular for acceptance of our positions, which coincided with those of many countries on our continent. The heroism of the people of Angola, the firm and timely support rendered to them by the socialist community of nations and the world anti-imperialist movement, coupled with the relative weakness of the forces of reaction, succeeded to save the People's Republic and thus further to shift the international balance of forces in our favour.

We should bear in mind that these events were taking place at a time when the Pretoria regime was engaged in its 'detente' offensive, using the Zimbabwe question in particular as a vehicle to gain acceptance for itself on the African continent. We opposed this manoeuvre, determined to ensure that, in the interests of our own struggle, the counter-revolution must not succeed.

We confronted the enemy offensive as a united movement, backed by our people inside the country, who had demonstrated their understanding, acceptance and support for the revolutionary perspective posed by Frelimo and the MPLA, by organizing the 'Frelimo rallies' for which some leaders and activists of the Black Consciousness Movement had been arrested, sentenced and gaoled.

Up to that time, these events represented the sharpest confrontation we had had with the apartheid regime in the struggle for the support of our region and of Africa as a whole. In a thousand battles and skirmishes, the question was being answered — would our continent march on from the victories in Angola, Guinea-Bissau and Mozambique to new successes or would we fall back in the face of the enemy counter-offensive, submit to neo-colonialism and the perpetuation of white minority rule. It is no exaggeration to say that our movement played a role, however limited, in getting our continent to decide against any retreat, in favour of a continued advance against racism, colonialism and imperialism. To prepare for this heightened confrontation with the racist regime, our movement had met in Conference from 17 to 20 March 1975. When we welcomed the delegates to that meeting we said: 'At no time have we at brief notice assembled such a representative meeting attended by delegates from such remote places.' We had timed our own Conference to precede the 9th Extraordinary Session of the OAU Council of Ministers which was being assembled to discuss southern Africa. We had to work to ensure that the positions we adopted at our Conference gained the acceptance of our continent as a whole.

The African ministers resolved that our continent has 'as its important prerequisite the maintenance and strengthening of unity and solidarity of Africa in confronting the new situation in southern Africa. The enemies of independent Africa realize that this unity is the most powerful weapon in the continent's arsenal. It is that unity and solidarity which Vorster, with his collaborators and supporters, is attempting to undermine. Therefore Africa's urgent need to close its ranks in facing South Africa's new tactics becomes self-evident.'

The ministers went on to reject Vorster's detente, reaffirmed their support for our movement and for armed struggle. They rejected the Bantustans and called for the complete isolation of apartheid South Africa and characterized her as 'the final major obstacle to Africa's march to liberation' .

All this signified that Pretoria's political offensive into Africa had been defeated. The continent and our movement adopted the same positions. Ten months later, Pretoria's military offensive into Africa, in this case its invasion of Angola, was also defeated.

The People's Republic of Angola had emerged victorious. Both these results were of great importance to our struggle. They demonstrated that the Pretoria regime could not impose its will on the people of Africa. The myth of the invincibility of the South African army of aggression and oppression was destroyed and buried for ever. Young white South Africans began to question themselves as to whether they should allow themselves to die in defence of the apartheid system.

These victories had also conclusively demonstrated that our movement and struggle enjoyed sufficient support among the peoples of Africa for our continent successfully to defend and advance the interests of our revolution regardless of the means and methods our enemy used to subvert us and regardless of the support it had from its imperialist allies.

The events of 1974-76, however, also confirmed the importance of independent Africa as our rear base and the need for us to ensure that at all times it remains a reliable rear base. The justice of our cause speaks for itself. At the same time, the ignominy of the apartheid system addresses itself directly to the hearts of the hundreds of millions of the African masses on our continent. And yet, we have to be with these masses continuously, maintain contact with their brother governments and in struggle retain Africa on our side as territory hostile to the apartheid regime. Any weakness on our part in this sphere inevitably raises serious complications for our struggle.

Conversely, during this period, the victories of the national liberation movement in southern Africa in particular acted as an important factor in raising the level of militancy among our own people and spurring them further into action. Great new possibilities emerged for us to reach into our country. Because allies with whom we had co-operated for a decade and more in the struggle for national liberation were now in power in Mozambique and Angola, a whole variety of other opportunities to increase our effectiveness emerged. One outcome of these developments was that, from 1975 onwards, we were able to establish an official presence in the Kingdom of Swaziland. Among the independent countries of southern Africa, Malawi was the only one with which we had and have no relations. At the same time, and as a consequence of these developments, the political crisis of the apartheid regime began to emerge into the open.

Building on what had been achieved in the past, we continued to expand our contact with the masses of our people as well as their democratic organizations, including the trade unions and the Black Consciousness Movement as well as the religious community within our country.

This is the appropriate occasion to disclose that in the course of this work we had, by 1976, arrived at the point where the time had come for us to meet that leading representative of the BCM, the late Steve Biko. By this time Steve and his colleagues had arrived at the following positions:

(a) That the ANC is the leader of our revolution;
(b) That the Black People's Convention should
    concen trate on mass mobilization;
(c) That the BPC should function within the context of
    the broad strategy of our movement; and
(d) That a meeting between the leadership of the BPC
    and ourselves was necessary.

Arrangements were made for us to meet Steve Biko in 1976. Unfortunately, it proved impossible to bring Steve out of the country for this meeting. Another attempt was made in 1977 but this also did not succeed. Subsequent arrangements also failed as, for instance, Barney Pityana was arrested when he was due to lead another delegation. Steve Biko was of course subsequently murdered.

These events might be of historic interest now, particularity as the BCM as an organized force was severely affected by the bans imposed by the Pretoria regime on the BCM organizations in 1977. However, this experience proved the correctness of the positions we had taken to deal with the BCM not in a competitive spirit but to relate to it as part of the broad movement for national liberation. The achievements made in building our relations with this movement and giving its members access to our policy, strategy and tactics were of great importance in enabling us to defeat a determined attempt by the forces of counter-revolution to build a so-called Third Force, especially in the aftermath of Soweto.

This uprising of 1976-77 was, of course, the historic watershed of the period we are reporting about. Within a short period of time, it propelled into the forefront of our struggle millions of young people, thus immeasurably expanding the active forces of the revolution and inspiring other sections of our people into activity.

Naturally, these heroic struggles had a profound impact on our organization as well. They resulted in the accelerated expansion of our movement both inside and outside the country. That process of course resulted in increasing the relative proportion of the youth and students within our ranks. It brought into our midst comrades many of whom had had very little contact with the ANC, if any. It put at the immediate disposal of our movement militant cadres who were ready and yearning to carry out even the most difficult missions that the movement wished to give them. It increased many times over the responsibility we had to maintain large numbers of people outside our country.

Conference will discuss the question whether, as a movement, we have built of this new army of our revolution the kind of cadre that the new situation and the tasks that we face demand. The issue of a proper cadre policy that takes into account our human resources and our perspectives is of fundamental importance to our further advance.

In this regard, we would like to take this opportunity to pay glorious tribute to the older cadres of our movement, those that fought in Zimbabwe in 1967 and 1968, those who were the delegates at the Morogoro Conference. These same cadres manned the operations structures of the Revolutionary Council. They are the ones who were sent back into our country to carry out the organizational tasks that the Morogoro Conference and the Revolutionary Council had elaborated. Many of these are now serving long sentences in Robben Island.

Indeed, we could say that had it not been for the steadfast commitment and loyalty of these comrades to our organization and our revolution, there might very well have been no ANC to join when the youth poured out of our country after the Soweto uprising. The new situation that confronts us, the tasks that this Conference will decide upon, requires that we pay attention to the question of utilizing to the full the experience and maturity of these outstanding cadres of our movement.

The message of the Soweto uprising was clear enough. It was that we had entered a new phase in our struggle, one that would be marked by an ever-sharpening confrontation between the masses of our people and the apartheid regime, one in which the mass offensive would, to all intents and purposes, be continuous and uninterrupted. It would also place the issue of the resumption of the armed struggle on our agenda, as an extremely urgent question in the face of the reality that the apartheid regime was using, and would continue to use, maximum force against our risen but unarmed people.

We have characterized the period we are discussing as one of Consolidation and Further Advance. As we have been trying to demonstrate, we had been consolidating our gains and on that basis taking further steps forward especially with regard to political work. We have also referred to the fact that from 1972 we had also been sending cadres of Umkhonto we Sizwe into the country to prepare exactly for the resumption of the armed struggle. In brief, we were getting better prepared to assume our place as the active vanguard force of our struggling people, within the country.

The Soweto uprising demonstrated that our country was a veritable powder keg. A decade and a half after the military suppression of the general strike of 1961, the pent-up revolutionary fury of the people rose to the surface. It became possible to conclude that such uprisings would become a permanent feature of our struggle. Our movement, as other revolutionary movements before it, has a responsibility to take advantage of such moments when the activity of the masses is increased a thousand-fold, when the masses are prepared to fight to the finish for the destruction of their adversary.

Understanding all this, it was however true that in 1976-77 we had not recovered sufficiently to take full advantage of the situation that crystallized from the first events of 16 June 1976. Organizationally, in political and military terms, we were too weak to take advantage of the situation created by the uprising. We had very few active ANC units inside the country. We had no military presence to speak of. The communication links between ourselves outside the country and the masses of our people were still too slow and weak to meet the situation such as was posed by the Soweto uprising. An outstanding role in this situation was, however, played by those of our comrades who were inside the country, many of them former Robben Island prisoners. Through their contact with the youth, they were able to make an ANC input, however limited, in the conduct of the bloody battles of 1976-77.

Some of them are with us in this hall today. But among them we would like to select for special mention the late Comrade Joe Gqabi, former Robben Island prisoner, member of the NEC and our first representative in Zimbabwe. This implacable enemy of the apartheid regime was assassinated in cold blood by agents of this regime in July 1981 because the racists knew what Joe was worth to our organization and our revolution. They could see that the seeds he had planted among the youth in Soweto in 1976, hardly a year after his release from prison, and in the subsequent years, were bearing bitter fruit for the oppressors and, for us, magnificent combatants for the liberation of our country.

The participation of the comrades we have spoken about, in assisting to guide the Soweto uprising, once more emphasized the vital necessity for us to have a leadership core within the country, known by us and in touch with the people, dedicated, brave, with clear perspectives and thus able to lead. The need further to strengthen our leadership structures within the country continues to press on us with ever-increasing insistence. It is an objective that must be realized without much delay.

We have said that the Soweto uprising also raised the urgent question of the resumption of armed struggle. Happily, in the period 1977-79, we were able once more to carry out military operations. This was thanks to organizational achievements inside the country, an improved organizational capacity outside and, not least, the availability of cadres whom we could prepare relatively quickly to return to the country. We should, of course, also mention that much of this we owed to the changed balance of forces in southern Africa brought about by the collapse of Portuguese colonialism and the capture of power by our revolutionary allies.

We cannot over-emphasize the importance of those historic blows struck by units of the June 16th and other detachments of the people's army, Umkhonto we Sizwe. The members of those units, such as Solomon Kalushi Mahlangu, have, despite their youth, left us with a tradition of combat and fearlessness which inspires both the young and the old to the acts of peerless bravery which our people are displaying today.

Those early actions signalled that Umkhonto we Sizwe lives, and lives among the people, within our country. They signified the defeat of the strategy of our enemy which, for more than a decade, had sought to ensure that no trained unit of our army ever entered South Africa and, if it did, that it would never carry out a single operation. They established, in action, the fact that there exist in our country two armies, one a people's army and the other an oppressor's army. They meant the defeat of all efforts to liquidate the armed struggle in our country.

By the same token, they signalled the inevitability of our victory. After all, both Frelimo and the MPLA had liberated their countries through armed struggle. In Zimbabwe, the Smith regime and its backer and ally in Pretoria were running into serious problems exactly as a result of the escalation of armed struggle. The apartheid regime was pouring more and more troops into Namibia in a vain attempt to halt the armed liberation struggle conducted by SWAPO. It was therefore obligatory that, from the small but historic beginnings of 1977-79, we should escalate the armed struggle by delivering bigger blows and on a continuous basis.

It would be a grave error on our part if we did not, at this point, refer, however briefly, to the socialist countries. The period we are discussing once more confirmed these countries as allies we can always rely upon, a secure rear base without which our struggle would be even more difficult and protracted. To this day, the socialist countries continue to play an important supporting role in many aspects of our work. Always willing to consider and respond to our requests, every day they demonstrate an unwavering commitment to see our revolution through to the end. As a movement, we need to be conscious of this all the time and protect our friendship and co-operation with the socialist community of nations very jealously.

The forces of reaction are always busy trying to detach us from these countries, knowing very well that, were they to succeed, they would weaken our organization and our struggle to such a degree that they could then defeat us. The conditions that US imperialism has arrogantly placed on the independence of Namibia aim specifically to achieve this objective, to deny the peoples of our region the enormous and disinterested support of the socialist countries and thus make us easy prey to continued imperialist domination . . .

4.2 MOZAMBIQUE IS LIBERATED
(Presidential Address to the Extended Meeting of the National Executive Committee of the ANC, April 1975)

Events across the globe in the past 12 months have moved at a new speed, in some instances, a dazzling pace. The period from the Lisbon *coup* to the installation of a transitional government in Mozambique, representing a rapid process of demolition of a colonial system, was characterized by a breathless succession of a historic transformation. The competition for time between the forces for progress, pressing hard for victory, and the forces of imperialism, seeking to gain time, for regrouping and for counter-offensive, raised

The liberation of Mozambique — celebrating with the late Samora Machel. *(IDAF)*

the whole tempo of conflict, and set a new urgency in the speed for executing political programmes — it introduced a kind of jet-era in the world of struggles for social transformations.

In relation to this new era of speed, we, the ANC, have to identify our position. Do we belong to the past? Are we properly marching with the times? I am glad to say that the ANC certainly has the potential if this meeting is anything to go by. For at no time have we at brief notice assembled such a representative meeting attended by delegates from such remote places.

This is a sign of vigour and vitality, if it is a sign of nothing else. It means we can rise in unison to respond to a challenge, to give answer to a clarion call to attack with massive might as our people have done before, as our own MK has done in the recent past. It means that, at least politically, the ANC is yet a force — it may be ill-managed, poorly directed and badly led — but still a force.

It is therefore with a feeling of strength and power that I wish, in the name of our beleaguered and fighting people, to congratulate you all for successfully solving all problems that stood in the way of your attending this meeting. Like an army of our people, you did not stop to reason why, you assembled as ordered.

. . . We must together assume responsibility for the leadership of our struggle and for the involvement of all our members and people. The ANC must be turned into an efficient and high-powered machine, able to lead a mighty and victorious struggle.

Having analyzed the situation and decided on the action to be taken, this meeting must address itself to the task of turning our movement into a power. The Revolutionary Council of the ANC met here last week. The Ministerial Council of the OAU meets in Dar next month. Both meetings focus exclusively on the struggle of our people in South Africa. The NEC must fortify and give political coverage to the former; it must give guidance to the latter.

This meeting, in its timing, has an element of inevitability.

It proved impracticable to hold it earlier: it would have been irresponsible to delay it further. It had to take place this week, on the 17th day of this month, rather like the inevitability of an infinitely greater event on the 17th year of this century. Let me invoke the revolutionary genius, discipline, determination, vision and sheer hard work which went into the Great October Socialist Revolution in calling upon you at this meeting to gear our movement for the accomplishment of the hardest task that has faced any people in the colonial history of Africa — a movement entrusted by history with a glorious and noble task — the conquest of power for the people from the high concentrate of racists, capitalists, colonialists and imperialists who have turned our country into a veritable bastion of reaction.

A rapidly changing balance of world forces has shifted the revolutionary battleground in Africa to our country, and has confronted us with an immediate challenge — complex in its content and global in its dimensions:

— Within our country, the meaning of a liberation struggle under arms, and the inevitability of its success, has been demonstrated afresh by Frelimo and other liberation forces, in addition to the examples of Vietnam, Algeria, Guinea-Bissau, Angola and the 1973 Middle-East October war.

— The masses have seen the great possibilities of their own liberation movement and look to us for guidance and leadership into action.

— Our great workers are spearheading the offensive and increasingly harassing the exploiters as part of the struggle for the seizure of political power.

— A new generation of young revolutionaries, embracing all races, is beginning to take to the political battlefield.

— The Bantustan policy is under challenge.

— Our gallant women are becoming restive, and those of them with us here have displayed a devotion to service which does great credit to the glorious record of our

fighting women in South Africa.
— The demand for the release of the peoples leaders from imprisonment has taken firm root in the country.

On the other hand, the white liberal politicians, ever ready to diffuse the tides of revolution, are sparing no energies in pursuing their accustomed reformist campaign — now given surprising encouragement from surprising centres in Africa.
An intensive, concentrated propaganda campaign with echoes in Africa, America and Western Europe has been unleashed on our people, designed to make them relax to false hopes of 'change' within the general context of a spirit of so-called detente, whereby fascism, with all its unchanging nature, is expected by some miracle to make a voluntary and even unsolicited surrender of its power and domination in peaceful response to demands by some spokesmen. But the fascist enemy — under the the SA Prime Minister, Vorster, during recent talks in Monrovia, capital of Liberia, smoke-screen of precisely this peaceful-solution talk, this talk of 'development', 'co-operation' 'financial aid' and 'detente', to mention but a few of its newly found slogans— is feverishly and rapidly strengthening its defences of the status quo in our country, recruiting allies from among our own anti-imperialist ranks, and moving out in a determined bid to break up, or sow confusion in, the international solidarity front which has contributed so massively towards the defeat of Portuguese colonialism and which has helped bring radical progressive transformations in other parts of the world.
In the situation in which we thus find ourselves today — in the interval of time since the Lisbon *coup* — it can be said our struggle stands at a temporary crossroads between, on the one hand, mounting an all-out and all-round offensive to carry forward and lead the struggle against the fascist regime: the mighty front of anti-imperialist forces which swept in our favour during last year, and on the other hand, yielding ground to the imperialist pressures symbolized in John Vorster. Is it within our present capacity to shift from the

crossroads and embark on a level of struggle in our country worthy of this time in history, in the history of southern Africa?

This is not a theoretical, or rhetorical question. It is a practical question to which this meeting must seek the most objective answer. It is a question about:

— The objective facts of the situation in South Africa;
— Our tactics in relation to the main areas of conflict in that situation;
— How we build support for the struggle among our people and among progressive forces in different parts of the world;
— How, as a revolutionary movement, we are organized for this great task.

Nothing has happened to justify change in our strategy of armed struggle. Much has happened to necessitate a review of our total effort in pursuit of the strategic objectives. Much is happening in Africa to require of us to re-state the objectives of our struggle. In this connection, let me emphasize that in its essence the forth-coming meeting of the OAU Ministerial Council is not a meeting about 'detente'. It is a meeting about the goals and future of our struggle, the future of a people colonized, oppressed, exploited and subjected to racial indignities. It is a meeting about the future of Africa.

From our point of view it is a meeting to initiate the onslaught on the stronghold of white minority rule in Africa. It is a meeting whose results will test anew Kwame Nkrumah's declaration, since adopted by all African states, that the independence of any one African country is meaningless — repeat meaningless — except in the context of the total liberation of Africa. This meeting of the NEC appropriately takes place before the OAU meeting, to let the voice of our people be heard on what we are fighting for, what support we need, and who we consider to be our comrades-in-arms and allies in that struggle.

. . . Having said this let me say once again that we have the inescapable responsibility to make the sacrifices necessary to bring us the Uhuru we demand for ourselves. It is sacrifices which constitute the best definition of what we want, the most persuasive and irresistible appeal for support, and the highest inducement to our brothers and friends to supplement our sacrifices with their own . . .

4.3 THE ANC AND THE MPLA
(Address to the First Congress of the MPLA, Luanda, December 1977)

We bring to this historic First Congress of the MPLA warmest and most fraternal greetings from the National Executive Committee of the African National Congress, from its militants and combatants, from the workers and peasants, the women and the youth; from the entire struggling people of South Africa . . .

The heroic anti-colonial struggles of the peoples of Africa for national independence, including, in particular, the armed struggles of the people of Algeria, Guinea-Bissau and Cape Verde, Angola and Mozambique, culminated in the epoch-making collapse of Portuguese colonialism in Africa. The earth-shaking victories of Frelimo and MPLA brought southern Africa to the crossroads. But the revolutionary experience accumulated during the liberation wars ensured that the people's advance towards social emancipation would not be halted.

Thus it is that as the year 1977 opened with the Third Congress of Frelimo, so it is ending with the First Congress of MPLA. Both Congresses are the collective voice of the Mozambican and Angolan peoples, proclaiming the continuation of the revolutionary struggle at a higher plain, more arduous but no less glorious than the earlier struggles. The historic significance of the First Congress of MPLA is precisely that, for southern Africa, like the Frelimo Congress, it blazes a new trail out of the crossroads towards the conquest of a socialist future for the peoples a future free of exploitation.

Our esteemed Leader, Friend and Comrade President Agostinho Neto expressed a key and important truth when he said in one of his statements that the victory of the Angolan people was 'a victory of the peoples advancing towards progress'.

This first Congress of MPLA is a victory of the Angolan people. It is also a victory of all the peoples, including the peoples of South Africa, who are pledged to fight for the creation of new socio-economic systems which will be characterized by the abolition of exploitation of man by man through ownership of productive wealth by the people themselves; characterized as well by the self-government of the ordinary working people through the institution of popular power and characterized also by a commitment to strive for a world that has been rid of the parasites that have imposed on all of us; fascism, racism and apartheid, deprivation and backwardness, ignorance, superstition and destructive wars.

Angola's orientation towards the social emancipation of her people has therefore, like Mozambique, brought to the fore, in our region, the confrontation between the liberating theory and practice of socialism and the oppressive, exploitative and anti-human system of capitalism. This latter social system is of course represented, *par excellence*, by racist South Africa itself. Hence today the open and sharp confrontations between People's Angola and Mozambique on the one side and fascist South Africa and colonial Rhodesia on the other.

Given such a juxtaposition of two diametrically opposed social systems within the same region of southern Africa, conflict and confrontation become inevitable. But of major importance for us in understanding the nature of this confrontation is the fact that the victories of the MPLA and Frelimo have become a key factor in the politics of the racist regime.

These victories have helped to deepen the general crisis of the apartheid colonial system: they have in the actuality of South African politics helped to strengthen the forces of progress and severely weaken the forces of reaction. In that fact lies the fundamental reason for the desperate determination of the Vorster regime to destroy these two People's Republics. In that also lies essentially the reason why we of the African National Congress join voices with Comrade President Neto in saying the victory of the Angolan people is indeed truly our own as well.

In the very first hours of its existence, people's Angola had to defend itself against the massive military onslaught of a mature but decaying imperialist system. The trials that confronted the MPLA even before 11 November 1975, right through to 1976 when the racist oppressor army of the Vorster regime was evicted from Angola, were not a test solely of the valour and military preparedness of MPLA and the people of Angola.

More significant in the longer term, the attempted military destruction of the People's Republic posed the question on the battlefield, had the time come for the birth of the new liberating social system in Angola? Or was the balance of forces still such that moribund imperialism, with its oppressive and exploitative system of social relations, would continue to hold sway, dictating to the people of Angola what kind of independence they should have?

The results of that contest have now become a matter of proud historical record. Progress triumphed over reaction, thanks to the heroic sacrifices of the people of Angola, supported by their progressive African allies, by Cuba, the Soviet Union and other socialist countries and by all peoples advancing towards progress.

What started as a triumphant march by the forces of reaction into the heart of Angola ended up with a deeper crisis for the Vorster regime inside South Africa itself: the humiliating defeat of Vorster's social system for which that army had been created, trained and armed to defend. The myth of the invincibility of the racist army was destroyed for ever. For the fascist regime of John Vorster, whose ultimate and principal means of survival is naked brute force, this was a stunning blow.

It proved to our own people, as well as to the more far-seeing sections of the oppressor population including especially the youth, that in the confrontation with the forces of progress, the fascist state is destined inevitably to lose, wherever that confrontation takes place, but above all, and especially, within South Africa itself.

Today the fascist regime is haunted by the spectre that large sections of the white population will, as the struggle intensifies, refuse to be used as cannon fodder to protect the interests of big capital and fascist domination. Already, thousands of white South Africans have left and are leaving the country. The regime stands in dread fear of the further narrowing of the social base of the system of apartheid domination. In this context, therefore, the so-called landslide victory scored by the Afrikaner Nationalist Party during the recent racist elections in South Africa can only be fragile and temporary.

Terrified at the prospect of the victory of the forces of progress within the country in the aftermath and as a direct continuation of the popular victory in Angola, the Vorster regime unleashed the bloody terror that is today symbolized by Soweto. By this brutal means the enemy thought he would solve that part of his crisis which is characterized by the ready acceptance among our people of the liberating ideas and the revolutionary practice of the MPLA.

The regime also thought that through the ruthless massacre of our people, it would once again re-establish the terrorist military and political authority that the regime's armed forces lost on the battlefields of Angola. Inevitably, the racist regime has failed dismally to achieve any of these objectives. So entrenched has the spirit of revolution among the people become that the enemy has been compelled to take extreme measures against even those who still preached peaceful transition to democratic rule.

The African National Congress with its allies is the representative inside apartheid South Africa of the kind of life that the people of Angola and Mozambique are striving to build, the kind of life that all peoples advancing towards progress aim for. Exactly because of this, its authority among the broad masses of our people has risen so high and has proved so indestructible that the enemy himself has had to admit this fact openly and repeatedly.

Instead of submitting to an already disproved invincibility of fascist arms, the best sons and daughters of our people have responded with enthusiasm to our call to them to swell the ranks of Umkhonto we Sizwe, our own people's army, the military wing of the ANC, and to confront the enemy with revolutionary arms now. The African National Congress therefore continues to find confirmation of the correctness of its positions from the historical experience of the MPLA.

One of these positions is that the victorious revolution cannot be defended successfully without arms. This condition is imposed on all revolutions by the fact that the forces of reaction never hesitate to attempt to reverse the historical process by force of arms. In building up our own popular army we aim therefore not only at the overthrow of the fascist regime, we aim also at building up a politically conscious and revolutionary army, conscious of its popular origin, unwavering in its democratic functions and guided by our revolutionary orientation. We know FAPLA [military arm of the MPLA] is such a force, and we know that that is why FAPLA is invincible.

We of the African National Congress visualize a South Africa in which the people shall govern, in which the wealth of the country shall be restored to the people and where the land shall be shared among those who work it. We aim to establish in our country a society free of the exploitation of man by man. We fight for a South Africa in which the people shall be guaranteed the right to work, in which it will be the duty of the people's state to ensure that the doors of learning and of culture are open to the working people. We seek to live in peace with our neighbours and the peoples of the world in conditions of equality, mutual respect and equal advantage. Those who monopolize political power, the land and the wealth of our country today, those who prohibit the distribution of everything that is progressive in literature and the arts, those who launch aggressive wars, will naturally do their best to ensure that we do not realize our goal of translating our liberation into a genuine people's liberation, leading to the radical social transformation of our country.

As revolutionaries it is our duty to deny these counter-revolutionary forces the possibility of victory. Part of that denial consists in our ensuring that no elements of the enemy's fascist state machinery, including his armed forces, remain as organized units within the new society. Angola and Mozambique have today ensured that. We also shall have to take the same path. In our view this is as true of Angola and Mozambique today as it will be true of Namibia and Zimbabwe tomorrow.

No element of the South African fascist state can be expected to defend or administer a SWAPO victory in Namibia. Equally, no element of the Rhodesian colonial state can be expected to defend or administer a Patriotic Front victory in Zimbabwe. For that reason, as in Angola and Mozambique, we support the demand for an unconditional transfer of power to SWAPO of Namibia and to the Zimbabwe Patriotic Front. The collective revolutionary experience of the peoples of southern Africa teaches us that where the enemy refuses to accede to this demand, then its realization has to be fought for. The imperialist proposals concerning Namibia and Zimbabwe are once again an attempt to ensure that the genuinely revolutionary forces of these countries are denied the possibility to bring about authentic people's liberation, to deny them the possibility of undertaking a radical transformation of their societies.

The MPLA, the organizer, the leader, the vanguard of the movement of the people of Angola for national and social emancipation, was itself confronted with similar imperialist attempts, and it successfully foiled them. But, to reach the point in the history of the Angolan struggle when it became possible to hold this First Congress, MPLA has had to fight for its very life against formidable enemies from within and from without. Imperialist reaction well understood that in order to defeat the Angolan revolution, it had to pierce the heart of that revolution, it had to smother its fountainhead, precisely, it had to destroy the MPLA.

The history of the MPLA therefore constitutes almost an encyclopaedia of the strategy and tactics of the counter-revolution against the revolutionary forces of southern Africa. We have seen attempts to cut the MPLA off from contact with the masses of the people of Angola. We have seen also attempts to drive wedges within the MPLA, to foment internal strife and discord through the exploitation of tribal differences, the use of racism, the encouragement of a rabid chauvinistic nationalism, the fertilization of blind personal ambition and the vilification of the best representatives of the Angolan people.

We have seen the instigation of extreme leftist elements who, while posing as the true defenders of the interests of the people within the MPLA, were in fact involved in plots to starve the people into a state of disaffection and rebellion against the people's own fundamental interests. We have seen attempts to encourage an anti-popular spirit of militarism among the armed cadres in an effort to denigrate the political leadership and political persuasion, and put on a pedestal the force of arms.

Imperialism along with its multi-national corporations also worked extremely hard to set up an alternative third force which would pose as liberation movements while at the same time remaining in the pay of exactly the forces against whom they would claim to be waging 'liberation wars'. We have seen imperialist attempts to Balkanize and dismember Angola itself. We have seen open assassination of leaders and activists.

We have seen the forces of counter-revolution try to create animosity between the MPLA and its most tested and natural allies, especially from the Soviet Union and the Socialist Republic of Cuba. Thus would the MPLA find itself weakened and isolated and therefore ready prey to imperialist attempts to liquidate it.

We have seen all this and much more. But we have also seen the MPLA emerge from this enduring crisis triumphant, stronger than ever before. Such a record of victories is a great tribute to the revolutionary maturity of the MPLA, of Comrade Agostinho Neto personally; it is a tribute to the veterans of two gruelling liberation wars, many of them present here today; it is a tribute to all those other heroes who have sacrificed their lives for the victory of the Angolan revolution and to ensure that once that victory was won, it was not lost again.

To see the MPLA as a target of imperialist attacks from 1956 to 1977 is to gain an idea of the experience of the ANC during the same period. In December 1956, the entire leadership of the organizations opposing the racist regime, led by the ANC, was arrested and brought to common trial on charges of attempting to overthrow the racist state. More than 150 leaders faced death sentences. This enemy act consolidated the unity of the revolutionary movement as never before.

In December 1961, like the MPLA in February of that year, we decided to embark on armed struggle and formed Umkhonto we Sizwe, the armed wing of the ANC. From then on, the MPLA and ANC have shared victories and setbacks, we have shared heroes and martyrs; we have marched arm-in-arm and no imperialist wedge will ever be allowed to interpose itself between the Angolan people and the mass of the South African people. And as with the Angolan experience, the victory of the South African revolution depends on the continuation of the ANC as the organizer, the leader, the vanguard of the movement for national and social emancipation in South Africa.

The South African fascist regime declared the ANC illegal more than 17 years ago, it committed Nelson Mandela, Walter Sisulu, Govan Mbeki, Ahmed Kathrada, Dennis Goldberg, Harry Gwala and other national leaders to terms of life imprisonment. It embarked on a wide range of tactics aimed at destroying the ANC. These have included attempts to strangle our revolution by isolating our movement from its allies, especially the Soviet Union and other socialist countries. The regime has now embarked on a policy of consistent assassination of the leading cadres of our revolution. But all this has served only to heighten the determination of the people and to deepen the political crisis of the racist regime, bringing ever nearer the day when these imprisoned leaders of the people will be free to assume their rightful place among the creators of a revolutionary democratic South Africa, arm-in-arm with the builders of the new social order in Africa and in the rest of the progressive world.

We are in unison with the MPLA when we say that the masses of our people, the workers, peasants, revolutionary youth and intelligentsia as a conscious and organized force, constitute the political army of our revolution, without whom, and against whom, victory is impossible. In their name, and in the name of its armed combatants, Umkhonto we Sizwe, the African National Congress renews its pledge to continue the struggle, to fight with arms until our strategic objective of seizure of power is achieved. The people of South Africa, led by the ANC and its allies, will not betray the victory of the Angolan people led by the MPLA.

The ANC places on record its profound appreciation of the consistent all-round support given by the MPLA with a willingness which fully confirms the fact that MPLA, the Government and people of Angola, regard as their own the revolutionary struggles of peoples for national and social liberation. In giving this support, Angola is being faithful to the highest aspirations of Africa, to the basic policy of the OAU and to the principles of proletarian internationalism . . .

4.4 BUTHELEZI AND INKATHA
(Extract from the Political Report of the National Executive Committee to the second National Consultative Conference, Lusaka, 16-23 June 1985)

. . . Throughout the period after the Morogoro Conference, we had been concerned about the organization and activization of the masses of our people in the Bantustans against the apartheid system as a whole, including its Bantustan creations. Consequently we were of the view that, among other things, it was of vital importance that we should encourage the formation in the Bantustans of mass democratic organizations where none existed, and urge that those which existed should be strengthened and activized. In pursuit of these aims we maintained contacts in such Bantustans as the Transkei, Lebowa, Venda and Bophuthatswana. We are happy to welcome to this Conference one of the stalwarts who, for so long, held high the banner of genuine national liberation in one of these areas, an outstanding leader of our people, King Sabata Dalindyebo.

It was also in this context that we maintained regular contact with Chief Gatsha Buthelezi of the KwaZulu Bantustan. We sought that this former member of the ANC Youth League, who had taken up his position in the KwaZulu Bantustan after consultations with our leadership, should use the legal opportunities provided by the Bantustan programme to participate in the mass mobilization of our people on the correct basis of the orientation of the masses to focus on the struggle for a united and non-racial South Africa. In the course of our discussions with him, we agreed that this would also necessitate the formation of a mass democratic organization in the Bantustan that he headed. Inkatha originated from this agreement.

Unfortunately, we failed to mobilize our own people to take on the task of resurrecting Inkatha as the kind of organization that we wanted, owing to the understandable antipathy of many of our comrades towards what they considered as working within the Bantustan system. The task of reconstituting Inkatha therefore fell on Gatsha Buthelezi himself who then built Inkatha as a personal power base far removed from the kind of organization we had visualized, as an instrument for the mobilization of our people in the countryside into an active and conscious force for revolutionary change. In the first instance, Gatsha dressed Inkatha in the clothes of the ANC, exactly because he knew that the masses to whom he was appealing were loyal to the ANC and had for six decades adhered to our movement as their representative and their leader. Later, when he thought he had sufficient of a base, he also used coercive methods against the people to force them to support Inkatha.

During 1979, in one of its sessions, our National Executive Committee considered the very serious question of how to respond to a request by Gatsha Buthelezi for him to lead a delegation of Inkatha to meet the leadership of the ANC. By this time, divergencies were becoming evident on such questions as armed struggle and disinvestment. After due consideration, the NEC decided that it was correct to meet the Inkatha delegation, once more to explain the position of our movement, and ensure unity of approach to the main strategic requirements of the struggle. An express and agreed condition for holding the meeting was that it would be secret and its deliberations confidential. However, Gatsha announced that we had met and explained the purpose, the contents and the results of the meeting to suit his own objectives, much to the delight of the commercial press of South Africa and other forces in the world that had, in fact, concluded that Buthelezi was possibly 'the Muzorewa' of the people of South Africa.

We have dealt with Chief Gatsha Buthelezi at some length because, although his efforts are doomed to fail, in a way he is our fault. We have not done and are not doing sufficient political work among the millions of our people who have been condemned to the Bantustans. The artificial boundaries purporting to fence them off from the rest of our country do not make them any less a vital and integral part of the popular masses fighting for national liberation and social emancipation in our country.

Certain advances have been made with regard to the creation of a mass democratic movement in the Bantustans, especially in the last twelve months. At the same time, it is true that, in the main, we have not succeeded in building this movement to the level of strength that is possible and necessary. We have not even succeeded to utilize fully the considerable experiences of such elders in our midst as Comrade Elijah Mampuru.

We have to build a mass democratic movement in the countryside and, in this process, separate any existing mass organizations from their diehard counter-revolutionary leaders, redirect them to the only correct path of revolutionary action by the people themselves and, for this purpose, solve the actual political problems posed by this population in terms of their organization and activization.

Bound as we are historically to work for the greatest possible unity of the oppressed masses, and without forgetting that these masses are our reliable base, we have to deal with any personalities within these Bantustans who display a democratic consciousness, however limited.

The storm that erupted as a result of our meeting with the Inkatha delegation in 1979 demonstrated the absolute need for a clear and common understanding and an acceptance of the basic strategic and tactical positions of our movement by the membership of the ANC as a whole, our allies, the broad democratic movement of our country and the masses of our people. It also became clear that, once more, whatever the ANC did was seen by the millions of our people as a matter of vital importance to their future and one over which they had a right and duty to intervene, to express an opinion, to influence. We had defeated the attempt of the apartheid regime to isolate us from our people and reasserted our position as the representative of these masses, recognized by them as such . . .

5

DECADE OF LIBERATION

Introduction

With the rising struggle the ANC's self-confidence grew proportionately. Throughout the country it was gaining in visibility and open recognition by wider sections of the population. The paradox of an external leadership able to influence events inside the country was unravelled as many former cadres of the ANC who had seemingly dropped out of politics emerged as key personnel in the new waves of struggle. By 1980 a network of community civic associations, student bodies and trade unions all over the country were organized around principles similar to those of the ANC.

The growth of independent black trade unions was particularly spectacular. The union movement was, however, divided by sharp disagreements over strategy between 'workerists', who emphasized a limited orthodox shop-floor approach to organization, and 'charterists', who wished to link economic to wider political struggle in the context of mass political mobilization reminiscent of the 1950s. The Government provided the grounds for a new wave of political mobilization by opponents of apartheid. Government proposed a new constitution for South Africa which would set up separate Parliaments for coloureds and Asians. Africans were excluded. In trying to whip up support for the scheme, the Government opened up the political space for a great wave of protest culminating in the formation of the United Democratic Front in 1983. The UDF was launched at a large open air mass rally reminiscent in its style of former ANC meetings. The UDF articulated sympathy with ANC aims and called for the unbanning of the ANC and the release of its leaders. This extraordinary event demonstrated that the regime could not permanently prevent the struggle from surfacing into the open. Despite a barrage of proscriptions a new period of public activity dawned.

Support within the country for the ANC was matched by increasing international support. Tambo was obliged to lengthen his strides as he and a team of experienced leaders travelled the world's capitals exhorting ever greater measures to weaken the apartheid regime. Even reluctant governments were obliged to establish contact with the ANC as it became increasingly clear that it was now the dominant influence in the anti-apartheid opposition. In part, the ANC's rising popularity was due to increased military effectiveness. Strengthened by its new recruits, Umkhonto embarked on a new phase of guerrilla activity in 1980-81. Targets of key economic or military importance were selected for attack. In July 1980 heavy damage was inflicted on the SASOL oil-from-coal refinery; in August 1981 the Voortrekkerhoogte barracks were bombed; in December 1982 the apparently tight security at the Koeberg nuclear power station near Cape Town was breached and the plant sabotaged; and in May 1983 a car bomb was detonated outside the South African Air Force headquarters in Pretoria. There were several attacks on police stations and Umkhonto actions now seemed to be undertaken in solidarity with and in support of mass protest. This highlighted ANC strategy of combining military and political struggle.

The regime was aghast at these bold actions and raised the level of repression to stamp it out. It engaged in cross border raids to intimidate its neighbours. These were, however, seen both inside and outside South Africa as the works of a desperate regime and international confidence in South Africa's capacity to withstand the strains of internal unrest and world hostility began to wane. On the other hand ANC confidence about the overthrow of apartheid rose accordingly.

5.1 MAKE SOUTH AFRICA UNGOVERNABLE
(Extract from the Political Report of the National Executive Committee to the second National Consultative Conference, Lusaka, 16-23 June 1985)

This day, the opening of the National Consultative Conference of the ANC, is a great and moving moment in the history of our struggle for national liberation. The days we will spend here will live forever in the records of that struggle as marking a turning point in the history of all the people of South Africa. Our Conference itself will be remembered by our people as a council-of-war that planned the seizure of power by these masses, the penultimate convention that gave the order for us to take our country through the terrible but cleansing fires of revolutionary war to a condition of peace, democracy and the fulfilment of our people who have already suffered far too much and far too long.

. . . The United Democratic Front, that outstanding example of the political maturity of our people, is a product of the years that our country's forces of progress have spent, first, to mobilize the masses of our people into action and to draw them into mass organizational formations, second, to ensure that these masses adhere to a common political platform and, third, that this political unity finds expression in the kind of organizational unity which enables the people to move as one mass political army of revolution, under one command, focussing on the central question of all revolutions, whether peaceful or violent, the question of state power.

We take this opportunity to salute the countless patriots of our country who acted correctly and at the right moment, to make the UDF a reality, as a mass instrument of democratic change which inscribed on its banners the fundamental issue which we are about, namely the struggle for the birth of a united, democratic and non-racial South Africa.

Over the years, as we worked to build this mass political amy of revolution, it became ever clearer that the entire progressive movement of our country had a responsibility to ensure that the women of our country should be active in this

Oliver Tambo addressing the second National Consultative
Conference in Lusaka in 1985. *(IDAF)*

political army in their millions. The ANC Women's Conference held in Angola in 1981 made an important contribution towards the realization of this objective.

During 1984, our Year of the Women, we devoted even more attention to this important issue. Further progress was achieved in the mobilization and organization of our women. The position has now been firmly established in our movement that the liberation of women is an essential element and an integral part of our struggle for national and social emancipation. The end of the Decade of Women, this year, does not and cannot mean the end of the struggle for the liberation of women. We must continue this fight and ensure the active and conscious involvement of the women of our country at all levels of our mass offensive.

In 1976, not long before the Soweto uprising exploded, we accepted an invitation by the Frelimo Party to tour parts of the People's Republic of Mozambique. The purpose of this tour was to help in the mobilization of the masses of the people to support the struggle for the liberation of Zimbabwe. The specific problem was that in the areas we had to visit, and did visit, the people wanted to mobilize for the liberation of South Africa and were happy to leave the task of the liberation of Zimbabwe to other areas of the country. Acting together with the Frelimo Party, we had to persuade these masses that the immediate task confronting all of us was the freedom of Zimbabwe.

We accepted the task we were given by our revolutionary allies because as anti-imperialists, as internationalists and as Africans we were vitally interested in the independence of Zimbabwe, a country in which many of our own combatants were buried and where many others had been serving imprisonment or had been in death cells for nearly ten years.

Some of these comrades are at this Conference today. We salute them and are happy to report to them that even as we seemed to be diverting the people of Mozambique away from our own struggle, we knew that the emancipation of the people of Zimbabwe would return them to our ranks. We wanted to receive them back into our midst with the honour due to them, as we receive them today, as combat veterans who would visit Mozambique to say to these brother people that Zimbabwe is free: now is the time to crack the hardest nut of all, the apartheid regime in Pretoria. These comrades, members of the Luthuli Detachment, some of whom had to endure many years as condemned prisoners, still have a journey to make — a journey to Mozambique to complete a task that could not be completed in 1976.

When Reagan spoke about the destiny of the United States in 1980, he spoke about the export of counter-revolution. Hammered and battered, bled slowly and having confronted the brutal face of the counter-revolution for many years, by 1984 the independent countries of our region had to take some important decisions. The question that confronted them was the same that had faced Africa ten years before.

The difference between 1974 and 1984 was, of course, that the frontiers of freedom covered almost the entire border of South Africa. With the forces of reaction on the ascendancy in the greater part of the imperialist world, the same question was posed in circumstances in which it was difficult to answer in the forthright manner that Africa had replied a decade earlier.And so the People's Republic of Mozambique signed the Accord on Nkomati in March 1984. At the height of the offensive of the revolutionary movement inside South Africa, externally the same movement had to retreat — and here I am not just referring to ourselves but to the entire liberation and progressive movement of our region and indeed of Africa. The forces of counter-revolution which had described the Mozambique revolution in 1980 as an affliction and which had thought in 1969 that the 'only hope (of the independent states of our region) for a peaceful and prosperous future lies in closer relations with the white-dominated states', could justifiably claim that they had scored a victory.

What had gone wrong? Why was it that in 1975 Africa could resolve that no matter how strong the enemy counter-offensive, we should not retreat and in 1984 be forced to accept retreat? The answer of course lies in the reply that Reagan had given to a journalist in 1980.

Given the offensive posture of US imperialism, the Botha regime also felt that, for the first time in five years, the balance of forces was shifting in its favour. Consequently, it resolved that the opportunity had come for it also to go on the offensive, to shift that balance further in its own favour, in keeping with the global drive of its most powerful allies. It thought it was possible to reverse the advances that the national liberation movement had achieved from 1975 onwards and set out to realize this result, acting in concert with the rest of the imperialist world.

The accomplishment of this task was made all the more urgent by the fact that within our own country our own actions and those of the masses of our people were further deepening the crisis of the apartheid regime which had surfaced with such drama a few years before. To change the balance of forces in favour of reaction therefore meant and had to mean that the ANC had to be weakened decisively if not destroyed altogether. By August 1983, we knew that the US Government was convinced that the ANC would be driven out of southern Africa or completely annihilated if it did not abandon armed struggle, surrender and join the so-called reform process in South Africa as a peaceful political formation.

The softening up process had started less than two weeks after Reagan was inaugurated as President of the United States. Our comrades were attacked and killed in Matola. Joe Gqabi was assassinated six months later. Griffiths Mxenge was murdered in Durban, the same city where Joseph 'Mkhuthuzi' Mdluli had been killed five years before. Ruth First, the Nyawoses and other comrades were killed in cold blood. Our people as well as nationals of Lesotho were massacred in Maseru on December 9th, 1982. One after the other, patriots such as Neil Aggett, Mohammed Allie Razak, Bheki Zachariah Mvulane, Sipho Mutsi and Andries Raditsela were to die in police custody, from attacks carried out by the Bantustan administrations, from repressive measures carried out by the Pretoria regime, in ambushes laid by counter-revolutionaries in Angola and yet others, not necessarily members of the ANC, but opponents of apartheid such as Frikkie Conradie and Joe Mavi, in mysterious circumstances.

The South African army returned to Angola where it remains to this day. The puppet forces went on the rampage throughout southern Africa, in Lesotho, Angola, Mozambique and Zimbabwe. Where none could operate, as in the Seychelles, the Pretoria regime sent in its own forces, reinforced by mercenaries. Swaziland signed a secret agreement with Pretoria.

The countries of southern Africa came under intense pressure to sign so-called non-aggression pacts with the express aims of compromising the independence of these countries and recruiting them to join Pretoria in carrying out police activities against the ANC. The offensive spread wide with the bombing of our office in London and demands by Pretoria that the various governments of Western Europe should close down our offices. In the United States, a veteran of genocidal war of aggression against the people of Vietnam, now turned Senator, chaired widely publicized hearings in the US Senate designed to stigmatize the ANC as a terrorist movement and an agent of the Soviet Union, exactly to justify a concerted imperialist offensive to destroy us.

Pretoria scuttled the ceasefire conference that it had agreed to hold with SWAPO. The implementation of Resolution 435 became impossible as the United States arrogantly sought to barter the independence of Namibia for the withdrawal of the internationalist Cuban troops in Angola.

From the most unexpected quarters we heard that South Africa was an independent state and the ANC no more than a civil rights movement with no right to engage in armed struggle. We were told that we should wage struggle exclusively by political means and seek an alliance with the big capitalists of our country. At the same time, we should distance ourselves from the South African Communist Party and the Soviet Union and reorientate our international relations towards the imperialist countries. And all this was diametrically opposed to the positions firmly held in southern Africa and throughout the continent that the solution to the problems of our region lay with the destruction of the apartheid regime and therefore with all-out support to the ANC and SWAPO to carry out their historic missions.

But fortunately, we had already alerted our people to what was likely to come and called on them to fight on. We had charged them with the task to make the country ungovernable and to defeat the cunning enemy manoeuvre represented by the amended apartheid constitution. And to that call and that challenge our people have responded with unequalled enthusiasm, persistence and courage. So we come to the perspectives that confront this historic Conference, our organization and our people.

It is clear to all of us present here that we have the possibility actually to make this our Decade of Liberation. That requires that we must in fact and in practice accomplish the strategic tasks that we have set ourselves and which our strategic objective of the seizure of power demands. We have spelt out these tasks before and publicly communicated them even to the masses of our people. As the general command of our revolution, we should carefully identify the decisive theatres of action on which we should concentrate in order to achieve purposeful movement forward . . . The apartheid system is in a deep and permanent general crisis from which it cannot extricate itself. The apartheid regime cannot rule as before. It has therefore brought its military forces into the centre of its state structures and is ready to declare martial law when the need arises. The widespread and increasing use of the army in the effort to suppress the mass struggle in our country, even before martial law is invoked, reflects the depth of the crisis engulfing the racist regime.

Despite massacres and murders that are carried out daily by Botha's assassination squads, the masses of the people are engaged in a widespread struggle which the enemy cannot suppress and which is driving the enemy ever deeper into crisis. Of decisive importance is the fact that this mass offensive is directed at the destruction of the apartheid state machinery, at making apartheid inoperative, at making our country ungovernable.

Internationally also, the movement of solidarity with our movement and our struggle is growing and increasing its effectiveness. Already, many countries consider the ANC virtually as a government and work with us as such. On the other hand, the process of the isolation of the racist regime is developing rapidly especially and notably in the United States.

In this respect, we should also mention the extensive political and material support that we enjoy from the Non-Aligned countries, the Nordic and other Western countries and the international anti-apartheid movement. Our relations with these important world forces have also contributed greatly in further weakening the Pretoria regime and strengthening our movement and struggle.

The key to our further advance is organization. Our NEC addressed itself to this question in its last January 8th statement when it proclaimed this the Year of the Cadre. The fact of the matter is that despite the enormous impact we have made in developing the struggle to the level it is today, our organization inside the country is relatively weak.

We need a strong organization of revolutionaries because, without it, it will be impossible to raise the struggle to greater heights in a planned and systematic fashion. Without such a strong revolutionary organization, we cannot take advantage of the uprisings we have spoken about and which are a reality of the mass offensive of our people.

We have to discuss carefully the question why we are not as strong as we can and should be, review our experiences and draw the necessary conclusions. One thing that is clear is that we have to realize that we have in fact developed many cadres inside the country who understand our policy very well, who are in daily contact with the situation and our people and are committed to our organization and struggle. It is vital that these cadres should be properly grounded in our strategy in its entirety, so that they can in fact advance all our strategic tasks.

It is very important that our leadership, by which we mean all those whom we consider the most mature among our ranks, must begin to involve itself directly in this work of internal organization. We have to be in daily contact with our people. We must also move with all due speed to tackle the tasks posed by our perspective of people's war. In this respect, we would like to mention in particular that we have to take the question of mass revolutionary bases very seriously. We shall also be discussing this issue when we consider the document on strategy and tactics.

As a result of the strength and tenacity of the people's offensive, many areas in our country are emerging, perhaps in a rudimentary way, as such mass revolutionary bases. The people are engaged in active struggle as a conscious revolutionary force and accept the ANC as their vanguard movement. They are organized in mass democratic organizations. They have destroyed the enemy's local organs of government and have mounted an armed offensive against the racist regime, using whatever weapons are available to them. What is missing is a strong underground ANC presence as well as a large contingent of units of Umkhonto we Sizwe.

We must correct this weakness in a determined and systematic manner because it is within these mass revolutionary bases that we will succeed to root our army. It is the risen masses in these areas who have to be organized into larger formations of Umkhonto we Sizwe, turned into organized groups of combatants, and who have to replenish and swell our military ranks. We have to bear in mind the fact that the comrades we are training outside constitute the core of our army. They are the organizers and the leaders of the mass army that we have to build inside the country. They are our officer corps. We cannot deploy them forever as combat units. For obvious reasons, no army in the world fights with combat units composed of officers. Ours will be no exception.

The question of the kind of cadre we are producing assumes greater significance with each passing day. The level of struggle demands that we deploy inside our country as many of our cadres as possible. As we succeed to do this, these cadres will constitute an important component part of our internal structures and therefore of the ANC as a whole. They must therefore be what the ANC wants them to be. This cannot be left to chance.

It is a good thing that Conference will be discussing the question of cadre policy. Our decisions in this regard will have to be implemented seriously and consistently. All other decisions we take at this Conference will only have real meaning if we have the cadres to implement them with the sense of purpose that everything we decide here will require.

We are raising questions which might be organizational. But they are central to the solution of the question of how we raise the struggle to higher levels. Anyway, they are issues which require our most serious reflection.

We would also like to raise the question of the release of political prisoners. But in the first instance the NEC would like to report at this Conference that, over the years, we have tried our best to keep in contact with these outstanding leaders of our people and activists of our movement. In this we were assisted by the great ingenuity and daring that these comrades showed in themselves ensuring that we kept in contact. When the need arose, we have consulted them on important questions of our revolution. Their constant steadfastness and their calibre as leaders was demonstrated only recently when they turned down Botha's offer to release them on condition that they renounced violence.

By its actions the Botha regime has admitted that it is finding it difficult to withstand the internal and international pressure for the release of our comrades.

We can take pride in the fact that, through consistent campaigning, we have utterly defeated all attempts by this regime and others before it to blot out the memory of these heroes of our people by keeping them behind bars for such a long time.

Our National Executive Committee is of the considered view that we must do everything in our power to secure their release. Their release would have an enormous impact on the advance of the people of our country towards a united, non-racial and democratic South Africa, apart from meeting the profound humanitarian concern that their return to the ranks of the people is long overdue.

As Conference knows, of late there has been a fair amount of speculation about the ANC and the Pretoria regime getting together to negotiate a settlement of the South African question. This issue has arisen at this time exactly because of our strength inside the country, the level of our struggle and the crisis confronting the Botha regime. The NEC is however convinced that this regime is not interested in a just solution of the South African question.

Rather, it is interested to use the question of negotiations to divide our movement, demobilize the masses of our people by holding out the false promise that we can win our liberation other than through its overthrow. It also seeks to improve its image internationally. In any case, it is clear that no negotiations can take place or even be considered until all political prisoners are released.

However, the NEC is of the view that we cannot be seen to be rejecting a negotiated settlement in principle. In any case, no revolutionary movement can be against negotiations in principle. Indeed, in our case, it is correct that we encourage all forces, particularly among our white compatriots and in the Western world, to put pressure on the Botha regime to abandon the notion that it can keep itself in power forever by the use of brute force.

The growing crisis of the apartheid system is, in any case, causing some sections of the white population to consider ways in which they can defuse the situation. Among these are elements from the big capitalists of our country, representatives of the mass media, intellectuals, politicians and even some individuals from the ruling fascist party. Increasingly these seek contact with the ANC and publicly put forward various proposals which they regard as steps that would, if implemented, signify that the racist regime is, as they say, moving away from apartheid.

This poses the possibility that our movement will therefore be in contact with levels of the ruling circles of our country that it has never dealt with before. It is absolutely vital that our organization and the democratic movement as a whole should be of one mind about this development to ensure that any contact that may be established does not have any negative effects on the development of our struggle.

Yet another significant result of the growing strength of our movement is that many Western countries are also showing interest in establishing and maintaining relations with us. Our policy on this kind of question has of course always been clear. In principle we can have no objection to establishing such relations. However, there are important tactical questions to consider about the timing of these developments and the form that the relations we may establish should take. The NEC would be happy to see us come out of this Conference with a consensus as to how our movement should handle these important questions of our revolution which, once more, confirm the centrality of the ANC in the solution of the problems of our country.

These events draw attention to the fact that we have to act in a manner that accords with the responsibilities that rest on our shoulders, with regard both to the short and the long term. If we seriously consider ourselves as the alternative government of our country, then we need to act and operate both as an insurrectionary force and a credible representative of a liberated South Africa.

With respect to the issues we have just raised, it is clear that we have to improve the quality of our diplomacy and therefore the training of our representatives and their staff. We need also to tap and utilize in a better way the intellectual cadres available to us, both inside and outside our country.

The scope, spread and intensity of our struggle have also thrown up a large leadership corps of our democratic movement. It is important that we pay close and continuous attention to the issue of maintaining close relations with these leaders, educate the masses of our people to understand and accept our own positions and at all times ensure that we are, as a movement, providing leadership on all major questions, in accordance with our position as the vanguard movement of our struggling people.

That, in any case, is the main lesson of our last 16 years of struggle since the Morogoro Conference.

It is that we must act as a vanguard force, the repository of the collective experience of our revolutionary masses in their struggle for national liberation.

We must be organized to act as such. We must focus on the offensive, instruct ourselves that we will win and enhance our position as the front commanders of our millions-strong army of revolution.

Through 16 years of persistent struggle, we have placed ourselves in a position where we can discharge this responsibility and finally achieve the great dream of our people, the liberation of our motherland

5.2 OUR BASES ARE INSIDE SOUTH AFRICA
(An interview with Carlos Cordosa of the Mozambique Information Agency, July 1983)

AIM: After the Pretoria car bomb there was much talk of a change in strategy on the part of the ANC. Has there really been any change?

Oliver Tambo: There has been no change in strategy at all. I think that, perhaps the idea of a change in strategy arose from the fact that the headquarters of the South African Air Force was an unfamiliar target: unfamiliar because it has been the policy of the regime to conceal the casualties they suffer in the conflicts we have had with them over a period of years now. for example, our rocket attack on the headquarters of the South African Defence Force in 1981 inflicted a great deal of damage, and there must have been so many casualties that steps were taken to suppress all information about it. The result was that the Pretoria bomb comes as something very new and suggests a change in strategy.

But there could be no change in strategy because there has been no change in the factors that constitute the basis of our strategy. That is why the Pretoria bomb attack must be seen simply as an instance of intensifying our action in the light of the continued intransigence of the apartheid system and of the brutality manifested in the methods used to maintain that system.

AIM: The ANC was criticized for the Pretoria explosion for the death of 'innocent civilians', including blacks. How would you respond to these criticisms?

Oliver Tambo: First, let me make it quite clear that the struggle which the ANC is leading is not a struggle in which we see people as our enemy, least of all civilians. We are not setting out to wipe out civilians. We are setting out to wipe out the enemy forces, the defenders of the system of apartheid, certainly the armed ones, those who maintain the instruments of oppression. So naturally, it must be a matter of regret that civilians were injured, some of them fatally. But I know of no war, no situation of conflict, which did not result in injuries to the innocent. The innocent were injured by the apartheid system itself, and as our struggle intensifies more innocent people are going to get hurt.

Having said that, let me add that the criticism you mention is not made by the oppressed sections of our population, the majority. They were jubilant over this action. The exploited masses accepted that those of them who died were simply casualties, the enemy takes casualties. It is important to recognize that this action was hailed by the majority of our people because the regime had created the impression that it is only blacks, the oppressed, who die even in the attempt to bring about justice in South Africa. So they saw this as a very welcome sign of the fact that all South Africans have got to carry the burden of liberating that country.

But who are the critics? Well, the regime invaded Maseru and killed a number of civilians there, women and children. We were informed that 86 per cent of the white population in South Africa rejoiced over that event, applauded the government's action: yet civilians had been killed. It is from among those people that the criticism of the ANC comes. Equally, when there was an attack in Matola in 1981 leaders of the white opposition parties in South Africa heartily congratulated the regime on that massacre. And it is significant that the criticism that the ANC action resulted in the death of civilians is not addressed also to the killing of civilians in Mozambique by the South African Air Force in its recent raid on Matola. They killed a child, an unborn child and its mother, they killed workers, they killed civilians. There wasn't a word of criticism about that. In fact the South African regime declared that they didn't care if civilians were killed in the attack on Matola. So what is this criticism all about? It is part of psychological warfare.

AIM: Then, in your view, the criticism itself is laden with racism?

Oliver Tambo: It is because, after all, thousands of Africans have been killed by the South African regime all over southern Africa, in Angola and Namibia, in Zimbabwe, in Mozambique, in Lesotho, in Botswana and in South Africa itself. They were civilians. Soweto children are civilians. Yet they were shot by soldiers. This is happening in South Africa all the time but no one ever complains about these civilians. A lot of crocodile tears are being shed about the black civilians in Pretoria. One is entitled to ask: when have Africans been considered civilians in the South African context? The clamour about blacks being killed is merely an attempt to recruit the oppressed against the ANC, a fruitless attempt because our people understand perfectly what is happening.

Defence Minister Malan says he is going to avenge every drop of blood whether it is the blood of a black or of a white person. Well, he didn't avenge the death of the Soweto children, or of those killed at Sharpeville. No one has been punished for that, no one has been taken to court for those massacres.

As I have said, the ANC and its struggle are not about civilians — though I must confess that it is becoming increasingly difficult to find a civilian in the South African situation because Malan is calling every white person to arms. This is creating a complicated situation for those who want to distinguish between army, police force, and simple civilians. But the ANC will remain committed to avoiding the impression that civilians are the enemy in our struggle.

AIM: Would you then say that the regime, by arming white civilians, is using them, not only as its ideological and social base, but also as a kind of buffer zone between itself and the ANC?

Oliver Tambo: Exactly. The regime is fighting with its back to the wall and it is pulling in white civilians as cannon-fodder. And they say so. They say it is the civilians who must tackle the guerrillas first and the army will come later. It should be the army which protects the civilians if they are in any danger — but the civilians are being drawn in to be 'the first line of defence'. Malan uses that expression.

That is creating problems. What are these civilians defending? They are defending a criminal, inhuman system. Do they really want to? Anyway, if they take up arms — and the law says they must — then that introduces limitations on our definition of who is a civilian. The ANC hopes that the movement to refuse to serve in the defence of apartheid will grow, and that the bulk of the white population will refuse to take up arms to defend a system which belongs to the past, a system that is going to collapse anyway.

AIM: Has the ANC got mechanisms to act upon the contradictions of the white community?

Oliver Tambo: Yes. How effective we are is difficult to say, but it is part of our strategy to get the white community to understand what the issues are. We work under the disability that the ANC is banned. Our statements do not reach the white public which is suffocated with lies about the South African situation. They are being misled, deliberately, constantly, consistently. They live in something of a false world. The ANC must break through this barricade, this *laager* which has been formed around the white population in terms of information, in terms of knowledge about the realities of our time. We are quite convinced that contradictions of a very serious nature are beginning to surface, are beginning to emerge among the ranks of the oppressing class.

AIM: Are there already many whites who are becoming patriots, in the sense of believing in one South African nation, free from all racial discrimination?

Oliver Tambo: Many whites are becoming patriots in that sense. Many more are refusing to serve the old order, and are therefore leaving the country or otherwise dodging the draft. Many of these subscribe to the principles embodied in our Freedom Charter, and they see in the Freedom Charter the hope of a different kind of South Africa, a peaceful South Africa as distinct from a South Africa of a mounting, worsening conflict. This is part of our battle area — to isolate the core of reaction and to get the whites to move into positions of support for the struggle to bring about a new order in our country.

AIM: Liberation movements, in southern Africa and elsewhere, have made major contributions to wiping out hundreds of years of racial preconceptions inherent in colonization. Is the ANC, in its internal composition and the way in which it operates, already an example of what a future anti-racist South Africa could look like?

Oliver Tambo: Yes, increasingly so. We think that the South Africa of the future is not created after a certain date. We think it has to grow organically. As our struggle develops, it begins to manifest itself in the forces that are participating in that struggle for a new South Africa, a non-racial South Africa. it should be the forces of non-racialism that in fact take over, instead of creating non-racialism afterwards. And this is the trend in our struggle. The ANC is encouraging our white compatriots to come into the struggle, to be part of it. Some are very much part of it already. The struggle itself is the embryo of the new South Africa. It is creating the new South Africa as it advances. It has to be like that.

AIM: Following the Pretoria explosion and the Matola air raid there was much talk about 'retaliation', 'cycle of violence' etc. What are your comments on this terminology?

Oliver Tambo: It is not, of course, the terminology of a liberation movement, of the ANC. These terms were promoted first of all by the regime itself and its supporters, by some of the leading journalists in South Africa who are clamouring for retaliation. We don't see developments in our situation as being those which one could describe as retaliation and counter-retaliation. We say we are involved in a continuing struggle to achieve our objective and we are not guided in this by actions which the enemy takes. Indeed, our reaction to any crime perpetrated by the regime is simply to intensify the struggle. Every crime is one more reason why the regime should be removed. When we strike in intensification this may look like an act of retaliation but this would be a misinterpretation because retaliation would mean that we sit down and do nothing after that. The cycle of violence is implicit in the fact of intensification of the conflict, the escalation of the conflict. This is the very nature of the conflict in South Africa. But it is not simply violence. An armed struggle is not simply isolated, individual acts of violence. It embraces violence but it involves political action of all types as well.

Those who commented on the Pretoria bomb, for instance, saw it as an act of retaliation for the massacre in Maseru. Of course, we can't close our eyes to what the enemy is doing. So it is not irrelevant to us that the enemy perpetrated this crime. We certainly must conduct our struggle in such a way that we are not seen to be taking blows and not returning them. It is a fight but that is not retaliation. It is part of the struggle.

We saw newspaper comments that incited the Pretoria regime to retaliate by invading neighbouring countries in an action that purports to be aimed at the ANC. There were many such actions during the liberation war in Zimbabwe, invasions across the borders into Mozambique and elsewhere. Those who talk about this kind of retaliation forget what the results were. The struggle grew until the Ian Smith regime was overthrown. We regard this call for retaliation simply as a statement made by people desperate about what to do. The answer is not retaliation. The answer is in the uprooting of the apartheid system.

The problem in South Africa is the apartheid system, and while it is there a thousand acts of retaliation will simply define a new level of conflict, and it could go on indefinitely, disastrously, with much of what has been created being destroyed, many lives lost as has happened in previous liberation wars. In actions of so-called retaliation they are not addressing themselves to the cause of what is happening, the cause of the cycle of violence they talk about. When that cause is removed there will be peace in the country. Otherwise the situation will continue to worsen, and they surely have not seen the last bomb explosion. There are bound to be many more, we hope with fewer consequences for civilians. But changing the South African system is going to call for sacrifices from innocent and guilty alike, civilians and non-civilians alike. As long as the system is there, that is the price that has to be paid.

WHERE ARE THE ANC BASES?

AIM: The apartheid government's military intelligence was undoubtedly aware that there are no ANC bases in Matola, or elsewhere in Mozambique for that matter. Why then do you think they launched their air raid on Matola?

Oliver Tambo: Their target was the minds of their supporters. This was to divert the attention of the white population in South Africa away from the real cause of the Pretoria explosion, to point to a false cause. Mozambique, the ANC somewhere in Mozambique. And that being the purpose, they did not even have to find the ANC. They simply had to execute an act, and then go to the public and say 'we have killed 64 terrorists'. They knew that they had not done anything of the sort. This was a psychological action for the benefit of the shocked white population.

The correct question was: what caused the Pretoria bomb? And the correct answer was not Maputo or Matola or even the ANC — because why did the ANC do it? The correct answer is in the whole system. One of the journalists did ask that question: What makes people carry out this kind of action? What is the matter with our system? That was the correct question.

It has been part of the regime's defence strategy to suggest that there is perfect peace, calm, stability and contentment within South Africa. Everybody is satisfied with everything: the only trouble comes from outside, from neighbouring countries, or from the ANC which, for them, is something different from the masses of the people, something external to the people of South Africa. South Africa is all perfect. All the trouble comes from outside from this 'total onslaught' which is being promoted by the Soviet Union. That is their explanation all the time. Therefore, when an explosion occurs inside, hurting even a lot of innocent people, the regime must react in terms of this legend, that the problem comes from outside. Therefore, attack outside. They have been doing this all the time, and they had to be consistent. I think that this myth about the ANC having bases in neighbouring countries will soon be disproved by reality.

AIM: Since the ANC has no bases in Mozambique, where then does it have its bases?

Oliver Tambo: In South Africa. A base for the ANC does not mean a place where you have an army and equipment in an independent country, and you go away and you come back there. We don't have that. Any such bases are inside South Africa, secret places we go to, we go in and out of, secret places from which we do our reconnaissance of targets and to which we return.

Our bases are the ordinary people themselves who are at work every day, who are cadres of our army. And a lot of training is going on in the country, not of the best sort naturally, in those conditions, but there are a lot of cadres around. They carry out these actions. A bomb explodes in Pretoria. The activists have never even come out of South Africa. They are trained in there, but the regime comes to Mozambique. Our bases are inside South Africa. The regime knows this. But of course they never concede it — except that now and then they find small caches of arms.

Well, who are those intended for? The people who use these arms, when the time comes, are in South Africa.

AIM: Many observers feel that in South Africa the ANC is opening new forms of military and political struggle without models ready to hand, notably with respect to urban guerrilla warfare. Could you comment on this? Secondly, do you consider workers' struggles and those of community groups to be more important than guerrilla struggle at this stage, or do they all have equal weight in the overall struggle?

Oliver Tambo: First of all, I think that although guerrilla struggles have been guided by certain models and have reflected a certain pattern, that did not alter the essential fact about guerrilla warfare — which is that it adapts to the objective and even subjective conditions in which it is being carried out. It must take into account and modify the situation that obtains.

Now it so happens that the other liberation movements have had the benefit of revolutionary rear bases provided by independent countries who were ready to provide camps and so on where the guerrillas could develop themselves, and after a period begin to clear liberated areas. In our situation, we are governed by the reality that the countries which have borders with South Africa do not have the possibility to provide us with bases, to give us revolutionary support to the extent that other liberation movements, virtually all of them, received. This affects our strategy. We must develop a strategy and tactics which correspond to our real situation. That is why there would be features in our struggle which have not been observed elsewhere. It is simply because we have had to adjust to our own conditions.

One of these conditions is, of course, that we have had to develop tremendous striking power, because the system is strong and it will take really heavy blows to destroy it. Also, because we could not rely on bases outside South Africa, we had to place more reliance on the popular masses in the country. We have had, as part of our struggle, to develop political organization and mass mobilization, and do this with concentration and consistency, building this political base to replace a base outside the country. So I think it is possibly true that the level of political activity inside South Africa, the level of mass mobilization, is higher than in most countries where liberation wars were fought except, perhaps, towards the end when victory was in sight.

Our country is highly industrialized. The oppressed population is the proletariat, the working people. The struggle for liberation is a struggle of the workers who constitute the proletariat. They constitute the most powerful contingent in our struggle, and we have had to devote attention to their organization and mobilization. It is clear to us, as it is to the enemy, that it is not enough to have a militant working class: it has to be well organized. This process of organization is developing rapidly. And it is clear to us, as it is to the enemy, that the workers, the black workers especially, constitute a force that could pose a serious threat to the regime.

But we don't see this as having exclusive importance. The armed struggle is indispensable, but strategically it would be a terrible mistake to rely on armed struggle alone. In our situation we have to attach equal importance, at this stage, to organizing the exploited workers, organizing the oppressed masses. Therefore we operate on three fronts: the labour front, the front of mass popular actions, as well as the front of armed actions.

AIM: Is there an organic link between these three?

Oliver Tambo: There is. Over the years we have developed this organic link and we think that they knit together to constitute a force which the enemy will find very difficult to contain.

AIM: Would you, then, say that the regime, as well as the more conservative forces around the regime, can no longer make an absolute separation between trade union struggles and the national liberation struggle?

Oliver Tambo: That is no longer possible. They have become part of the same broad front of action.

AIM: What about guerrilla struggle in the rural areas? Is the ANC also developing armed actions there?

Oliver Tambo: Yes, that is developing. Of course, the trouble about that is that there is a policy which bars any disclosures about what is happening in this area of armed struggle. So activities in remote areas would not get known until they reach a certain level of intensity. Then they become public knowledge.

This is developing also because the Bantustans are a real injustice. People understand that the enemy is not even the administrations set up there. They are obviously brutal agents of the regime but the people understand that the real enemy is the Pretoria regime. There is a lot of activity in the Bantustans which addresses itself to the regime.

AIM: Could you mention some examples of this?

Oliver Tambo: For example, some of these administrations, like the one in Vendaland, are really isolated. In the first instance there was resistance to this so-called independence, resistance to Pretoria. But Pretoria simply imposed its stooges on the people. So there is hostility to this administration all the time, and it is basically hostility to the forces which installed it on the people.

Another example is the Ciskei where you have two brothers who are open agents of Pretoria. There again, a commission went into the question of whether the people wanted independence or not, and the bulk of the people rejected this independence. But the regime installed its agents all the same. The opposition was to the independence as imposed by the South African regime.

AIM: Has resistance in the Bantustans grown to a point where Pretoria can no longer create a structural break in the liberation struggle?

Oliver Tambo: That is not going to happen. The problem for the regime is that it is taking people from the urban areas to the Bantustans. In fact, the policy of migration is such that you have people going into the Bantustans and then back into the towns and back again into the Bantustans.

AIM: So they carry the idea of one South Africa. . .

Oliver Tambo: Exactly.

AIM: So it is impossible for the regime to develop peripheral nationalism . . .

Oliver Tambo: It is trying to do this, but I think that as the struggle develops these are going to disappear. As the struggle develops with increasing participation from people who have been compelled to live in the Bantustans, the unity of the people is going to emerge. The regime has failed to break up the people into these tribal nationalisms.

AIM: The ANC's political and military actions in the rural areas include also the Bantustans?

Oliver Tambo: In the Bantustans our action is largely political because we don't want to conduct a struggle between the oppressed people. The Bantustans are largely populated by the discarded who are a potential force in the struggle against the regime. They are squeezed there in a small portion of the country in their millions, starving there. There is vast territory which is reserved for the whites where the enemy is exercising direct control. We want to conduct an armed struggle where the enemy is — which is outside the Bantustans. In the Bantustans you do have these administrations which may be forced to defend the apartheid system, and to that extent they bring themselves up against the wrath of the masses. But that is not really our starting point, to engage the oppressed among themselves. Even these Bantustan leaders who are traitors have been created by the main enemy.

The Bantustans are ground largely for political organization and for preparing our armed struggle, for strengthening it. A number of people from the Bantustans are in our armed forces, and they come precisely because they rejected the Bantustans and because of the conditions there.

DESTABILIZATION

AIM: How do you view South Africa's destabilization of the SADCC region? Do you consider destabilization to be some kind of pathological behaviour on the part of the regime incapable of long term survival, or do you think destabilization is becoming a sort of business, comprising a cycle of destruction and reconstruction, and the resulting profits for many companies? Would it be reasonable to assume that destabilization is becoming a part of the South African sub-system of economic hegemony?

Oliver Tambo: I think you have something of each. There is an element of the pathological in the behaviour of the regime because there is an element of desperation. Sometimes the basis for the threats to invade neighbouring countries can be absurd, like the case of two or three guerrillas of the ANC who land in Harare from somewhere; they make their way through the country and enter South Africa, and at some point they are found by the regime's forces. It is a very small incident but they turn it into such an international issue that you would think it was not just two or three guerrillas who came through Zimbabwe but a whole army complete with tanks.

But I think we must see destabilization as part also of the attempt by the South African regime to carry out their old ambition of dominating southern Africa economically and politically. They have been making attempts to achieve this over a long period. Smuts did it. Verwoerd did it. He came up with the idea of a commonwealth of southern African states. John Vorster was pursuing the same objective, and then comes Pieter Botha with his idea of a constellation of states. The idea is the same in all of these, that is, that South Africa is the centre, surrounded by countries with weaker economies which it continues to exploit, and they are all tied to the South African economy. It is an old dream. They are trying to weaken these countries economically, to keep them economically underdeveloped so as to increase their dependence upon South Africa.

There is a struggle going on. It is the question of how long these countries can resist. Destabilization is intended to force them to surrender to South Africa, to appeal to South Africa for sustenance, to accept economic aid from

South Africa, to accept capital and therefore, in practice, to re-establish the constellation of states, which is so far confined to the Bantustans. The formation of SADCC was a rejection of the constellation idea. So part of destabilization is pursuing the goal of making these countries part of the economic empire of the South African regime.

But there is more to destabilization. It is also resistance to the very fact of political independence of neighbouring countries. One recalls that during the liberation war in Zimbabwe, the Ian Smith regime had established this 'MNR', but in March 1980 when it became clear that the Smith regime had been demolished, the MNR was taken over by the South African regime. From that time on, this whole army of bandits began to receive increased support from South Africa.

South Africa was continuing to resist the countries of southern Africa as it had done all the time, for example, when its troops had served with the Portuguese army against the liberation struggle in Mozambique and Angola. As far as South Africa is concerned, this is a continuing struggle to prevent the true independence of these countries, which is seen as a threat to the South African political, economic and social system.

But in part — and one cannot ignore this aspect — this is also a defence strategy for the survival of the regime itself, as distinct from an attempt merely to gain control. It is part of this survival strategy to deny these countries the possibility of developing in such a way to expose the character of the South African capitalist system. There can be no doubt that the oppressed, and even the whites, in South Africa must be affected by the knowledge that a neighbouring country is prospering, is stable, and that the standard of living of the people is improving. South Africa would constitute a contrast. Therefore, South Africa must prevent, for example, Zimbabwe, from being a success, a non-racial state. They have got to destabilize it so as to be able to say: 'Look, this is what liberation means; so let's keep what we have here — it's better than anything else we could have.

Let's keep the whites horrified about what happens around South Africa'.

There are two ways in which destabilization could stop. One is total surrender, total acceptance of South Africa and all its racist policies, acceptance of apartheid by everybody, submission, in which case South Africa gets its constellation, a whole network of Bantustans related to South Africa. The other is simply to remove the regime itself, remove the apartheid system. Then there will be no destabilization. There is nothing in between. I see what is happening as a combination of an aggressive posture and a strategy for survival.

AIM: What is your assessment of P.W. Botha's 'reforms'? Are they a sign that Pretoria has lost the initiative?

Oliver Tambo: I think so. I think Botha is on the defensive. These reforms do not arise from a change of heart. They are an adjustment to a new reality which consists in the ever-growing effectiveness of the liberation struggle. I am not talking now only about pressure from the masses in South Africa, but also about the other development in southern Africa, the struggle in Namibia, international pressures, the growing isolation of the regime. Botha himself said that it was necessary to adapt to the new reality. That meant that they were going onto the defensive.

Of course, they are going about it in a very zig-zag kind of way. Why are they called 'reforms'? They are reforms maybe in form, in so far as there is the changing of the wording of the constitution and other things, but in substance there is no change. Still, the fact that Botha has to manipulate the constitution, the fact that he has to get results from the black community, and try and win over Indians and the so-called coloureds, means that he is in desperate need of their support. The situation has changed against him. The Indians and coloureds are not forthcoming, because they also understand that Botha has lost the initiative, that he is on the defensive. He is trying to use them to defend the very system they have been fighting against. Because of these pressures contradictions have emerged in the ranks of the ruling class, again making Botha's task increasingly difficult.

We have the initiative in broad strategic terms, and what is required is simply that we intensify our offensive. Indeed, the fact that Botha has had to shift his ground is a challenge, an opportunity for the forces for change to step up the offensive and keep them on the run. That's how we see the so-called reforms. They are not reforms, and precisely because of that they are being rejected, and it is easy for our people to reject them. But they do indicate a feeling on the part of the regime that they can't continue ruling in the old way. They've got to change at least the outer forms of the way they are ruling. And this change is not being accepted.

AIM: Basically, then, apartheid cannot be reformed?

Oliver Tambo: It is not possible. You either have apartheid or you don't. You can't amend it from the top.

AIM: How do you see the contradictions within the regime?

Oliver Tambo: Once they reach a position when they can't continue in the old way, then these contradictions arise. Some are feeling that they will be destroyed if they change nothing. Others feel that they will be destroyed if they change anything. So that's a crisis that has overtaken them, and I think it is going to lead to splits and sub-splits. Objectively they are being broken apart by the pressure of the revolutionary struggle.

AIM: Would you say that they are living through a crisis of confidence which is affecting even people like Botha as individuals?

Oliver Tambo: It could. There is speculation as to what will happen to Botha as an individual if he can't carry out these proposals, if the thing is a flop, or if he has a referendum in which his own supporters reject the proposals. There is a view that that could spell the end of his political life. That is the kind of crisis in which he finds himself. He can't go back, but he is unable to go forward.

AIM: In some quarters there seems to be an attempt to revive the PAC. What do you think of this? What relations, if any, does the ANC have with the PAC?

Oliver Tambo: My attitude towards the PAC is that it is not really worth even discussing.

There is a very serious situation in South Africa at the moment, affecting all the countries of the region. It is all about the ANC. Lesotho is expecting anything to happen. There is a very vicious campaign against that country's government, and it is all about the ANC. The enemy is talking about the ANC all the time, and the ANC is the subject of discussions between the regime and the leaders of this region. In this situation I don't think there is room to discuss the PAC at all. It is not a factor.

AIM: You recently visited the People's Republic of China. What were the results of the visit? Was this the first ANC visit to China?

Oliver Tambo: It was the third time that the ANC has sent a delegation to the People's Republic of China. The first time was in 1963. Then there was another delegation in 1975. I was leading both. Between 1975 and 1983 is quite a bit of time, and over that time relations have not grown. So part of the purpose of this invitation was simply to strengthen relations between the ANC and the People's Republic of China. That's how we saw our visit. We think we emerged from our discussions feeling that our relations had been deepened and we got assurances of China's all-round support: political and material. In fact, as I have said elsewhere, we asked for support related to our armed struggle and got a promise of weaponry and generally a willingness to assist and support.

AIM: Did you have talks with the leadership?

Oliver Tambo: We had talks with representatives of the Central Committee as well as with the foreign minister and the premier.

AIM: Is this the first time that China has promised material support for the ANC?

Oliver Tambo: It isn't. I think they have whenever we have been there.

AIM: But did they ever materialize these promises?

Oliver Tambo: They did. It's just that there have been long gaps. On the first two visits we didn't ask for armaments, but if we had, they would have given them to us.

AIM: Do you think the ANC's relations with China have been affected by the Sino-Soviet conflict?

Oliver Tambo: I think that in the 1960s and early 1970s this was a factor, but in 1975 we resolved that question. The Chinese accepted the fact that we have nothing against the Soviet Union, that the Soviets were close friends of ours, and that friendship with anyone else was not conditional upon our weakening relations with the Soviet Union. They accepted that in 1975.

5.3 THE CHURCH AND OUR STRUGGLE
(Address to World Consultation of the World Council of Churches, Holland, 16-21 June 1980)

We have been asked to contribute to the process of consultation on how the churches should be involved in the struggle to combat racism in the 1980s. Of necessity we have to approach this subject both in a spirit of humility given the size and importance of the world Christian community as well as a spirit of frankness in recognition of the urgency of the need to abolish racism in all its forms.

Our own historical origins and our continued commitment to liberate ourselves make it inevitable that in the main we shall speak on the basis of the Christian experience in our country. We believe however that this experience is universal rather than national. Our words are therefore directed at the world community rather than the local.

In its extreme forms, racism is an institutionalized system of inequality between people who differ in genetic origin, skin colour and other inherited physical traits. Generally, it is a system of discrimination against black and brown people that came about when the countries of Western Europe invaded America, Asia, and Africa, conquered the indigenous populations, and enslaved some. As it affects the peoples of Africa,

Oliver Tambo with the Rev. Jesse Jackson and the Rev. Alan Boesak of the UDF in the USA. *(IDAF)*

Asia and the Americas, racism therefore presents itself as a by-product of colonialism, an integral part of the process that led to the domination by European peoples of the rest of mankind.

Racism is thus not an autonomous social phenomenon. It is a product, a component part and a reflection of exploitative social relations, a form of expression of these relations and a means for their justification and perpetuation. It encompasses actual structural relations between people as well as psychological attitudes which pretend to explain these structural relations.

Therefore it would be logical to conclude that the struggle to combat racism must aim fundamentally at the elimination of all exploitative social systems and at the eradication of racial prejudice. But does this mean that the call for a struggle against racism constitutes a false perspective?

Our own national experience of racism leads us to answer this question in the negative, to affirm the necessity and urgency of the struggle against racism. Apartheid in South Africa illustrates the point clearly that racism as a system of structural relations among people and as an ideology has developed historically to the point where it has acquired its own internal dynamics which give it its own self-perpetuating existence.

The fact however remains that whenever it occurs, racism serves to justify exploitative social relations and is nurtured and entrenched by these relations. Therefore while it is perfectly justified and correct to speak of and wage a struggle against racism, it is also important at all times to seek a deeper understanding of this anti-human phenomenon the better to be able to remove its root causes rather than focus solely and exclusively on the effects.

Racism in South Africa is also a product of the colonization of our people by European powers. In all the phases of its development, from the settlement of our country by Dutch mercantile interests, through the stage of direct British colonial rule to the post-1910 period of administration of our country by a white settler minority, racism has served three principal purposes. The first was to justify the seizure of our country, our land and wealth by the colonizers. The second was to establish the basis for the transformation of the dispossessed millions of our people into instruments of labour for the enrichment of the colonizers. The third was to legitimize the exclusive concentration of political power in the hands of the colonial and settler oligarchy.

The system has allowed of no overlapping between the colonizer and the colonized. The owners of wealth, the exploiters of our labour and the governors of our country are drawn exclusively from among the colonizers . The colonized constitute the masses of the impoverished, the exploited and the voiceless. The colonizers are of course white and the colonized, black. This system is unique in world politics in the clarity and rigour of its racist demarcations, its pursuit as consistent and deliberate state policy and the brutality of both the conception, its implementation and results.

From the earliest days to date successive colonial and settler regimes have pursued as a principal objective of state policy the defence, entrenchment and extension of this racist and colonial system. Any changes that have taken place in it have been those in the direction of its further refinement to improve its effectiveness for the further promotion of white minority interests. The changes so loudly proclaimed by the Botha regime today also pursue this objective.

While the World Council of Churches and the rest of the world anti-apartheid movement must of necessity continue to respond to the new brutalities committed by this regime, we believe it would be wrong for us to start looking for 'qualitatively new features' of apartheid in the 1980s with the aim of directing all or most of our attention at combating these features. The principal aim must remain still that of the destruction of the system as a whole.

We are convinced that the churches at home and abroad have an important role to play in the accomplishment of this aim. It is however common cause that in the period of imperialist expansion the church accepted as legitimate the concept of a civilizing mission and for that reason justified the imposition of white colonial domination over many peoples throughout the world, including South Africa.

What was arrogantly described as a civilizing mission in South Africa was in fact the genocidal destruction of the Khoi and the San people, the land expropriation of the rest of the indigenous people, the obliteration of their culture in all its forms, the application of a consistent policy for the impoverishment of the black people and their transformation into labour units for the enrichment of the colonizer and the political domination of the majority by a white settler minority.

It is this brutal reality of colonialism and racism which the Christian church in South Africa and the metropolitan countries accepted as a civilizing mission. Pursuing its purely evangelical mission, the Christian church continued to hold out the promise of the good life to the poor, the suffering and the despised, but only after death. By refusing by and large to do anything about the life of these poor masses before death, it got itself further involved in what looked increasingly like a conspiracy to convince our people to bear their earthly tribulations patiently and submissively in the hope of a better future in the world to come.

In the midst of the great upheavals that the process of colonization brought about, with centuries-old social systems destroyed overnight, it was inevitable that many of our people would reach out towards whatever seemed to offer them peace, stability and human fulfilment in the new conditions. Of all the institutions that came with colonial rule, the Christian church seemed the only one that offered peace, stability and human fulfilment. Our people in good numbers therefore placed their faith in the Christian church.

From this moment onwards and again almost inevitably, the history of the Christian church in South Africa is the history of a faith betrayed. We say almost inevitably because the church continuously refused to recognize the fact that the fulfilment of its black congregation lay in their liberation both from colonial domination and from what the church describes as sin.

While denouncing as sinful the coveting of their white neighbour's possessions by the black people, the church did not condemn as sinful the reduction of the black by the white into homeless and propertyless beggars. While issuing injunctions of forbearance to the black, urging them to eschew violence, it avoided condemning colonial state violence against the black people.

Many Christians among our people accept the meaning in its literal and direct sense that God made man in his image and gave him dominion over the earth. From the stand-point of these Christians, it must be obvious that the first and decisive task of a Christian and all ecclesiastic organizations, such as the church, whose *raison d'être* is the defence and propagation of God's purposes, as reflected in the Bible, must be the accomplishment of this equal dominion of all men over the earth.

Looked at from this Christian perspective, colonialism and racism must surely be seen as seeking exactly to remove the colonized and discriminated against from the exalted throne on which God placed the whole human race at the very beginning of creation. Colonialism and racism in South Africa as expressed in the apartheid system have placed in dominion both over nature and the black masses a white minority which claims it to be its divine mission to exercise this dominion over the black majority. Thereby not only does this white minority deny the universal validity of the thesis that 'all men were created equal', more fundamentally, by appropriating to itself the right to subdue and by actually subduing the black people, the white minority in South Africa appoints itself to a station in the universe higher than that of God Himself, and transforms the Creator into a handmaiden for the fulfilment of its own diabolical aspirations.

For apartheid is truly diabolical, embracing as it does all systems of inequality — discrimination against all black people on ground of race, denial of our right to self-determination, and our subjection to harsh and excessive forms of economic domination and exploitation — systems of inequality which are consciously and systematically maintained and reinforced, aimed at ensuring that the whites do in fact multiply and fill the earth on the basis of the debasement and enslavement of the blacks.

The more the church avoided placing on its agenda the uprooting of this system as an inalienable component part of its divine mission, the more justified the conclusion seemed that the Christian church was ineluctably doomed to betray the very faith which it professed. To their credit, there were a few among the Christian leadership in South Africa who refused to take this path. These are men and women who read in the Scriptures a clear message that it was impermissible that he who had been made in the image of God should be debased and enslaved. It is part of the proud history of the African National Congress that among its founders and early leaders are to be found such true Christians as:

— Rev. John Dube, first President of the ANC, minister of the Congregational Church;
— S.M. Makgatho, second President of the ANC, Methodist leader and lay preacher;
— Rev. Z.K. Mahabane, third President of the ANC, minister of the Methodist church and president of the Interdenominational African Ministers Federation (today known as IDAMASA);
— Rev. W.B. Rubusana, one of the four original vice-presidents of the ANC, co-translator of the Xhosa Bible and Vice-Chairman of the Congregational Union of South Africa.

Finding it impermissible in the context of their Christian beliefs that he who had been created in the image of God should be debased and enslaved, these men and women, and others of their time and since, saw clearly that their own efforts to secure human fulfilment and salvation lay also in their personal involvement in the struggle for liberation.

As early as 1906, one of the predecessors of the ANC, the South African Native Congress, passed a resolution which, inter alia, said:

Congress believes that Ethiopianism (the African independent church movement) is a symptom of progress, brought about by the contact of the natives of Africa with European civilization making itself felt in all departments of the social, religious and economic structure.

It is therefore little wonder that among the leaders of the African National Congress and its official chaplains are to be found the leaders of this 'Ethiopian' movement. For this movement represented not only a struggle for equality within the church, but more significantly a struggle to reorientate the Christian church as a whole such that by espousing the anti-colonial and democratic aspirations of the majority of the people, the church would once more bear true witness to the greatness of man.

It is a measure of the profundity of the damage that the church brought upon itself during the process of the colonization of our country that even today we still have to make the same point that was made by our predecessors 75 years ago that Christianity must inevitably concern itself with progress 'in all departments of the social, religious and economic structure'.

Yet another organization that preceded and laid the foundations for the formation of the African National Congress, Imbumba yama Afrika, formed in 1882, drew attention to another issue which remains with us to this day. To quote one of its founders writing in 1883:

Anyone looking at things as they are, could even go so far as to say it was a great mistake to bring so many church denominations to the black people. For the black man makes the fatal mistake of thinking that if he is an Anglican, he has nothing to do with anything suggested by a Wesleyan, and the Wesleyan also thinks so, and so does the Presbyterian. Imbumba must make sure that all these three are represented at the (forthcoming) conference . . . In fighting for national rights we must fight together. (S.W. Mvambo in Karis and Carter, *From Protest to Challenge, Vol. 1, 1971, p 12*)

The question that was raised then, and which we raise today, is the necessity of the unity of the Christian community in the struggle against colonialism and racism. Looked at from a different dimension this constitutes a call for the practical recognition of the ecumenism of the Holy Scriptures as opposed to their separate, denominational interpretation.

Given our historical experience, which has made the African National Congress play the role of virtual incubator of the ecumenical movement in our country, certainly among black Christians, it is natural that we should make this call for Christian unity in the struggle against racism. It is also natural that we should raise our voice against those within the Christian community who intentionally or otherwise are working to undermine the degree of unity achieved around the WCC's Programme to Combat Racism.

Even more disturbing is what seems to us a veritable offensive on the part of certain Western church circles to disengage the world Christian community from the struggle to combat racism; to separate and oppose one to the other, the temporal and the sacred, the material and the spiritual; to deny that the church has a task to create such conditions that mankind can, without distinction of race or nationality, 'be fruitful, multiply and fill the earth and subdue it'.

As a people we know that this constitutes a reversion to the principles and practices of the colonial church, justifying the perpetuation of racism and inequality and resurrecting the concept of a civilizing mission. This is a church which exhorts the slave to remain on his knees and on his knees to pray for the peace and prosperity of the slave master.

We are of course not surprised that it is at this moment that the principles and practices of the colonial church are being raised anew. We are not surprised because it is at this moment that it has become clear to all that real change in South Africa is both imminent and inevitable. Therefore powerful political, economic and military forces in the West feel that their interests in an African country which is central to the success of their global strategy are threatened.

These forces are naturally fully aware of the role that the

church played in the colonization of our peoples when ministers of religion blessed the arms of the colonizer and damned the indigenous people for bearing arms to resist the rape of their country. At this moment of crisis for the apartheid regime, these Western circles hope to activate the church to play the same role all over again — to bless the arms of the oppressor and to damn the oppressed for bearing arms in the struggle for liberation.

These Western forces feel an even greater sense of urgency to achieve this goal given that the church had at last begun to identify itself with those who fight for freedom and thus added enormously to the strength of the active forces of change. Yet the present epoch calls for a church that is closely allied with the poor and the oppressed. It demands Christians of the calibre of Camillo Torres, the heroic Colombian priest who joined the guerrilla forces of that country in struggle against the tyrannical Colombian oligarchy of the 1960s. This is a church which must exhort the slave to rise from his knees and to assert what the Bible bestows as a right 'to fill the earth and subdue it'.

The victories that have been scored in southern Africa which have left Namibia and South Africa as the only countries which are as yet unliberated, as well as the heightened offensive of our people within South Africa and those of Namibia, are forcing the Pretoria regime to devise new strategies for the preservation of the apartheid system. By bringing about peripheral and inconsequential changes, the Botha regime hopes to give the apartheid system a more acceptable face as well as to delude our people and the rest of the world that the racist regime has started a process of amending this criminal system out of existence.

In other words, Botha and his henchmen want to project an illusion of change in order to ensure that the substance remains unchanged. That substance is national oppression, the super-exploitation of the black people and fascist repression to ensure that the people do not rise to regain their right to determine their political, economic and social destiny without let or hindrance.

The church that the oppressed people of our country demand is one that openly, publicly and actively fights for the political, economic and social liberation of man, as part of the world forces engaged in the process of bringing into being a new world order for those who are discriminated against, for justice, peace and social progress.

In this year 1980, the 25th anniversary of the adoption of the Freedom Charter, which contains the demands of the vast majority of the people of South Africa, it would be appropriate that the WCC adopts the Charter as its own perspective of the future South Africa which it is committed to help bring about. By this act the world Christian community would have taken an important step forward in joining hands with the world forces for genuine change in South Africa and helped to reaffirm the right of our people to determine their future.

The struggle for the realization of the demands contained in the Freedom Charter means that the church has to reassess its role with regard to the South African struggle. That process of reassessment must lead towards the conclusion that it is insufficient and indeed wrong for the church to view its participation in the struggle for the eradication of racism as that of a philanthropic institution.

Our movement and our people deeply appreciate the aid given to us by the WCC for maintaining refugees and other forms of humanitarian assistance within South Africa and would like this aid to continue and increase. But we are arguing that for the WCC to stop at this form of assistance is to renege on its tasks. Indeed there is a sense in which the continuing handing out of alms to alleviate suffering is encouragement to the recipient to acquiesce in his condition. On the other hand this gives opportunity to the alms-giver to avoid confronting and changing the fundamental situation which gives birth to the need for alms.

The Christian church in South Africa is called upon to produce its own Camillo Torres. It is called upon to join in with other patriots to mobilize the masses of the people, including the millions of worshippers, to engage in struggle to change the fundamental situation which has given birth to the need

(above) Oliver Tambo with Rev. Jesse Jackson and life-long friend
Archbishop Trevor Huddlestone, President of the British Anti-
Apartheid Movement, at the biggest march against apartheid ever
seen in London. *(Stefano Cagnoni, Report)*

(below) Oliver Tambo receives the Jawarlal Nehru Award on behalf
of Nelson Mandela from the Prime Minister of India, Indira
Gandhi. *(IDAF)*

for alms. The Christians of South Africa have need to recall the example of a Christian liberator represented by John Dube, Sefako Makgatho, Z.R. Mahabane, W.B. Rubusana, A.J. Luthuli, Ambrose Reeves, Trevor Huddleston, D.C. Thompson and others and follow in their footsteps.

Many among the present generations of South Africa, whom it is perhaps unwise to mention by name, have already heeded this call and are to be found at home and abroad among the ranks of the political and military fighting forces of our people. They and all of us will both feel and be stronger if we know that the rest of the world Christian community stands with us and is actively engaged in striving to accomplish the following programme in addition to what we have already mentioned:

— increase moral and material support to the African National Congress and other patriotic forces of our country, for the transfer of all power to the people;

— severance of all political, economic and cultural links with the apartheid regime of South Africa;

— ensure strict observance and enforcement of the UN Security Council arms embargo against racist South Africa;

— urge member churches of the WCC and all countries to withdraw investments from South Africa;

— encourage member churches of the WCC to contact and co-operate with one another at regional and local levels with the purpose of enhancing and strengthening the Programme to Combat Racism;

— the education and activization of every single Christian throughout the world to raise their level of personal and collective involvement in the struggle to eradicate racism;

— encouragement of the church in South Africa to be fully involved in all aspects of the struggle against apartheid, for a democratic South Africa.

The masses of our people have risen in their millions in defiance of the brutal terror of the apartheid regime to wrest power from the racists. The young and the old, men and women, rural and urban people, believers and non-believers are waging political, military and economic battles to bring about the future which they themselves described in the Freedom Charter.

Through the Free Mandela campaign they are asserting their right to decide who their leaders are and are thereby expressing the total rejection of leaders appointed for them by the oppressor.

It is these masses, the main and decisive force of genuine change in South Africa, that we are asking the WCC and the world Christian community to encourage, assist and support in all their endeavours. Only thus can the church be true to its professed ideals, tend to all the needs of its flock, both material and spiritual, and once more claim with justification to personify the body of Christ the Liberator. When those who worship Christ shall have, in pursuit of a just peace, taken up arms against those who hold the majority in subjection by force of arms, then shall it truly be said of such worshippers also: blessed are the peacemakers for they shall be called the sons of God.

5.4 MANDELA AND NEHRU
(Address on presentation of the 1979 Jawaharlal Nehru Award for International Understanding to Nelson Mandela, 14 November 1980, New Delhi)

Today, as Nelson Rolihlahla Mandela moves around the restricted confines of his prison cell on Robben Island, his mind is tuned in to the proceedings in Delhi. He shares this pre-occupation not only with his beloved wife, Winnie Mandela, herself the subject of heartless restrictions and bans, but also with Walter Sisulu, Ahmed Kathrada, James April, Toivo ja Toivo and other national leaders and fighters for liberation, for democracy and justice — fellow inmates of the notorious Robben Island prison. The thoughts of the entire membership of the ANC and of its allies and friends converge today on Delhi. The vast majority of the people of South Africa, from all walks of life and all strata and race origins — the young no less than the old — regard this day in New Delhi as a national occasion for them.

It is therefore my pleasant duty, on behalf of the National Executive Committee of the African National Congress, to express the deep appreciation and gratitude of all the national leaders and patriots incarcerated in the prisons of apartheid, all the members, allies and friends of the ANC and the great masses of the people engaged in the liberation struggle of our country, for the great honour bestowed on Nelson Mandela in nominating him for the 1979 Jawaharlal Nehru Award for International Understanding.

It is equally and especially my pleasant duty, although a much more onerous one, to convey to Your Excellency, Mr. President, to your Government and people, the heart-felt thanks of our colleague, brother and comrade, Nelson Mandela. He received the news of the Jawaharlal Nehru Award with a mixture of disbelief, surprise, profound gratitude and excitement. But the excitement quickly mellowed into a deep sense of humility. For he understands the full meaning of the Award, its enormous significance and its challenging implications for him and his people.

He understands, because he knows Pandit Nehru's imposing stature as a world statesman, he knows his revered place in the hearts, minds and lives of the 650 million people of India; he knows, too, the esteem and deep respect Pandit Nehru enjoyed among the peoples of Asia, Africa and Latin America. Nelson Mandela, therefore, accepts the Award with full awareness of its historic message. He accepts it as a supreme challenge to him personally and to the leadership of the ANC and the people of South Africa of all races. He accepts it as an honour less for him than for the people of Africa.

We of the African National Congress wish to pay special tribute to the penetrating vision of the jury of the Jawaharlal Nehru Award for International Understanding: the recipient Nelson Mandela is beyond the reach of society. For more than 18 years he has travelled and appeared nowhere, his voice has remained unheard and his views unexpressed. In that time, momentous world events have occurred sufficient to put into complete oblivion anyone not involved in the main current of development. We mention a few of these developments, limiting ourselves to Africa only.

A long-cherished dream of the ANC came true with the formation of the OAU in 1963. The continent has torn asunder almost every chain of colonial bondage and joined the world community of nations as a full and equal member, contributing with great effort to the solution of international problems. Southern Africa has undergone geopolitical transformations and social upheavals in the course of which colonial foundations, some of them laid 500 years ago, have been reduced to a heap of ruins. New names have appeared on the international scene and now stand out as great landmarks defining the geopolitical landscape of southern Africa: Samora Machel, Kenneth Kaunda, Agostinho Neto, Seretse Khama, Julius Nyerere, Joshua Nkomo, Robert Mugabe, Sam Nujoma.

The South African Defence Force, mighty in its arms and proud of its record, has had a traumatic defeat for the first time in its history by the armed forces of a newly independent state, and barely three months later, the same army was unleashing its might upon small children who confronted bullets with dustbin lids and stones in Soweto. South Africa has suffered the staggering 'Information Scandal' which climaxed in the fall of Vorster and Van den Bergh, of whom it could be said: 'No two South Africans have been more faithful to Hitler and his ways, and none more identified with the naked inhumanity of the apartheid system.' Their place has been taken by P.W. Botha and Piet Koornhof, who, fighting no less relentlessly for the permanence of white minority rule in South Africa, have given fresh impetus to the dynamics of revolutionary change by their remarkable and disastrous failure to distinguish between the forgotten era of J.C. Smuts and Jan Hofmeyer — when the African giant was still lying prostrate, in chains — and the present hour, when the people's demand for power enjoys universal support and can no longer be compromised.

For the question in South Africa today is no longer what amendments should be made to the law, but who makes the law and the amendments. Is it the people of South Africa as a whole or a white minority group with not even a democratic mandate from the majority of the people? An organ like the so-called Presidential Council is wholly objectionable, not because Africans are excluded from it, but because it is a studied insult to the black people. It represents a policy decision for, and not by, the majority of South Africans. If this is the practice today, it was the practice in 1910 and since. But today, the people of South Africa are challenging the very constitutional foundations of the Republic of South Africa. Hence the struggle for the seizure of power.

The stormy succession of tumultuous events of the kind you have mentioned were sufficient to drive Nelson Mandela and his Robben Island colleagues out of our minds. Yet he and the other jailed national leaders have a presence in the consciousness of our people and of the world public, so powerful, that it cannot be explained except in terms of the indestructibility of the cause to which they have surrendered their liberty and offered their lives — the cause of the oppressed majority in South Africa, the cause of Africa, the cause of progressive mankind.

The unique significance of the 1979 Jawaharlal Nehru Award is that, displaying a delicate sensitivity to this enduring presence, it has identified in Nelson Mandela the indomitable spirit of a people, the supreme justice of their cause and their resolute determination to win final victory. In our humble opinion, the jury of the Jawaharlal Nehru Award for International Understanding could have made no better choice among the people of South Africa for such an honour at this time. For if the immediate reaction of racist Prime Minister P.W. Botha to the victory of the Patriotic Front Alliance in Zimbabwe was to invite the people of South Africa to a multi-racial conference to discuss the future of that country, the oppressed millions, supported by white democrats, responded by demanding the release of Nelson Mandela from imprisonment.

The fact that P.W. Botha was evidently only trying to diffuse an explosive situation in South Africa subtracts nothing from the centrality of Nelson Mandela's past, present and future role in the struggle to unite the people of South Africa as fellow citizens in a democratic, non-racial and peaceful country. His entire political life has been guided by the vision of a democratic South Africa, its people united across the barriers of race, colour and religion, and contributing as a single nation to the pursuit of international peace and progress. For this reason, he knows no distinction between the struggle and his life. Having chosen the law as the avenue through which he could best serve his people, he soon found that the legal system of apartheid was itself an instrument of oppression. His conscience dictated that he place the quest for justice above the administration of unjust laws. This concern for justice led him into politics, into the leadership of the African National Congress, and ultimately to Robben Island and even more politics.

It is opportune to recall, and Nelson Mandela's captors may wish to ponder the fact, that Jawaharlal Nehru, who was no stranger to imprisonment and was in no way destroyed by it, served the world community, including the British, far better as a free man than as a political prisoner. Nelson Mandela's 18 years' imprisonment has in no way destroyed him, and will not. Indeed, a striking feature of political imprisonment in South Africa is that the morale of the prisoners remains intact, notwithstanding the harsh brutality of the prison conditions and the long duration of the prison sentences.

The demand for the release of Nelson Mandela and all political prisoners is world-wide, and is made more in the interests of all South Africans than out of any sense of unwanted pity for those imprisoned. But, overwhelmed by their iniquitous past and present, and lacking in true courage, the self-appointed rulers of our country fear the future; they are frightened of democracy, scared of social progress and suspicious of peace. That is why Nelson

Mandela and some of the best known of our leaders remain in prison.

It is fitting that on this day, I should recall the long and glorious struggle of those South Africans who came to our shores from India 120 years ago. Within two years of entering the bondage of indentured labour, Indian workers staged their first strike against the working conditions in Natal. This was possibly the first general strike in South African history. Their descendants, working and fighting for the future of their country, South Africa, have retained the tradition of militant struggle and are today an integral part of the mass-based liberation movement in South Africa.

But the striking role of India in the development of the struggle for national and social liberation in South Africa has its firm roots in the early campaigns led by Mahatma Gandhi in that country, coupled with the continuing and active interest he took in the South African situation. All South Africans have particular cause to honour and remember the man who was in our midst for 21 years and went on to enter the history books as the father of free India. His imprint on the course of the South African struggle is indelible.

In the 1940s, in South Africa and India, our people voiced the same sentiments: to wage a war in the name of freedom and democracy, they said, was a hollow mockery as long as the colonial peoples were not free. We applauded the 'Quit India' demand against the British, for, as the Congress resolution in August 1942 so correctly said: 'India, the classic land of modern imperialism, has become the crux of the question, for by the freedom of India will Britain and the United Nations be judged, and the peoples of Asia and Africa be filled with hope and enthusiasm.' And so we were filled with hope and enthusiasm as we watched events unfold in India.

If Mahatma Gandhi started and fought his heroic struggle in South Africa and India, Jawaharlal Nehru was to continue it in Asia, Africa and internationally. In 1946, India broke trade relations with South Africa — the first country to do so. In the same year, at the first session of the UN General Assembly, the Indian Government sharply raised the question of racial discrimination in South Africa — again the first country to take this action. Speaking at the Bandung Conference in April 1955, Jawaharlal Nehru declared: 'There is nothing more terrible than the infinite tragedy of Africa in the past few hundred years.' Referring to 'the days when million of Africans were carried away as galley slaves to America and elsewhere, half of them dying in the galleys', he urged: 'We must accept responsibility for it, all of us, even though we ourselves were not directly involved.' He continued, 'But unfortunately, in a different sense, even now the tragedy of Africa is greater than that of any other continent, whether it is racial or political. It is up to Asia to help Africa to the best of her ability because we are sister continents.'

To her great honour, India has consistently lived up to this historic declaration, which constitutes one of the cornerstones of the Non-Aligned Movement. The tragedy of Africa, in racial and political terms, is now concentrated in the southern tip of the continent — in South Africa, Namibia, and in a special sense, Robben Island.

Quite clearly, we have all come a long way from 1955. Jawaharlal Nehru's clarion call has already translated itself into a partnership of the peoples of Asia, Africa and Latin-America, who have joined hands with the Socialist community of nations, the progressive forces of the world and the national liberation movement, in an anti-imperialist front to eradicate the last vestiges of colonial domination and racism in Africa and elsewhere, to end fascism and exploitation, and promote a new world economic order that will ensure true democracy, social progress and peace.

Nelson Mandela, who gained political maturity in the company of such household names in South Africa as A.J.Luthuli, Moses Kotane, Yusuf Dadoo, J.B.Marks, Elias Moretsele, Z.K.Matthews, Monty Naicker, Walter Sisulu, Lilian Ngoyi, Bram Fischer, Govan Mbeki, Helen Joseph and many others, has been confirmed by the Jawaharlal Nehru Award as a leader of men, ranking among the great international leaders of modern times. In their struggle for the seizure of power, the people of South Africa — its youth, workers, women, intelligentsia and peasants — led by the African National Congress and its allies, will not betray this great honour to our country. Nelson Mandela, with the rest of the leadership of the ANC, will remain worthy of the great Jawaharlal Nehru — today, tomorrow, ever.

5.5 THE ANC AND THE SACP
(Address on the occasion of the 60th Anniversary of the South African Communist Party, 30 July 1981)

Let me commence by thanking you, Comrade Chairman, and the SACP for inviting the African National Congress to be a party to this occasion and in particular, for the opportunity of sharing a platform with the Communist Party of Great Britain, represented here by the General Secretary Gordon McLennan, and with the Communist Party of Ireland, represented by Comrade Michael O'Riordan. These are our allies; they are part of the international movement of solidarity which gives us strength and confidence in the certainty of our victory. These parties, together with other communist and workers' parties around the world, are parties which we can always appeal to for solidarity in the conviction that they will respond. It is a great pleasure for us, a great honour to participate with them on an occasion of great significance in our struggle in South Africa.

You, Comrade Chairman, and Comrade General Secretary of the SACP have shared hundreds of platforms together in our lifetime in South Africa and in many parts of the world outside our country. Today, we share a platform on an occasion which takes our reflections back across a span of 60 years, in which we can recall great names that have ensured that our struggle shall continue and is continuing today — names that shall always be honoured in our history.

We share this platform in another significant context, for me in particular. I have the great pleasure today of repeating on behalf of the African National Congress and our people in general, our congratulations to Comrade Moses Mabhida on

his election some while ago to the position of General
Secretary of the SACP.

We utter these congratulations with a sense of confidence,
knowing his background, knowing his role in our struggle
especially in the discharge of his tasks in the ANC, his absolute loyalty and his understanding — profound understanding — of the character of the South African situation and its
problems. Confidence, because he succeeds one of the great
giants of our struggle in the position of General Secretary of
the SACP — Moses Kotane, whose contributions alone to the
building up of the forces that can resist fascist onslaught on
any scale is acknowledged by all who have worked with him,
such as I have, by all who have read about him. We are confident that you, Comrade Moses, will prove yourself a worthy
successor, and perhaps in the fullness of time we shall likewise
name you among the giants of our struggle.

Comrade Chairman, I should like to pay a special tribute to
you today. It is 60 years since the SACP was formed. It is several decades since you have been involved in the front ranks of
our struggle, inspiring everyone around you, inspiring youn-
ger generations: first among the volunteers in situations that
threaten arrest, torture, imprisonment; never missing where
there is struggle to be waged. You were awarded the title Isitwalandwe by our nation not as a formality but in recognition of
your services. This was more than 25 years ago. Your presence
here, and chairmanship of this particular meeting, enables us
to recall with great clarity the various revolutionaries with
whom you associated in your period of service to our people
and our country. On this the 60th anniversary of the founding of the South African Communist Party, I bring the greet-
ing and felicitations of the NEC of the African National
Congress, and the good wishes of all those engaged in the liberation struggle and all the oppressed in South Africa.

This year also marks the 25th anniversary of the women's
great march to Pretoria — the march of our gallant women.
It is the year that carries with it the 20th anniversary of the
founding of Umkhonto we Sizwe. It is the Year of the Youth of
our country. We hail the SACP in the name of these

contingents of our army of liberation which together with the SACP comprise a fighting alliance that represents the power of the South African revolution in the making.

We salute the SACP, particularly in the name of the combatants who have fallen in the course of our struggle as well as on behalf of the national leaders and militants presently held in the enemy's prisons. We congratulate the SACP on this occasion, particularly for the dedication and commitment of its leaders and cadres that has ensured its survival these 60 years, despite intensive repression and desperate attempts to destroy it. We applaud your achievements, for the SACP has not only survived, but is today stronger, and increasingly makes more significant contributions to the liberation struggle of our people.

The ANC speaks here today not so much as a guest invited to address a foreign organization. Rather we speak of and to our own. For it is a matter of record that for much of its history, the SACP has been an integral part of the struggle of the African people against oppression and exploitation in South Africa. We can all bear witness that in the context of the struggle against colonial structures, racism, and the struggle for power by the people, the SACP has been fighting with the oppressed and exploited.

Notwithstanding that it has had to concentrate on thwarting the efforts to destroy it, cadres of the SACP have always been ready to face the enemy in the field. Because they have stood and fought in the front ranks, they have been amongst those who have suffered the worst brutalities of the enemy, and some of the best cadres have sacrificed their lives. And so your achievements are the achievements of the liberation struggle. Your heroes are ours. Your victories, those of all the oppressed.

The relationship between the ANC and the SACP is not an accident of history, nor is it a natural and inevitable development. For, as we can see, similar relationships have not emerged in the course of liberation struggles in other parts of Africa. To be true to history, we must concede that there have been difficulties as well as triumphs along our path, as, traversing many decades, our two organizations have converged towards a shared strategy of struggle. Ours is not merely a paper alliance, created at conference tables and formalized through the signing of documents and representing only an agreement of leaders. Our alliance is a living organism that has grown out of struggle. We have built it out of our separate and common experiences. It has been nurtured by our endeavours to counter the total offensive mounted by the National Party in particular against all opposition and against the very concept of democracy. It has been strengthened through resistance to the vicious onslaught against both the ANC and the SACP by the Pretoria regime; it has been fertilized by the blood of countless heroes many of them are unnamed and unsung. It has been reinforced by a common determination to destroy the enemy and by our shared belief in the certainty of victory.

This process of building the unity of all progressive and democratic forces in South Africa through united and unified action received a particularly powerful impetus from the outstanding leadership of Isitwalandwe Chief Albert J Luthuli, as President General of the ANC. The process was assisted and supported by the tried and tested leadership of such stalwart revolutionaries as Isitwalandwe Yusuf Dadoo and Isitwalandwe the late Moses Kotane, revolutionaries of the stature of J. B. Marks and Bram Fisher.

Today the ANC and SACP have common objectives in the eradication of the oppressive and exploitative system that prevails in our country: the seizure of power and the exercise of their right of self-determination by all the people of South Africa. We share a strategic perspective of the task that lies ahead. Our organizations have been able to agree on fundamental strategies and tactical positions, whilst retaining our separate identities. For though we are united in struggle, as you have already pointed out Comrade Chairman, we are not the same. Our history has shown that we are a powerful force because our organizations are mutually reinforcing.

It is often claimed by our detractors that the ANC's association with the SACP means that the ANC is being influenced by the SACP. That is not our experience. Our experience is that the two influence each other. The ANC is quite capable of influencing, and is liable to be influenced by, others. There has been the evolution of strategy which reflects this two-way process. In fact the ANC was quite within its rights to tell the SACP that we are sorry we cannot release Comrade Moses Mabhida from his tasks in the ANC — find another comrade to be General Secretary. Yet we agreed he would make a good General Secretary for the SACP. He was not grabbed. This kind of relationship constitutes a feature of the South African liberation movement, a revolutionary movement, a feature of the SACP which helps to reinforce the alliance and to make it work as it is working. It is a tribute to the leadership of the SACP.

We are therefore talking of an alliance from which, in the final analysis, the struggle of the people of South Africa for a new society and a new social system has benefited greatly. Within our revolutionary alliance each organization has a distinct and vital role to play. A correct understanding of these roles, and respect for their boundaries, has ensured the survival and consolidation of our co-operation and unity.

As stated in its programme, the SACP unreservedly supports and participates in the struggle for national liberation led by the ANC, in alliance with the South Africa Indian Congress, the Congress of Trade Unions, the Coloured People's Congress and other patriotic groups of democrats, women, peasants and youth. The strategy of the African National Congress sees the main content of the South African revolution as the liberation of the largest and most oppressed group: namely the black population. And by black I do not mean what our enemies have elected to designate as black — namely just the Africans. By black, we mean all the oppressed. Those who were formerly called Non-whites and which we prefer to call black.

Of course, it does not suit the enemy to club all the oppressed and exploited together. It is better for the enemy that this vast majority be split up into what they call blacks and then Indians and coloureds. That fits their strategy —

serves the interests of their strategy best. But I am talking about the oppressed population as the blacks. Whilst concerned to draw in, and unify, all progressive and democratic forces in the country, including those amongst the whites, our priority remains the maximum mobilization of those who are the dispossessed, the exploited and the racially oppressed.

That is only a priority, for we recognize that victory requires that we build up maximum unity of the forces for progress. Indeed we need to break up this white racist clique, win friends from among the ruling class and isolate the fascists. Then a united people of South Africa can deliver the final blow, crush the colonialist structures and move to a new South Africa.

The poverty of our people, the incidents of malnutrition, unemployment and other manifestations of the criminal policy, the criminal system under which we live, demand that our people should fight with everything they have, all the time, to destroy the system. To this end the ANC has called upon the people to resist this oppressive and exploitative system at every level, using every occasion and every means at their disposal. And the response has been nationwide. People in all walks of life and races have banded together in opposition to the fascist regime. Almost every township has been faced with rent strikes and other forms of resistance. Fare increases are met with boycotts. Youth and students have maintained their action against the education system and found widespread support from parents. Though many of these actions are local and focus on immediate issues, they are not directed at seeking piecemeal and at best temporary redress. These actions are not an end in themselves but they are part of the struggle for a new social system in our country.

The ANC has called upon and encouraged workers to use their labour power, not only to improve wages and working conditions, but also to destroy the exploitative system itself. Workers have been and are responding to this call. In the process, employers have been dismissing large numbers of the poorly paid and brutally exploited strikers. The right of the workers to withhold their labour is universally recognized as fundamental. The ANC is determined to defend the right of South African workers to strike — especially the black workers. Firms which victimize strikers do so at their peril. They must be made aware that they dismiss their workers at the risk of dismissing their profits. The ANC intends to see to it, that the workers' right to strike is defended.

The objective of our struggle in South Africa, as set out in the Freedom Charter, encompasses economic emancipation. It is inconceivable for liberation to have meaning without a return of the wealth of the country to the people as a whole. To allow the existing economic forces to retain their interests intact is to feed the roots of racial supremacy and exploitation, and does not represent even the shadow of liberation. It is therefore a fundamental feature of our strategy that victory must embrace more than formal political democracy; and our drive towards national emancipation must include economic emancipation.

Mr Chairman, exploitation and repression are brutal. But they have not deterred or cowered us. On the contrary, throughout the country, the struggle is generating a climate of defiance, in which people are going into action without thought of torture, arrest or even death. They are asserting their right to freedom of association and speech, their right to strike, and most importantly their right to govern. They do so in the context of a mass struggle which demonstrates the success of our strategy of reinforcing popular actions with armed force — as was shown most forcibly during the nationwide campaign of boycott and rejection of the white republic in May of this year.

The ANC and its allies recognize that in our situation in South Africa armed struggle is an absolute imperative. But we have always seen mass mobilization as essential to the growth and development of armed struggle. We acclaim it is an achievement, that in both areas of activity — the mass struggles as well as armed action — there is now ample evidence of growth and expansion.

Umkhonto we Sizwe has emerged as a force to reckon with.

And yet, we all know that before we can hope to bring the enemy down, the scope and scale, as well as the quality of the operations, of this our people's army must be greatly stepped up. Umkhonto we Sizwe has won its first great victory — namely, that the enemy has proved unable to stop its growth, its expansion and the increasingly effective striking powers of our guerrilla army. That is a victory which we must build on. To say that, is to pronounce the challenge posed for our revolutionary alliance. Unless we build on that victory we will lose the victory itself. For even as the unity of the oppressed has grown and strengthened so too has the offensive against us. As we stand poised for new advances, the onslaught grows more fierce.

As the apartheid regime has sought ways to preserve itself, power in South Africa has increasingly become concentrated in the hands of a particularly dangerous and authoritarian politico-military clique, which tries to retain control through the unashamed and overt use of institutionalized violence and the escalation of brutal repression. Not content with waging war against the South African and Namibian people, the regime has embarked upon an undeclared war against neighbouring states. In repeated breaches of the UN Charter and of international law, the territorial integrity of Angola, Botswana, Mozambique, Swaziland, Zambia and Zimbabwe is violated by the regime, the political stability of independent states subverted, and economic development retarded and sabotaged.

In opening this meeting, Comrade Chairman, you have drawn our attention to the new crime of aggression against the People's Republic of Angola. We should like to especially associate the ANC with the resolution adopted here today. And to add, that in our view Angola's closest friends should rally to her defence, and that Africa must act against the aggression against Africa. We consider the situation demands an emergency meeting of the OAU to decide upon concerted measures to be taken to drive South African troops out of Angola and out of Namibia.

We should not omit to emphasize and underscore the

special role of the new administration in the US, in relation to this aggression. There has been some consistency in the behaviour of the South African regime ever since Mr Reagan appeared on the scene. The first sign of a new arrival in the arena of international relations was the fact of the Geneva Conference being torpedoed.

A state had been reached when all concerned had agreed including South Africa and at that moment the Reagan Administration appeared on the scene. The first evidence of that was the collapse of that Geneva conference. It was succeeded by an attack on Angola; an attack, an invasion against Mozambique when our people were butchered and assassinated in Matola.

Now as pressure grows for the implementation of Res. 435 to resolve and finalize the Namibian question, the greatest ever invasion is mounted against Angola — the greatest, certainly, since the mid-1970s. Backing all this up is surely that administration which proclaims itself as an ally of South Africa, which labelled the national liberation movement as international terrorism to be eliminated and liquidated. It is in pursuance of that policy that by way of liquidating SWAPO, the South African regime is being assisted and encouraged and equipped to try and destroy Angola.

. . . The ANC has received and continues to receive international support and solidarity from a variety of sources. We must today acknowledge especially, with appreciation, the very significant support we receive from the socialist countries. You have mentioned many of these countries — all of them without exception have given freely by way of supporting our struggle and meeting our demands.

We appreciate in particular that they and some African countries have not hesitated to deliver weapons to peoples fighting for their liberation. The enemy likes to squeal that we have been fighting with either Soviet made weapons, or communist made weapons. It does not matter what weapons they are. But we are glad to have them, and shall continue to use them if they are effective — and they are. This support has been given during the liberation struggles in southern

Africa and the rest of Africa and has been extended to the independent states that have been forced to defend their own victories . . .

Dr Yusuf Dadoo, Chairman of the South African Communist Party, chats with Oliver Tambo. (*DIP*)

6

PREPARING FOR POWER: REVOLUTION AT HOME, SOLIDARITY ABROAD

Introduction

A renewed uprising began in the black townships in September 1984, sparked off by the decision of some of the new local councils to increase rents. Harsh police action to suppress the protests exacerbated the violence and between September 1984 and January 1987 over 2,200 people died. In 33 out of 38 town councils, designed to offer urban blacks a limited measure of local self-government, government authority became inoperative. The councils collapsed in the wake of attacks on black councillors and policemen, who were deemed to collaborate with the regime.

Black defiance hardened into a radical call for political power and the release of Nelson Mandela. On 20 July 1985 a State of Emergency was imposed on 36 of the country's 265 magisterial districts, the first since 1960. The uprising continued unabated — extensive school and consumer boycotts were combined with successful strikes and stay-aways — surpassing post-Soweto proportions. The regime resorted to thousands of arrests and detentions, the banning of the Congress of South African Students (COSAS), the deployment of the army in the townships, and a clamp-down on the international press. In an effort to mislead world opinion the Government lifted the partial State of Emergency in March 1986 only to impose a new nationwide State of Emergency on 12 June.

It was in this context that the ANC called a Consultative Conference — a 'Council of War' — in Lusaka in June 1985. Oliver Tambo presented the report of the National Executive, which was a major survey of the movement's past history and an assessment of the current situation in South Africa. At the conference and in subsequent statements Tambo called on the people to launch a determined offensive to make the country ungovernable, to prepare the conditions for the seizure of power, and in one powerful phrase 'to engulf the apartheid system in the fires and thunder of a people's war.' The conference took a number of important decisions: non-blacks were admitted to full membership, including the right to sit on the National Executive (five non-blacks were elected); the working class was acknowledged as the 'ideological lodestar' of the liberation movement; and negotiations with the South African government were rejected unless tied to a discussion of the transfer of power.

Despite rising international pressure, Botha's government refused to unban the ANC and to release Nelson Mandela and other leaders The crisis brought other groups to undertake the journey north to the Lusaka and Harare offices of the ANC. In September — soon after the Rand collapsed in the face of both the French Government's restriction on future investment and the announcements that international banks would not renew loans — a group of businessmen led by the Chairman of Anglo-American Corporation met a nine-man ANC team at President Kaunda's lodge in Luangwa National Park in an historic rendezvous. Corporate capitalists set about distancing themselves from the ideology of apartheid in an exploratory attempt to secure their survival in a future democratic South Africa. Their visit also served to confirm the leading role of the ANC in the black liberation movement.

Hot on the heels of the businessmen went representatives of the white Progressive Federal Party, the Soweto Parents' Crisis Committee (SPCC), the Federated Chamber of Industries, the National Convention Movement, Roman Catholic and Protestant churches, the Kngwane Inyandya movement (a homeland based organization), the National Union of South African Students (NUSAS) and the National African Federated Chambers of Commerce (NAFCOC). Most importantly, the Congress of South African Trade Unions (COSATU), a federation of 33 trade unions formed in

November 1985, held long discussions with the ANC and the South African Congress of Trade Unions (SACTU) leadership and the resulting statement revealed an identity of policy. A coalition of legal organizations was rapidly emerging in the country with common positions linked to the Freedom Charter. Equally important, there was a momentum of opinion outside of these organizations, including liberal whites towards these positions. The prospect began to emerge of a certain disaggregation and splitting off in the white camp and the accumulation of support to the anti-apartheid forces. The meeting in Dakar in July 1987 of Afrikaners and ANC was unprecedented.

The State of Emergency and its associated repression received widespread condemnation throughout the world. Tambo was called to explain the policies of the ANC in numerous international fora and reiterated his demands for sanctions with growing success. An important catalyst in the international arena was the role of the Commonwealth Eminent Persons Group, created in early 1986 to report on the situation in South Africa. The ANC expected the group to propose mild palliatives and perhaps even to give some credibility to the Government's claims of reform. However the Group made a great effort to investigate real conditions. Its visit was punctuated by South African raids into Zimbabwe and Botswana, showing even greater intransigence and contempt for international opinion. The report of the Eminent Persons emerged as a damning indictment of reform in South Africa and a clear indication that dialogue with the Botha government was futile.

But Western business and political interests foiled attempts within the Commonwealth to impose sanctions, and the influence of Britain, combined with West Germany and Portugal, led to a watered-down sanctions package being adopted in the European Community. However, despite resistance by President Reagan, the United States Congress passed an Anti-Apartheid Act in October 1986 which contained a set of sanctions that have placed the United States ahead of all other Western countries.

International interest in the policies of the ANC required an intense effort by Oliver Tambo and his colleagues to meet world leaders of all kinds to explain its policies in far greater depth than previously. Questions had to be answered about its organizational structure, its allies in the struggle, its international policies, its views on violence, and most pressing of all, on its vision for a post-apartheid South Africa. Tambo met these challenges on policy with remarkable consistency which has won wide international respect and which has made a remarkable impact within South Africa.

At the same time the crisis in the country has polarized society even more, creating a scenario for revolution. In this one of the most critical factors is the quality of leadership provided by the ANC to both foster the process of revolution, yet guide its overall direction towards the establishment of a non-racial democratic state. Oliver Tambo's wisdom and vast experience has placed him in a crucial place at what is undoubtedly a vital moment in South Africa's history.

6.1 DESTROY THE OLD ORDER
(Address to the nation on Radio Freedom, 22 July 1985)

Forty-eight hours ago P.W. Botha announced a State of Emergency affecting the Eastern Cape, the Witwatersrand and the Vaal Triangle. Already in these areas many people have been arrested. Combined military and police units have moved to occupy certain townships such as Kwa Thema. People have been murdered by these forces of occupation. The truth about the criminal misdeeds of these bands of marauders has been kept out of the public eye through tightened press censorship.

Inevitably the fascist measures of extreme repression that Botha has imposed will be extended to other areas of our country. Botha has at last decided to impose martial law. He has granted full powers to his armed forces to govern certain areas of our country. This is an eventuality for which the Botha regime has prepared and about which we have repeatedly warned. This regime can now no longer conceal its true face. What has become plain for all to see is the reality of military dictatorship and not the comforting but spurious image of a reformer that Botha had sought to cultivate and project.

The Pretoria regime speaks about law and order. It says it has imposed martial law on large parts of our country in order to re-establish order and stability. In cynical disregard of the interests of the majority of the people of our country, the United States government, the principal ally of the apartheid regime, has not hesitated to approve of the new measures of repression that its friends in Pretoria have adopted. The Reagan Administration has openly said that it hopes that these measures will succeed in their purpose. Botha and Reagan hope and pray that the intensified campaign of terror against the people and our democratic movement will succeed to stop our march to liberation. They are intent to ensure that racist law and apartheid order continue to hold sway. That is the hopeless mission that the Pretoria regime and its supporters have given themselves.

Our own tasks are very clear. To bring about the kind of society that is visualized in the Freedom Charter, we have to break down and destroy the old order. We have to make apartheid unworkable and our country ungovernable. The accomplishment of these tasks will create the situation for us to overthrow the apartheid regime and for power to pass into the hands of the people as a whole.

We have achieved a good deal of progress in making South Africa ungovernable. Correctly, we concentrated on the weakest link in the apartheid chain of command and control. For months we have maintained an uninterrupted offensive against the puppet local government authorities in the black urban areas, as well as other state personnel in the townships such as the police and their agents.

By declaring a State of Emergency in these areas, Botha has admitted that his organs of government have collapsed. He has conceded that the only way he can restore apartheid rule in these townships is through martial law. He could no longer govern in the old way. The perspective ahead of us is to intensify the struggle exactly in these areas that are under martial law. In struggle, we must make it impossible for our enemy to govern even in the new way. We must confront its new organs of government in the townships — the combined army and police units which have been brought into our midst exactly to reassert apartheid rule and therefore to perpetuate our oppression and suffering. This is the first task we have to accomplish in the light of Botha's State of Emergency — to confront and defeat his new organs of government.

While saluting those among our people who have responded so magnificently to our call to make our country ungovernable, we must also draw attention to the fact that not all areas of our country and not all sections among the oppressed responded with the same level of activity and determination. This has enabled the enemy to concentrate its forces on certain areas of our country. Even now, under its State of Emergency, the apartheid regime has the possibility to concentrate its attack on a selected number of areas in our country.

This is a situation which we must correct. It is vital that all areas of our country should join in the general offensive to make the apartheid system unworkable and South Africa ungovernable. There is not a single black person anywhere in our country who can say that he or she lives in conditions of freedom. We are all subjected to domination by organs of government imposed on us by the apartheid regime. This is the case whether we live in the towns or the countryside.

In the past, all of us have joined together to reject apartheid rule, whatever form it took. Accordingly, we have consistently rejected the Bantustan system and the community councils. We have also overwhelmingly rejected Botha's tri-cameral parliament as well as the organs of local government visualized in the latest apartheid constitution. But, as we had foreseen, all these institutions have been imposed on us despite the fact that we do not want them. As usual, the apartheid regime has refused to act in accordance with the will of the people.

We, for our part, have no cause to submit to the dictatorship of the racists. We have said we are opposed to its apartheid institutions. These have been imposed on us against our will. We have no choice but to destroy them. This is what we have done in the Eastern Cape, on the Witwatersrand, in the Vaal Triangle and the Free State. We must spread this offensive to reach all other parts of our country. In all our localities, wherever they may be, we must rise now and destroy the apartheid organs of government that are used to hold us in bondage. We make this call to all black people — African, Indian and so-called Coloureds.

Our people in some parts of the country are suffering under the iron heel of military dictatorship. They are facing the full might of the apartheid state because they dared to stand up to fight for our liberation. Regardless of what the martial law administrators do, the masses of our people in these areas will continue to fight for our emancipation. The time has come that the rest of the black masses of our country, all 25 million of us, should join in one determined offensive to make all of our country ungovernable. If needs be, let us force the apartheid regime to deploy its armed forces in every village and township in our country. Let us act together to make all of South Africa ungovernable.

Racist white South Africa is, without doubt, applauding P.W. Botha for declaring the State of Emergency. These hidebound white supremacists see this act of desperation on the part of the apartheid regime as a demonstration of firmness and a determination to protect white privilege at all costs. They are convinced that Botha will succeed to suppress our struggle and save the apartheid system from collapse.

White South Africa will not awaken from this dream world while our struggle is concentrated in the black areas of our country. We cannot and should not allow a situation of relative peace and tranquillity to obtain in the white areas of our country while the black townships are in flames. We must take the struggle into the white areas of South Africa and there attack the apartheid regime and its forces of repression in these areas which it considers its rear.

For many years, the Pretoria regime gave its white supporters a false sense of security by deluding them into believing that the battlefront of struggle was drawn at the borders of our country. We have shattered that myth and brought the struggle to the very doorstep of the colonial oppressor. The enemy, however, continues to hope that it will manage to hold our struggle to that line of battle, outside of the white towns and cities. As we buried the illusion of a confrontation taking place at the borders of our country, so must we now put paid to the notion that our struggle will remain confined to the black areas. No longer should white South Africa live with the idea that it can continue with its business as usual, while our people are perishing in their hundreds, out of sight of the white families that have sent their sons into our townships, armed to the teeth and with one intention only, to kill, kill and kill.

Our task, to take the struggle into the very midst of the enemy, presents all revolutionaries of our country with the challenge of devising the correct tactics to realize this objective. It is a challenge that all of us, workers, women and youth, must meet. It however also places a special responsibility on all our white compatriots who are committed to bring about a democratic South Africa to act now to show the white population of our country that, however much it might try to close its eyes to what is happening, the fact of the matter is that our country is in crisis.

White South Africa must be made to realize that Botha cannot guarantee its security. The greater the repression that he resorts to in defence of white minority rule and in the name of the whites of our country, the greater becomes the level of insecurity facing these very same whites. To guarantee its own security, white South Africa has to come over to the side of the forces fighting for a democratic and non-racial society. The alternative that Botha offers them — that of pitting themselves against the overwhelming majority of the people of our country — is nothing but a death trap. Nothing will come of it except grief for the whole of white South Africa. We offer our white compatriots the only way out of the crisis which will surely engulf them, and that, in the near future — renounce Botha and his apartheid republic: join the anti-racist forces in the struggle for a democratic South Africa.

The time has also come that those who serve in the apartheid tri-cameral parliament and claim to stand for a democratic South Africa should abandon the illusion that this parliament can do anything to solve the problems of our country. This institution is as much a part of the structure of apartheid rule as are the racist army, police and the prison service. It is an instrument for the perpetuation of white minority rule. To hold out the hope that it can do anything to bring about a just social order is to attempt to hoax the people and to aid and abet the Pretoria regime in perpetuating its rule of terror. If there is any genuine anti-racist left wing within Botha's parliament, now is the time for them to abandon this house of iniquity and join the masses of the people in struggle for a truly just society. Large parts of our country are under a publicly proclaimed State of Emergency. Others are treated as though they are under such a State of Emergency. This situation no longer allows for the playing of inconsequential games presented as an effort at reform. It demands that each one of us should choose sides: one is either on the side of genuine change or one is on the side of continued repression. There is no middle road.

Those among the black people who have persisted in refusing to stop serving the army are now faced with the inevitable consequences of their mercenary stubbornness. They have now been turned into an army of occupation and administrators of martial law. If, in the past, they considered their duties as normal, they can no longer do so. There is nothing normal about an emergency. Neither will the actual tasks that they will carry out be normal. Their masters will demand of them the most heinous acts of brutality against their own people. On them will fall the greatest burdens in Pretoria's campaign of extreme repression. Once more we call on these black people to leave the ranks of the enemy which is using them to terrorize their own mothers, fathers, brothers, sisters and children. We call on those whom the enemy has armed to turn their guns against those who have invaded our townships and not point them at the unarmed black masses of our country who are fighting to liberate themselves.

There are some black people in our country who, claiming to be leaders and representatives of our people, have joined the clamour for the maintenance of apartheid law and order. The enemy is using these so-called law-abiding blacks to justify the intensified campaign of repression it has launched under the State of Emergency that it has proclaimed. We call on these misguided individuals to direct their anger against those who have brought our country to the situation in which it is today. Only recently, Afrikaner intellectuals at the state-funded National Council for Social Research correctly laid the blame for the conflict in our country on the apartheid system. It is the height of servility for the black people who call themselves leaders to refuse to acknowledge this truth and instead seek to secure a livelihood for themselves by blaming the victim of terror for the injury done to him.

The apartheid system is in crisis. The State of Emergency will not extricate the racists from this situation. All it will do is further to deepen that crisis and increase the cost in human lives of ending white minority domination in our country. We have advanced a great deal towards the realization of our goal of a united, democratic and non-racial South Africa. There can be no stopping now. There can be no turning back.

Let us therefore mobilize and march together in even greater unity towards freedom. At all times we must expect that the enemy will respond with even greater repression. We must withstand these campaigns of terror with the same determination that we have displayed over so many months. But more, we must defeat these campaigns and raise our struggle to even higher levels.

Our watchword must be mobilization, organization, struggle. All our people must be mobilized into action. All our people must be organized for action. All our people must engage in struggle. That must be our reply to the enemy's desperate counter-offensive.

In that struggle we have to set up our armed offensive. In a situation of martial law, the need for the oppressed masses to resort to people's war becomes plain for all to see. Therefore the order of the day to all units of Umkhonto we Sizwe is that they must strengthen their links with the people. They must act together with the people to inflict the greatest possible number of casualties on armed enemy personnel. They must take the battle to the enemy and, side by side with the heroic masses of our country, defeat the enemy's efforts to rule in a new way, seize the initiative from the enemy and drive him into retreat.

Thousands upon thousands of our people have been engaging the enemy in armed confrontation, using primitive means to deliver their blows. Now is the time for them to face the enemy using modern weapons of war.

At this hour of a heightened enemy counter-offensive, progressive humanity has rallied behind us as never before. The whole world has denounced Botha's State of Emergency and pledged its support for our struggle. The international community will adopt new measures to isolate the apartheid regime which has declared war against our people. Drawing strength from this international support, we must march with even greater confidence to victory. Botha's State of Emergency is an admission of defeat. Each desperate act he adopts is a sign that we are approaching our goal.

6.2 THE COMMONWEALTH AND SANCTIONS
(Address to the Royal Commonwealth Society, London, 23 June 1986)

Exactly eight months ago to the day, in Nassau, the capital of the Bahamas, heads of states and government of the Commonwealth countries assembled to debate the South African issue, strictly from the point of view of what the Commonwealth wanted to do to bring about an end to the apartheid system. The question was whether sanctions or no sanctions. Part of the reason why we are gathered here today is that that question has not yet been resolved. We meet to

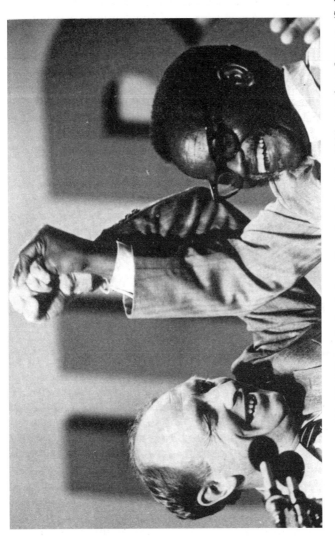

Oliver Tambo being greeted by Neil Kinnock, the Labour Party Leader, at the 1985 annual conference. *(Stefano Cagnoni, Report)*

address the same question that the Commonwealth faced in the Bahamas. The invitation to us to address you on this occasion, which we greatly appreciate, and your presence, demonstrate the profound interest and concern of the Royal Commonwealth Society over developments in southern Africa.

It would seem to us clear that in the recent past a good deal of progress has been made towards the clarification of various issues. This relates not only to the issue of what should be done to end apartheid, but also to the question of what should take its place. The current international debate hinges, therefore, on the question of how to make this country, Britain, take its proper position among the countries of the Commonwealth and the majority of the international community of nations.

As we know, in its recalcitrance, Britain is not alone. The problem of how to act effectively on the South African situation boils down to the question of how to win, how to compel the support of the United States, Great Britain and the Federal Republic of Germany for the cause of the victims of apartheid. The positions that these countries take are supportive of a crime against humanity, the permanence of white minority domination over the black majority.

Recently the debate has come to concentrate on the question of the effectiveness of measures to be imposed upon Pretoria in order to bring about as peaceful a resolution of that country's problems as possible. Questions are being raised about the effectiveness of economic measures, the possibility of their adoption universally, their impact on a liberated, post-apartheid South Africa, their effect on the independent sovereign states of southern Africa and related issues. All these questions are part of the on-going debate.

But there are pointers, very clear pointers, to the direction that this debate is taking. I have referred to Nassau, the striking unanimity of the Commonwealth countries, save for the position of Britain. From Nassau came the Commonwealth Group of Eminent Persons. They were directed to examine that situation and see whether the Pretoria regime was ready to behave in such a way as to make it unnecessary, perhaps, to consider sanctions. The Eminent Persons have passed their judgment, and it is in the hands of the international public.

Twice in the recent past, the United Nations Security Council has met, again to consider action arising out of developments in southern Africa. Twice, resolutions intended to see the international community take action were defeated by the veto exercised against those resolutions by the United States and Britain.

Last week, a World Conference to discuss sanctions against South Africa met in Paris, attended by many countries of the world, with delegations led by foreign ministers. That Conference came to the conclusion that the demand of the situation in South Africa on those who want to see a resolution of that problem is sanctions.

And we think it is important that, as we debate these questions, we should never forget that there is a horrendous situation in which violence is being perpetrated against millions of our people every day — as a matter of course. We refer here not only to the daily shootings, the bestialities inflicted on demonstrators and detainees and the vicious campaign of terror carried out against all who are opposed to the apartheid system — churchmen, whole religious communities, students, professors and teachers, workers, peasants, mothers and even children. No one is excepted.

Nor is this the end. It is certainly not the beginning. This is the situation we have endured since the beginning of the apartheid era. It simply gets worse and worse. Thousands, hundreds of thousands of people have perished under the apartheid system, and because of it. The suffering has been massive and it worsens day by day. The imposition of a State of Emergency is evidence of a worsening situation.

And so in a sense the international community does not have the leisure to be taking its time, debating inconsequential issues such as the fact that action in the form of sanctions will affect all the people of South Africa, including the victims of the apartheid system. It is idle, in the face of the destruction in terms of life which the apartheid system has caused, to be saying nothing should be done, because blacks will suffer. That kind of argument displays lack of knowledge, lack of appreciation of what apartheid has been and continues to be. It is the pain of apartheid that we want to stop by ending apartheid. We are not asking for pity for our suffering. We are asking to be supported for the sacrifices we are ready to make and are making. The burdens that sanctions will bring upon us are a sacrifice we are prepared to make.

The death that we suffer in the course of struggle is a sacrifice we are ready to make. We ask for no pity. We ask for support from those who, we believe, in our position would feel compelled to do what we are doing to seek to end the pain of apartheid.

It should also be remembered that as long as the apartheid system and the apartheid regime feel free to take their own time over what should be done, for so long shall we wait, before those of our people who have been consigned to prison for more than two decades shall be released. Outstanding leaders of our people and many others are being held this minute as caged animals simply because they dared to demand the liberty of our people. They were caged, Mr Chairman, when I came into this hall. This minute they are still there.

To their credit, their morale is as high as it ever was before, because they continue to have faith that the international community is on their side, not simply by way of declarations, but by using its great potential to change the fortunes of the apartheid system in favour of the majority of the people of South Africa and southern Africa as well.

We speak also of the inhuman burden imposed on millions of our people who have been banished to the Bantustans, the countless numbers of children who die from sheer hunger, the tens of thousands at Crossroads and others like them who are being forcibly uprooted and literally shot and butchered to compel them to live elsewhere to satisfy the apartheid designs of the Botha regime. When we talk about sanctions, we are addressing the current, on-going misery that these people must bear.

In addressing the question 'what is to be done?' it should be borne in mind that as each day passes and no action is taken, so an extra day is added in the perpetuation of this crime against humanity. Those who refuse to act accordingly make the resolution of the South African problem more complicated. But because our people are not sitting passively, but are suffering bravely, they are challenging the apartheid monster. They are seeking to do and achieve what the international community would want to, see an end to the crime against humanity.

There is no need for us here to go over the ground that has so brilliantly been covered by the Commonwealth Group of Eminent Persons. It should suffice that we emphasize only some of its conclusions. These are that the Botha regime is determined to maintain the apartheid system of white minority domination by force; that its so-called reforms constitute an attempt to strengthen this system; that violence against the people is an inherent feature of this system, and that the firm belief that the leading Western powers will not impose sanctions has encouraged the Botha regime to pursue its apartheid policy regardless of its complete rejection by our people and the rest of the international community.

white rule in 80's

The Group of Eminent Persons has also recognized the fact that, in the light of all this, we have no alternative but to fight and has correctly warned of an impending catastrophe of immense dimensions. To avoid that eventuality, the EPG has called on the Commonwealth, and indeed the rest of the world, to impose effective economic measures, which means sanctions, against apartheid South Africa.

One of the most pressing questions that arises from all this is what the British government should do in response to this Report, to the situation which obtains in South Africa and to the demands of the public, both here and abroad. We believe that the British government can no longer shirk its responsibilities to act decisively in support of the democratic, anti-racist forces of our country. The fact that this country also has the honour to be one of the permanent members of the Security Council imposes on its government an obligation to act for justice and peace in South and southern Africa. Failure to do so not only lowers the prestige of the Security Council but also puts in question the usefulness to the world community of the institution itself. It surely cannot help to strengthen the Commonwealth, of which the people of this country are justly proud, that one of its leading members, the United Kingdom, should treat its collective view with contempt.

MANDATORY SANCTIONS

What we are calling for, and have been urging for decades, are comprehensive and mandatory sanctions now. We are convinced, advisedly, that a long drawn-out conflict in South Africa will most certainly result in the destruction of the economy, to say nothing of the scale of death of which the EPG and leaders of the Commonwealth such as President Kaunda have so repeatedly warned.

The argument for selective and incremental sanctions is flawed exactly because it perpetuates Pretoria's belief that this country and South Africa's other trading partners will only act merely to defuse pressures for meaningful action. It is also an argument for imposing sanctions in such a manner that South Africa should be permitted the possibility to adjust and to weather the consequences of each specific action.

Take, for instance, the call for a ban on new investment. The fact of the matter is that new investment in South Africa has all but dried up because of the obvious crisis in the country and the related parlous state of the economy. Simply to impose such a selective measure would be to send a signal to the Botha regime that the British government is still resolved not to act in any serious way.

The argument for comprehensive and mandatory sanctions is, of course, that such a massive blow would make it almost impossible for the apartheid regime to continue in power for much longer. Such comprehensive measures would naturally include financial and trade sanctions, an oil embargo, the termination of air and maritime links, ceasing of all

[handwritten margin notes: "not an alternative for the government"; "doesn't show support as investments were drying up anyway"; "ANC feel loss of government power would weaken regime."]

co-operation in the nuclear field and the closing of all loop-holes with regard to the embargo on arms and other materi-als related to the military capacity and the repressive state machinery of the Pretoria regime, as well as other measures within the sphere of comprehensive sanctions.

It will certainly be argued by some that we are being exceedingly unreasonable to make such a call. To this we can only reiterate the point that the alternative to all this is that we will be left with nothing but the inevitable choice to fight it out with everything we have. Indeed, we will always be doing this. The consequences of this are, as was once said, too ghastly to contemplate.

And yet, the prospect of something too ghastly to contem-plate can be no deterrent to a people who are determined to have their freedom. It is not the power of the apartheid machinery, or even its efficiency, that is the determining fac-tor. It is our humanity. It is the fact that we are people, we are human. We have decided to liberate our country and our-selves, to get rid of a crime against us and humanity. We will make all the necessary sacrifices to achieve that end.

Those who equivocate on the question of economic sanc-tions are preparing conditions which will ensure that what most people would want to avoid does in fact occur. It has been called a 'bloodbath' and 'the reduction of South Africa to a wasteland'. Prospects of a bloodbath and the reduction of South Africa to a wasteland will not stop this struggle. We would much rather that no blood was lost, that the country was left intact. But not at the expense of our continued enslavement. It is in the hands of the international communi-ty, perhaps today I should say in the hands of the Commonwealth, especially the head of the Commonwealth, to intervene on our side, on the side of humanity.

In the light of this it will not do to persist with arguments that the black people and the neighbouring states will suffer from the imposition of sanctions. We have dealt with that. The key factor is that in the absence of sanctions, the conflict with all its consequences will multiply itself a hundred-fold, and more. We believe also that the time has come for an end to the interminable debate about the effectiveness or non-effectiveness of sanctions.

Practice itself has answered this question. To add to this, the Pretoria regime has admitted publicly how much it fears sanctions, exactly because of their effectiveness. According to the Proclamation declaring a State of Emergency earlier this month, it is an offence to 'encourage or promote disinvestment or the application of sanctions or foreign action against the Republic'. If sanctions were of no consequence and would have no effect, it would not have been necessary for Pretoria to adopt such a position.

We are at war against the apartheid system and its inhumanities, for the right to be human in a land of humans. We, therefore, are determined to fight, alone if necessary. In that sense we view sanctions as a complementary form of action to the struggle we are waging, and must intensify, within the country. We do not see sanctions by themselves as ending the apartheid system. We see them as aiding the speedy end of the apartheid system.

An important element in that struggle is the mobilization of all our people, including our white compatriots, to act against the apartheid regime. The argument that sanctions would drive whites into a *laager* fails to take into account the fact that many whites are in fact joining this struggle. We are convinced that as the price for maintaining the apartheid system rises, so will it be clear to many more of these white South Africans that the time for change has come.

We are convinced that a consensus in favour of sanctions has emerged in this country. We are encouraged by the positions that various sections of the British public have taken, including some among the business community. We are convinced that given the political will there exists today the possibility to oblige the British government to act in a meaningful way.

At the same time there still exists a great reservoir of opinion in this country which cannot be described in any other way than racist, I'm afraid. This was reflected in a newspaper yesterday which made bold to state that 'African blacks, inside and outside the Republic, (are) for the most part so backward'. 'African blacks' means black people in Africa. Some, of course, are in South Africa. They are all 'backward'. And the point that is being made in the article is that the international community tends to forget the factor of race — they are 'backward' because they are black. The writer concludes that they are backward and 'white supremacy (in South Africa) is there to stay'.

These comments are made in the context of explaining the positions of the British Prime Minister in opposing sanctions, and suggests that she appreciates this fact of 'backwardness'. But the writer also believes — we submit wrongly, we wait to be proved wrong — that the majority of the British public are also aware of this 'backwardness' and therefore the permanence of white supremacy in South Africa. And if that is the position, who would want to oppose white supremacy, if it is going to be there forever? This is given in explanation of the position of the British government. It is an opinion credited to the British public.

If the Commonwealth breaks up because of the intransigence of the British government, it would be an unfortunate but inevitable conclusion that those who have the power to decide will have been influenced by such racist notions as were reflected in the newspaper to which we have referred. The impression we have, that the British government considers as not very important the views of the Commonwealth as opposed to those of its NATO and EEC allies, emphasizes the need for the British government to act correctly if it is not to be seen to be contributing to the exacerbation of world racial tensions.

And we trust that the countries of the Commonwealth will not allow themselves to be dragged into an alliance against the people of Africa, however 'backward' they may be, into an alliance against the people of southern Africa, into an alliance with apartheid. The time calls for great firmness.

We have, in the past, said that the unconditional release of all political prisoners is a prerequisite to any consideration on our part of a negotiated settlement of the South African question. Nothing has happened in this regard except a continuing and stubborn insistence by the Botha regime that these leaders, as well as the ANC as such, must renounce violence — and this in a situation in which the most massive violence against our people is being perpetrated every day, violence which is being hidden behind the most comprehensive news blackout that our country has ever seen.

media hides violence

We are convinced, as the EPG was, that the Botha regime is not ready for negotiations. Nevertheless, we remain of the view that the campaign for the immediate and unconditional release of all political prisoners must continue to build up to even higher levels of intensity.

Surely it should be obvious to everybody that once these patriots are released unconditionally and the situation thus created for all our leaders, across the entire spectrum of the democratic movement, to come together and have the possibility of discussing the situation as it is today, and its demands, as well as the way forward, this would also provide the possibility for us to address even the question of negotiations as a leadership. Once this happens, we can then address the question of negotiations, on the basis that a demonstration has been made by the Botha regime of its seriousness about negotiations.

Those of us who have lived in southern Africa over the past ten years have experienced the attitude of the Pretoria regime towards negotiations. The record is dismal. It has never negotiated anything seriously, not with the Mozambicans, not with the Angolans, not with the Namibians. We do not want a repetition of so-called meaningful negotiations.

Pretoria must prove its bona fides. It is not possible to negotiate with someone you totally distrust in regard to his aims about negotiation. We will not participate in giving the Pretoria regime the possibility of extending its lease of life by pretending to be negotiating. But it can demonstrate its serious intention to negotiate. Its words do not add up to anything. It is its actions that must speak.

The next few weeks are very important to us because, by

their concrete actions, the government of Great Britain, the rest of the EEC and the United States will demonstrate whether they are ready and willing to take sides against apartheid by imposing sanctions or whether they insist on continuing to underpin white minority rule, which prevails in our country.

If the Botha regime, as it claims, has not used a tenth of its might against those who want to see a new order in South Africa — a non-racial, democratic and united South Africa — if they have not used one tenth of their might against us, then neither have we used a tenth of our strength.

We count on all who are present here to act in support of our cause; to push the British government to join those who would want to stop the Botha regime from pushing South Africa over the brink.

6.3 DISCUSSIONS WITH GORBACHEV
(An ANC delegation, led by President Tambo, visited Moscow in November 1986 at the time of the celebration of the 69th anniversary of the 1917 Revolution. Tambo spoke to the Press in Moscow on 6 November)

As you know, we have already met the General Secretary of the Central Committee of the CPSU, Comrade Mikhail Gorbachev. We have also held discussions with Comrade Anatoly Dobrynin, Secretary of the Central Committee of the CPSU. We have also met the leadership of the Soviet Afro-Asian Solidarity Committee, whose delegation was headed by its first Vice-Chairman, Dr Vladimir Totstikov. Our Secretary-General, Comrade Alfred Nzo, is currently having conversations with the Deputy Foreign Minister, Comrade Anatoly Adamishin.

Later today we shall participate in a public meeting organized to commemorate the October Revolution. We will, of course, be present at Red Square tomorrow. Until we leave over the weekend, we shall be holding further informal discussions with our Soviet colleagues.

An historic meeting—Oliver Tambo with President Gorbachev in Moscow, 1986. (*IDAF*)

Tomorrow is 7 November, a very important holiday for the Soviet people and an historic date on the world political calendar. We would like today to extend our greetings and congratulations to the people of this country and wish them the best as they celebrate the 69th anniversary of the revolution.

The few days that we have spent here have helped us to understand better the tasks that the Soviet people have set themselves, including the central objective of achieving disarmament and world peace and radically improving their own material and spiritual well-being. We wish them success in all these endeavours and are certain that progress on these issues will benefit not only the Soviet people but humanity in general. Therefore we 'Sprazdnikom' to all the citizens of this country and many thanks for having us as your guests as you rejoice over your hard-won success during the last 69 years.

We have held what was, for us, an historic meeting with the General Secretary of the CPSU, Comrade Mikhail Gorbachev. We emerged from this meeting greatly strengthened by the knowledge that the Soviet Union stands firmly with us in the struggle for a united, democratic and non-racial South Africa, an independent Namibia and a peaceful region of southern Africa. We draw immense satisfaction and inspiration from the fact that the Soviet Union is resolved to contribute everything within its possibilities and, within the context of our own requests, to assist the ANC, SWAPO and the peoples of our region to achieve these objectives.

We would like to state it here as our firm conviction that in taking these positions, the Soviet Union is acting neither out of considerations of selfish interest nor with a desire to establish a so-called sphere of influence. We are therefore more than ever certain that in the CPSU, the government and the people of this country we have a genuine ally in our struggle against racism, colonial domination and aggression. We are honoured that Mikhail Gorbachev could find time in his busy schedule to receive us and wish to thank him most sincerely for this.

During our visit we have also had occasion to listen to a moving account of the efforts of the Soviet leadership to help rid humanity of the threat of nuclear war. We believe that no thinking person can avoid being partisan for disarmament and world peace, because to guarantee the survival of humanity demands that all of us must act for peace. The Reykjavik Summit has come and gone. But it would seem to us that the promise it held for the human race must remain a factor motivating all peoples to fight even harder for disarmament, because Reykjavik demonstrated that peace is possible, thanks to the extraordinarily bold, but necessary, proposals that the Soviet Union put on the table. The promise of peace must be a spur to its realization.

We understand the urgent need for peace because we are ourselves victims of repression and war. Throughout southern Africa people are dying daily because of a desperate effort by the apartheid rulers to maintain themselves in power. Only recently, this untenable situation claimed the life of the President of Mozambique, the late Comrade Samora Machel, who died in circumstances which have yet to be explained.

The Pretoria regime is caught in a deep crisis from which it cannot extricate itself. Whatever it does, including the imposition of a vicious state of emergency and the latest reshuffle of the apartheid cabinet, will not save it from defeat and destruction. Our people and those of Namibia, led by SWAPO, are set on an unstoppable march to liberation. Similarly, the peoples in the rest of southern Africa are determined to resist apartheid aggression and destabilization and to contribute what they can to the total liquidation of the apartheid system.

Clearly, the US policy of so-called constructive engagement has not succeeded in saving the Botha regime nor in strengthening the positions of its authors, the Reagan Administration. We are entitled to conclude that the Congressional elections in the United States, two days ago, in part represented a vote against the pro-apartheid policies of the US government.

The result creates even better possibilities for us and the world anti-apartheid movement further to advance the campaign for comprehensive and mandatory sanctions against the apartheid regime. We are certain that in this area we shall continue to score new victories resulting in the further isolation of apartheid South Africa and, accordingly, an improvement of our possibilities to bring into being a democratic South Africa without bloodshed and destruction.

On 8 January next year we shall be observing the 75th anniversary of the ANC. We believe that this will provide a uniquely appropriate occasion for the world community to implement programmes of action designed to ensure a speedy end to the apartheid system. East and West, North and South can and must act together in a decisive manner for the triumph of democracy in South Africa, the emergence of a society in which black and white will live together as equals, in which all our people will have the right and possibility to decide as free men and women how to shape their destiny.

This is one of the great imperatives of our time. We are glad that we have found complete understanding and support for these positions in the Soviet Union.

6.4 OLOF PALME MEMORIAL LECTURE ON DISARMAMENT AND DEVELOPMENT
(Address in Riverside Church, New York, 21 January 1987)

Tonight is a most moving occasion — for me personally, for the leaders of the African National Congress who are here with me, for all South Africans who live in this country. We are moved by the rapturous reception accorded us by this great assembly of friends and supporters, and more particularly by the cause which brings us together tonight. I should like to express my most profound thanks to the Riverside Church Disarmament Programme and the great honour accorded the African National Congress in inviting me to deliver the first Olof Palme Memorial Lecture.

Five weeks from today the Swedish people and the rest of democratic humanity will be observing the first anniversary of the assassination of Olof Palme. On a winter's day in February, this supremely humane man died because he had dared to seek the birth of a humane world. His death will forever remain a poignant and noble plea for the healthy human condition he sought to construct across the face of the globe.. . . We are honoured to be here today to try to amplify with our weak voices the message which Olof Palme can no longer convey himself. But we speak only as some of those who would have gained liberty and happiness from the realization of his dream, beneficiaries of his vision of a world redeemed.

How much better it would have been if his life partner and companion, Lisbet Palme, were standing here, speaking to us. More than all of us present, she would have conveyed to us something of the making of that vision which she, too, helped to form. She would have shown us the portrait of an outstanding statesman, whose inner being she helped to model. We would have been happy if she were with us today, attending a meeting that is as much a tribute to Lisbet as to Olof Palme.

The violence of our century took her husband's life. It succeeded in claiming him as its victim because he abhorred that violence with a singular intensity and sought to lead a life that, by its example, would be an argument against violence. He died because he believed that to protect his person with the instruments of war would itself constitute the fostering of the use of force to which he was implacably opposed. He perished as he did because the offspring of the violence of our century remain as yet steeped in the idea that brute force can vanquish reason.

Each of the nearly nine decades of the twentieth century has contributed its share to the blood-letting. Like the proverbial Prince of Darkness, each has seemed to require its portion and elixir of human blood to feed on. Along the path of its ghastly and fearsome logic are strewn graves that had to be dug to accommodate its demands. Among the fresh sepulchres of the last five years are those of Olof Palme of Sweden, Indira Gandhi of India, Mozambique's Samora Machel and Grenada's Maurice Bishop.

The assassination of all these who were to us friends — our

leaders and comrades-in-arms — served to re-awaken our sensitivity to the horror of man's violence to man, to the enormity of the crimes of violence that were and are being perpetrated daily against people in many parts of the world. Their deaths constituted a stern rebuke to us: that we can never afford to give encouragement to the killers by getting accustomed to their deeds, by coming to accept that the blood in the streets is as much part of the human reality as the signposts on the highway. They were a reminder confirming the continued virulence of the forces that spawned the murderers of Salvador Allende of Chile, of Martin Luther King, Jr, and of Robert and John F. Kennedy.

Olof Palme hated and despised the assassins. He would, if he could, have broken up their murderous conspiracies by the force of argument, challenging all cabals to a contest of intellects and a confrontation of ideas. But even he knew, with a great depth of understanding, that the hands that fire the shots are the products of a century that has seen two world wars and a great number of bloody local conflicts.

They, like all of us, are part of the same humanity from among whom sprang the Nazi criminals who carried out the indelible horror of the attempted genocidal extermination of the Jewish and Slavic people. In common with us all, the killers are heirs to a past over which hang the mushroom clouds of the hydrogen bombs that devastated Hiroshima and Nagasaki.

Olof Palme knew that to end the use or the threat of the use of force in international relations, to secure and guarantee a just and stable world peace, requires a determined struggle to overcome the tradition of a ready resort to arms. He was aware that the triumph of world peace would have to be achieved against the resistance of those who have a vested interest in the manufacture of weapons, whose place in society obliges them to argue that world peace is a utopian hope of the simple-minded.

Those of us who have a vested interest in world peace — and the African National Congress and the people of South Africa count themselves firmly among the world peace forces — those of us who are involved in this struggle, as Olof Palme was, need to be clear about the obstacles we have to overcome. One of these, which we have to stop and reverse, is a tendency which has characterized the present century.

When this period began, our own country was going through the agonies of the Anglo-Boer War, with its own measure of brutalities. When the First World War started, the rate and the manner of the slaughter of human beings in the battlefields of Europe made the Anglo-Boer War look almost like a gentlemanly affair. In its turn, the Second World War marked an even higher level of savagery, including the use of nuclear weapons, while the Vietnam War was accompanied by newer and yet more horrifying methods of war.

In other conflicts, such as those in some Latin American countries, the use of secret murder squads and the practice of kidnapping and assassinating opponents of tyranny added new dimensions to the repressive use of state power. These methods, tested out in Argentina, Guatemala, Chile, and other countries, are now being used by the Pretoria regime in our country. They would undoubtedly be used in any larger international conflict that may break out.

The point we are making is that throughout the last nine decades, there has been a consistent tendency towards the improvement of the destructive capacity of weapons of war. This has led to the development of nuclear weapons and the means for their delivery. At the same time, and as a necessary corollary, the forces whose task it is to plan for and conduct war have worked to improve these and all other elements of their destructive enterprise.

The struggle for world peace is about the direct opposite of all of that. Its objective is to dismantle what the proponents of such concepts as 'the balance of terror' view as outstanding achievements. When all of us join forces to demand an end to nuclear tests, it is because we are opposed to the improvement of nuclear weapons. We want to keep space free of any weapons of any kind, because we do not wish to see mankind with a better capacity to fight. In the end, we would rather that humanity had neither the incentive nor the means to engage in a conflict that would end the human race itself.

When Olof Palme convened the Commission on Disarmament and joined the Five Continent Peace Initiative for disarmament and world peace, it was because he knew that these fundamental questions of our time could not be left to those who have nuclear weapons and to experts. To save themselves from destruction, the ordinary people who know nothing about trajectories of missiles or the techniques of splitting atoms have to take their destiny into their own hands.

Today, the mass peace movement occupies an important place in international politics as an expression of that resolve. As the millions march for world peace, with flowers in their hands, they reaffirm the message that Olof Palme tried to convey to all of us, that people can and must walk with no weapons in their hands to demand that everybody else should have no weapons of mass destruction at their disposal. His death can serve only to encourage us to fight on, defending ourselves from the assassins by our unity, our numbers and the justice of our cause.

The question of the activation of the ordinary people in the struggle for peace is also very important with respect to another issue which was of deep concern to Olof Palme. This is the matter of the democratization of the decision-making process both nationally and internationally. Confident that open debate was a necessary element in the striving of all peoples to determine their future, Olof Palme was a champion of real democratic practice. He was not satisfied with the mere forms, but was deeply concerned to see the substance.

The technological and scientific revolution has transformed questions of war and peace into a complicated affair. This has enhanced the role of experts and specialists and thus concentrated power into even fewer hands than in the past. Given the nature of modern non-conventional weapons, this means that these professionals and a handful of politicians in fact have the power of life and death over the whole of mankind. The peace movement constitutes a historic struggle to democratize international relations with specific reference to the decisive questions of war and peace.

Olof Palme sought to achieve this result with regard to the entirety of the system of international affairs. As much as he understood that the world needs peace, so did he comprehend and engage in struggle against underdevelopment and poverty. He saw the connection between disarmament and development not only in terms of the option of turning swords into ploughshares. He also understood that the achievement of peace itself requires that the world community should abolish underdevelopment and guarantee the social progress of all peoples. While the world is divided between the super-rich and the abjectly poor there can be no peace. As long as the super-rich pour enormous resources into the development of weapons of mass destruction, it will be impossible to banish hunger both within the developed countries themselves and in the Third World.

Forever concerned to promote democratic practice, Olof Palme was unswervingly committed to seeing the poor stand up and speak for themselves. Proud as he was of the political, economic, and social achievements that the Swedish working class had won for itself in struggle, through its trade unions and his own Social Democratic Party, Olof Palme wanted to see the poor of the world stand up and speak for themselves. Accordingly, he held the Organization of African Unity and the Non-Aligned Movement in high esteem. In particular, he entertained an abiding hope that the United Nations Organization would thrive, as an effective voice of the nations of the world, especially the weakest. He viewed it as an instrument that should serve mankind to redress all grievances, to give power to the weak, to marry the two imperatives of world peace and the fastest possible development of those most in need.

Historical circumstance, which has included the colonization of whole continents, has resulted in the concentration of economic and military power in a few countries. The issue of redressing this imbalance hinges on the requirement which Olof Palme saw so clearly: that it was necessary to fight against all attempts to deprive the underdeveloped nations of their potential and actual political power. At a time when the

Third World is rendered more vulnerable to pressure and blackmail because of its considerable economic problems, the task of strengthening the bargaining power of the poor, of giving proper meaning to their right to self-determination, assumes a new significance.

Our own people will always remember Olof Palme as one of us, an unswerving opponent of the apartheid system, one who took sides by supporting the oppressed and our organization, the African National Congress. Apart from his deep-seated revulsion at the theory and practice of racial domination in our country, he was determined to ensure that we too should have unrestricted access to political power and thus put ourselves in the position where we could take our own sovereign decisions about the future of our country.

Proceeding from this same fundamental thesis, he sided with the Vietnamese people against the attempts of the various US Administrations to impose their will on Vietnam. A consistent ally of all who fight for national liberation, Olof Palme played an important role in reducing the negative impact of those who sought to define our struggles within the parameters of the East-West conflict. Representing as he did a small, neutral West European country, his ideas and his practice carried considerable weight. They confirmed what to us seems obvious: that, being an act of rebellion against domination, the struggle for national liberation cannot be predicated on serving a new master.

Were he present today, Olof Palme would surely have said that the struggling people of South Africa, as those of Namibia and the rest of southern Africa, should be supported on their own terms. He would have argued, as we must, that a democratic country such as the United States must promote democracy in South Africa in part by upholding our right to have our own history, to have our own national experience, to decide what is best for us.

We recognize the fact that in the real world in which we live and in which we have to conduct our struggle, countries and various factions within these countries place our country as it is today and will be tomorrow, in the context of what are described as national interests. Olof Palme thought the national interests of his own country would best be served by the genuine liberation of South Africa and Namibia and the guarantee of peace, stability, and social progress throughout southern Africa.

Elsewhere, others are making it a condition for the support of the national liberation and democratic forces of our country that we must reproduce ourselves in their image. In the process, they have borrowed and taken over from the opponents of democracy in our country a characterization of us which is naturally intended to serve the purposes of the oppressors. On the other hand, we must of necessity define ourselves and our purposes in a way that negates our present condition of slavery in all its forms. For us, the process of the negation of the apartheid system must mean that we oppose the arguments and the practices that led to the banning of the African National Congress, the dissolution of the Liberal Party, and the proscription of the Communist Party. We must create the conditions in which it will be possible for any among our people to form a social democratic, Christian democratic or any other democratic party of their choice. Without underestimating the difficulties, Olof Palme understood our resolve to set ourselves free — free to think and act independently, free to differ with him without losing his support, free to expand the frontiers of liberty universally by asserting our own right to live as a liberated people in an emancipated world. I think we can say truthfully that he was as happy to be associated with us as we were honoured to count on his support. It is our prayer to the future that those who count themselves as democrats anywhere in the world will pause for a brief moment to reflect on the example that Olof Palme set.

We have spoken of Olof Palme's abhorrence of violence. That attitude was also reflected, among other things, by his promotion of Sweden's traditional neutrality and his timely opposition to military blocs. And yet he was not a pacifist. Neither would he allow hypocritical positions about the issue of violence to pass as immutable and inherited wisdom.

On occasion, when he addressed the question of armed struggle against racist and colonial domination in southern Africa, he referred to the history of his own country and party. Referring to the period when Sweden had colonized Norway, he said there could never have been any peace between the peoples of these countries until Norway was free. The oppressive Swedes of the day could not demand peaceable behaviour of the Norwegians until Norway had become decolonized. Nobody has the right to demand peaceable behaviour of us within our own country until we are free. Furthermore, as Olof Palme argued, drawing on the history of his party, nobody should demand of us that we should seek change by non-violent means when we are denied all constitutional possibilities to redress the grievances of the majority.

We yearn for the day when these issues, as they affect us in southern Africa, will be treated by the rest of the Western world with the same honesty with which Olof Palme approached them. We know that the American people went to war to achieve their independence and to suppress slavery. We have been taught that modern Britain and France, the Soviet Union, China, Mexico, and many other countries owe their being in part to armed rebellions due to the oppression the ruling classes of the day imposed on the respective peoples of these countries. We also know that these people took up arms because they valued life, as we do.

Our own manifesto proclaiming our resort to arms was no different in its meaning and its intention from the proclamations that the peoples of Europe issued when they took up arms against the genocidal Nazi regime. Why, then, does the West treat us as an exception? Whence the new-found argument that the use of armed force to achieve political purposes is impermissible?

A formidable debater, Olof Palme always sought to cut through the cant and hypocrisy of those who wield power. We too must cut through the cant and hypocrisy as a result of which apartheid is condemned by word while it is given material sustenance. We must expose for what it is the description of white minority violence as the maintenance of law and order. We must spread the understanding that all talk about minority rights is a disguised demand for white privilege. We who know from experience have to cut through the cant and hypocrisy to explain that to reform oppression is to maintain oppression in an amended form.

Liberty is an act of liberation both for the oppressed and the oppressors, a condition for the peaceful coexistence of peoples and individuals.

No words, however clever, no concepts, however profound in their appearance, can reconcile the conflict between freedom and oppression, between truth and falsification. Nothing could ever persuade Olof Palme that he must reconcile himself to the inevitability of world war, the permanence of want among millions of human beings and the oppression of people on any grounds, such as those of race, colour, sex, religion or nationality.

Every age has its prophet. The immediate conditions of life demand of the peoples that they act in particular ways. And yet each day carries both the burden of its past and the seeds of the future. Our day bears both the scars of yesterday and the potential for human development whose basis has been laid by the present and earlier generations. To understand and overcome the former as well as to appreciate and exploit the latter requires men and women with the honesty, courage, intelligence, and instinct of an Olof Palme.

As a prophet of our age, Olof Palme showed us a vision of a world free of oppression, hunger, and war. He spoke for millions of people who readily responded to the imperatives of our time to be free, secure, and not threatened by poverty. To achieve these objectives the ordinary people must still overcome a desperate resistance from those who view the striving for these inalienable rights as an act of treason.

In the course of this struggle, some of us will die as Olof Palme did. Others will sacrifice as Nelson Mandela, Walter Sisulu, Govan Mbeki and others are doing. And yet we know that, as surely as their names will never be forgotten, all they stand for will certainly triumph. In the face of the risen people, let all tyrants tremble. In the interests of all humanity, we will insure that the cause for which Olof Palme sacrificed his life emerges victorious.

6.5 STRATEGIC OPTIONS FOR INTERNATIONAL COMPANIES
(Address to the Business International Conference, London, 27 May 1987)

I am told that it is inherent in the business of businessmen that they live with uncertainty. At the same time it is part of your everyday tradecraft to talk of such issues as investments, economic growth rates, profits and losses and to back up your technical arguments by many statistics.

For my part I shall try to avoid technical arguments and statistics but I shall grapple with some certainties. South Africa is trapped in an irreversible crisis. The struggle of the black people has reached the point of no return. Since the onset of the current phase in the crisis which set in in the latter half of 1984, thousands of black men, women, and children have been gunned down by the racist army and police in the black townships. In the life-span of the present state of emergency more than thirty thousand have been detained without trial, including over 2,500 children.

Apartheid has long become intolerable to our people. We have spilt too much blood and lost too many lives to stop our forward march. Apartheid tyranny has forced us to become accustomed to injury and death. Everything that the racist regime does now in an attempt to suppress and defeat our movement becomes an added spur to us to act with an even greater sense of urgency to terminate a system which is capable of such gross evil. When millions of people are inspired by this degree of determination then victory is inevitable.

On the other hand, the regime of P.W. Botha has driven itself into a corner. He has no coherent strategy except to tighten the screws of repression. Of course he dresses up this naked and increasing spiral of brutality with the contention that 'law and order' are a necessary precondition for his brand of 'reform'. One wonders: is there anyone who is still prepared to buy such an empty package of meaningless promises?

Because of the truism that business executives live with uncertainty it is perhaps understandable that you constantly hanker after certainty and are therefore tempted by Botha's promises. And change that does not disturb the existing order is sometimes alluring, however much it may be illusory.

The African National Congress, together with the overwhelming majority of the people of our country, do not consider as meaningful any changes aimed at reducing the brutalities of apartheid or ameliorating its effects whilst the shackles that bind the black people are left intact. Liberation in our country requires the destruction of the apartheid system in its entirety: its ideological roots, its institutional branches, its violent seeds and its bitter fruits of oppression, racism and exploitation.

Liberation must therefore entail the transfer of power to the people of South Africa so that we can collectively determine and shape the society we desire, create the institutions and structures required and decide by whom and how they will be operated. Our struggle is for the creation of a non-racial, democratic and united South Africa founded on the principle of one person, one vote — a principle which must be untainted by any concepts based upon racial and ethnic categories, which Botha uses to ensure the survival of white domination and by means of which he denies the oneness of all South Africans.

Reform of apartheid is a meaningless concept. It is a stratagem by which Botha tries to retain control over the lives of our people, to arrest the process leading to fundamental change and to steer this process away from the fulfilment of our people's aspirations. The bottom line of this stratagem can be summed up as sharing power while retaining control over the destiny of our people in the hands of the white minority. Those who still insist that change in South Africa can only come through reform, in effect accept that apartheid must continue, albeit in a different guise, and that the white minority should retain their monopoly of decision-making. And more. Bereft of any strategy for real change Botha seeks acceptance that he, his party and the all-white parliament are the agents for change in our country.

Let it be said clearly: the African National Congress is committed to bringing about fundamental change to the entire socio-economic and political formation which constitutes the South Africa of today. In case anyone should be tempted to ignore these realities, let us remind ourselves that almost 40 years ago, and before the present Nationalist regime came to power, the historian Arthur Keppel-Jones concluded 'that the salvation of the country can only lie in the reversal of historic tendencies, a reversal so thorough as to constitute a revolution'.

Through unrelenting struggle the democratic forces of our country, under the overall leadership of the African National Congress, have now become rightfully the locus of change. The responsibility for destroying apartheid and liberating our country rests with our people. The persistent tyranny of the apartheid system, which had often been proclaimed by its architects as a variant of Fascism and Nazism, forced us to take up arms to end this crime against humanity. Then, as now, we were conscious of the awesome potential for bloodshed and destruction inherent in the character of the South African conflict. Nothing that has happened since that historic decision in 1961 has altered the validity of that choice. Every move by the Botha regime underlines our need to intensify the armed struggle side by side with our mass political offensive.

APARTHEID'S INTERNATIONAL CONNECTIONS

Within this strategy we see the need for international sanctions even more urgently than before. We conceived of sanctions and the isolation of the apartheid regime as a weapon which would complement our people's efforts, and not as a substitute.

The efficacy of this complementary weapon flows out of the

fact that South African society has, to a considerable extent, been the product of foreign influence and that, to a significant degree, its political and socio-economic character has been determined by outside interests. And more. Over the years Western companies and finance houses have helped to build and continue to prop up the apartheid system: trade and foreign investment have bolstered the apartheid economy and added to the resources which the apartheid State has recklessly wasted in the pursuit of inhuman schemes of so-called social engineering founded on racism; furthermore, this trade and investment has enabled the apartheid economy to fund ever-increasing expenditure on the State's coercive machinery which is aimed at internal repression and external aggression; the flow of technology from outside helps to refine that apartheid machinery and make it more efficient; military collaboration has enabled the Pretoria regime to gain access to arms and build an armaments industry despite the mandatory arms embargo. These international connections have helped sustain, and continue to sustain, the very system we seek to abolish.

It should be clear by now that there can be no peaceful resolution to the struggle we are engaged in. One cannot even begin to address the issue without recognizing that violence is inherent and endemic in the system of white minority rule. Violence emanates from the apartheid system. What is on the agenda today is the extent to which determined action to terminate these international connections will help minimize the amount of bloodshed and destruction that is unavoidable before freedom, democracy and justice prevail in South Africa.

We are encouraged that the business community within as well as outside our country, and governments, have begun to rethink their positions in relation to the South African struggle. And we believe that the dialogue arising from this process will positively reflect upon our struggle and the future of our country, as well as upon the entire southern African region. Encouraging as these tendencies are, they are as yet wholly inadequate. Today no one dares defend apartheid. But statements of rejection and condemnation are not enough.

Within South Africa the business community persists in believing that reform is a realistic path to change. Their programmes of reform, however boldly they have begun to challenge the credos of apartheid, shy away from the fundamental political demand of the black people, namely one person, one vote.

Internationally, business executives and bankers are becoming less confident of the status quo in South Africa that they have been defending, and more reluctant to invest any more. If one may be permitted to characterize the present stage of re-thinking, the tendency is one of beginning to hedge your bets, rather than to change sides.

Disinvestment and economic sanctions have emerged as an unmistakable tendency. As the crisis deepens and the struggle in South Africa intensifies, this tendency will grow. The majority of the people throughout the world, and in particular the Western world, recognize that apartheid is a crime against humanity and that investment, trade, technology transfer and military collaboration with the Pretoria regime are indefensible. In the meantime, the escalating struggle inside South Africa, combined with a stagnant economy moving towards bankruptcy, necessarily increases the risk to investments and inexorably whittles away the profit ratios that have hitherto made collaboration with Pretoria and investment in the apartheid economy such an attractive proposition.

Many companies and some banks have in the recent period begun to disinvest. And many governments have imposed limited and selective sanctions. Whilst the tendency is encouraging, it is also true that the process is much of a mixed bag. Essential to the support that we are seeking is not only a stoppage of the flow of funds into the apartheid economy, but an effective withdrawal of funds from that economy. Secondly, we insist that the flow of technology into the apartheid economy be arrested and frozen. Whilst some of the pullouts are clearly genuine, most are highly problematic and it is understandable that we should look at these with a high degree of suspicion. While some of the creditor banks claim that the three-year rescheduling agreement was unilaterally forced on them, some of them are actively considering converting their short-term loans to longer-term claims that will be repaid in ten years, thereby diluting the pressure potential that had been built up by the initial refusal to reschedule. Some companies have gone so far as to transfer money into South Africa and arranged for purchasers to repay out of future profits on extremely favourable terms! Is this not a case of business-as-usual, except in name? Perhaps this is more a case that illustrates the capacity of those in business to acknowledge back-handedly the growing power of the campaign for disinvestment and sanctions.

MULTINATIONALS AND THE MILITARY

It is difficult for us to accept the argument of business both inside and outside the country that it is politically impotent. Business has chosen, until now, to align itself with and benefit from the economic and military state that is part of the apartheid system. Let us for a moment pause to look at the ways in which business is enmeshed in the repressive machinery of the State by legislation and practice.

All companies in South Africa, including multinationals and subsidiaries of foreign concerns, are integrated into Pretoria's strategic planning and directly into the repressive machinery. This is done institutionally by their participation on Committees and Boards, by complying with legislation, and by financial and other support.

In addition to taxes and purchase of defence bonds, most companies top-up the salaries of their white employees while they are doing their national service in the South African Defence Force. No law requires them to do so. It would appear that only a few small companies have desisted from engaging in this practice. From a study of the national service pay scales, it is clear that business enterprises are directly and voluntarily subsidizing the South African Defence Force. This practice means that some of the SADF soldiers occupying the townships and Namibia and engaged in aggressive military actions, particularly against Angola, are being paid in part by the companies that employ them in civilian life. Though there is widespread concern about the role that the South African Defence Force is playing in the black townships and against internal so-called unrest, it would seem that business prefers to rationalize its direct subsidizing of the SADF on the grounds that it also has to take into account the so-called needs of employees who are performing national service!

Representatives of 21 employers' organizations sit on the Defence Manpower Liaison Committee, which succeeded the Defence Advisory Council in 1982. The 1982 Defence White Paper states that this Committee 'meets regularly and consists of the Chief of Staff Personnel, the Chiefs of Staff Personnel of the four arms of the Service and representatives of 21 employer organizations, and its aim is to promote communication and mutual understanding between the SADF and Commerce and Industry with regard to a common source of manpower'. The Defence Manpower Liaison Committee is reproduced at the regional levels and it has been easy to establish that the regional committees deal with a variety of issues including intelligence briefings aimed at placing, and I quote, 'controversial subjects into the correct perspective'.

In addition to the Defence Manpower Liaison Committee, business leaders also sit on the various key policy-making bodies of the country — all of which place many of them at the heart of the South African military-industrial complex, both profiting from it, and indebted to it. In terms of the National Procurement Act there are ministerial powers to compel any company to supply, manufacture and process goods. In most cases the minister does not have to use his powers. Their mere existence has been sufficient for companies to supply whatever is requested, be it vehicles, tents or oil for the SADF.

Hundreds of installations and areas have been designated national keypoints under the National Keypoints Act. Owners of these factories or plants are required to train and equip their own militia. Usually, but not always, made up of white employees, these are trained in 'counter-insurgency and riot control'. The companies have to provide access for SADF units to their premises and to incorporate their own militia in regional so-called Defence Planning. They also have to provide storage facilities for arms. In terms of this act the whole process is kept secret and there are severe penalties for even disclosing that a given plant, mine or installation has been designated a keypoint.

Some multinationals initially protested about having to bear the costs, but there is no evidence that any have refused to comply. In fact, there is reason to believe that the overwhelming majority of identified keypoints were co-operating fully with the Pretoria regime. It cannot be denied that international companies are co-operating with the South African military establishment not only in instances where they are required to do so by law. As the case of the topping-up of salaries of employees who are doing national service shows, their co-operation is extensive and indefensible, particularly before their black labour force which is so grossly exploited.

We have taken some time to dwell on these aspects because we believe that statements rejecting apartheid must be accompanied by concrete action which visibly breaks the intimacy that characterizes the relationship between international business and the apartheid state and economy. The co-operation that exists in relation to the repressive machinery of the State tends to be ignored by those who justify their refusal to disinvest on the grounds that by their presence they are helping to bring about change in the interests of the black man.

With apartheid universally condemned and disinvestment and sanctions vigorously resisted, international business has turned to justify its presence by promising to provide so-called neutral support in the form of black education, housing and welfare. It is strange indeed that support for the cause of the black man has to be neutral while support for the apartheid system is as positive as emerges in the connection to be found in relation to the repressive machinery of the State. In any event, the issue is not simply about black education, housing or welfare, notwithstanding that these are grossly neglected by the apartheid State. The point is that such neutral support will always be compromised by the apartheid system. In fact, such neutral support will further enmesh international business in the apartheid system.

If the preponderance of evidence points to the fact that hitherto corporations have undermined their own future by assuming political impotence, today it has become far more urgent that they define their political alignment. This, necessarily, means that corporations have to distance themselves from and resist the short-term pressures that lock them into Pretoria's embrace. It is our firm view that the true interests of the business community lie not in continuing to identify with a system doomed to disappear, but in relating to the forces for change which are destined to take charge of the socio-economic life of a non-racial, democratic South Africa.

Such a perspective is, in our view, the only way to peace, stability and progress in not only South Africa but the entire southern African region. Accordingly, we consistently maintain that support for our struggles in South Africa and Namibia in the form of sanctions and disinvestment should be part of a larger effort of disinvestment and assistance to the independent states of the region who are engaged in constructing their own economic infrastructures and resisting Pretoria's aggression and destabilization of the region.

I should like to conclude with a few words about the perspectives of the African National Congress with regard to a future non-racial, democratic and united South Africa. South Africa today is a country of immense inequalities. The bedrock of our perspective is our commitment to the establishment of democracy in a South Africa that belongs to all who live in it, black and white. In keeping with this commitment to our people, our policy positions enshrined in the Freedom Charter have been formulated with the fullest participation of our people. Every word, every line of that Charter is permeated with the concrete realities of oppression, exploitation and racism that our people have endured for centuries.

No one can deny the economic realities of the apartheid system. Ownership of the land is a virtual monopoly of the white community. While starvation and malnutrition plague the majority of the people of our country — the black people — the white community knows neither hunger nor poverty. Ownership of the mines and industry is so concentrated that it is difficult to conceive of a parallel. Some writers describe South Africa as a First World country in the case of the whites, and a Third World country in the case of the blacks.

A future and free South Africa must break that monopoly of white power and privilege. All formations are entitled to their own prescriptions as to how to achieve this. The African National Congress has its perspectives, deriving from the people, which are embodied in the Freedom Charter adopted in 1955. The Charter embodies the aspirations of our people and does not prescribe the formulas for their realization. In the context of its parameters, we believe that the issues as to how the wealth of our country is redistributed for the benefit of all our people, how the economy of our country is remoulded in order that all South Africans may thrive and prosper, are of prime importance and should find their solutions in the context of democracy. These are matters requiring the participation of the people; issues to be settled by informed debate and discussion in a democratic and sovereign parliament rather than through street battles.

Victory in our struggle is certain. As the vanguard movement of our people, the pre-occupation of the African National Congress is, and should be, the relentless prosecution of the all-round struggle to achieve freedom and democracy in our country. At the same time, we have begun to face the responsibilities that flow from having to lead our people in the restructuring of our society under the conditions of freedom. At the heart of this process is the need to ensure that the hopes and aspirations of our people find realization through programmes based on concrete socio-economic facts. This process involves systematic examination of each aspect of our society from the point of view of developing guide-lines and programmes which can be put before our people for the purpose of consultations. This is an enormous task but our approach has, as its starting point, our commitment to democracy. There are no glib answers and we are not about to provide any.

We have welcomed this opportunity to address you frankly and forthrightly. We believe that if the international community, governments and corporations in particular, play their part, racist South Africa will soon cease to exist. But the condition for you to play such an honourable role is that you choose sides now. That choice is between the apartheid system led by P.W. Botha and the alternative power of a future South Africa, at whose head stands the ANC, and which is already being moulded in the heat of struggle.

Are we expecting too much when we ask you to incorporate in the dry equations of profits and losses the balance of suffering and sacrifice that is inevitable for the realization of a free South Africa?

6.6 SOUTH AFRICA AT THE CROSSROADS
(Canon Collins Annual Memorial Lecture, 28 May 1987)

It is now almost five years since Canon John Collins passed away. With his departure, many of us lost a dear friend. As a people, we lost a fellow-combatant for justice and liberation, a dependable ally in the struggle to abolish the system of apartheid. Yet such was the durability of his good works that it was inevitable that they would outlast the short life that is given to us all and thus serve to turn the memory of the man into a material force that will continue to transform the destinies of the living.

As early as 1954, when he visited South Africa, he had the possibility not merely to study the situation as it then was, but more, to understand the nature of the apartheid system. From his assessment at the time, it was clear to him that South Africa, which he described as a 'madhouse', was heading for disaster. Even when some members of his own church within South Africa denounced him for being a foreign, meddling priest, Canon Collins did not waver in his involvement in the struggle against racist domination, precisely because he understood the dementia of this system.

We meet here today to pay a continuing tribute to him. Some of us have come here as his disciples. As such, all we can do is try to reflect on the message he left us, in the hope that we can communicate something of his example so that one or more among us can be inspired to act as he did and thereby contribute their tithe to the banishment of evil.

Canon Collins came into our lives at the inception of the crisis which the imposition of the apartheid system was to bring to the people of South Africa. In 1952 and from 1955 onwards, he intervened in the persisting drama of South African politics to comfort the persecuted and to help save some of the most outstanding representatives of our people from possible death sentences or long terms of imprisonment. He came to our aid not in pity but in solidarity. He stretched out his hand to our people because he saw that what was happening to us was an unacceptable attack against humanity itself. He acted because he could not stand aside.

When the racist regime arrested and charged with high treason 156 leaders of our democratic movement in 1956, it hoped that it would destroy that movement and create a situation in which it would expand and entrench the apartheid system without opposition. John Collins took the side of those on trial, as he had supported the patriots who joined our Campaign in Defiance of Unjust Laws in 1952. His actions carried the message that in the struggle between the forces of democracy and those of racism, there can be no neutrality.

The crisis which was in its early stages when Canon Collins joined us for the emancipation of our people has matured. The septic boil caused by the apartheid system is ready to burst, as the brutally repressive casing which contains the putrefaction of this system ruptures irrevocably and for all time. South Africa is at the crossroads.

It has taken many years of struggle to reach the point at which we are today. In that period, tens of thousands have been killed, injured and imprisoned within South Africa. Thousands of others have suffered a similar fate in Namibia.

The rest of southern Africa has also seen enormous numbers of people die, economies forced to the verge of collapse and social programmes brought to a halt.

Precisely that scale of destruction has only served to confirm the view among the victims of apartheid violence that they dare not give up, but have to fight with everything they can lay their hands on, to end the system that has brought about so much suffering. Above everything else, it is that resolve and determination by millions of people which guarantees the defeat of the Pretoria regime and the liquidation of the apartheid system. And yet there are those in this country who, unlike John Collins, doubt the certainty of our victory. These calculate that the racist regime is so powerful, and the white minority so steadfast in its commitment to the maintenance of its domination, that the oppressed are condemned to a futile and self-destructive battering at the ramparts of the racist fortress. But, of course, these doubting Thomases also profess an abhorrence for apartheid and declare a desire to see it brought to an end.

WESTERN APPEASEMENT

These positions have resulted in a policy which amounts to appeasement of the apartheid regime. Of central importance to the logical integrity of this policy is the notion that the Pretoria regime can and must be persuaded to turn itself into its opposite. Accordingly, it is required and expected that the racists should themselves dismantle the oppressive system they have instituted and over which they preside. Thus would we see the miraculous conversion of oppressors into liberators and the consequent transformation of the liberation movement into an irrelevance.

Another important element in this equation is the definition of the essence of the policy that the white minority regime must follow, as repression and reform. In terms of this perspective, it is required that this regime should gradually reform the apartheid system out of existence. To do so, it is considered necessary that the supposed reformers should work their wonders in a situation of stability. Consequently, it is viewed as a *sine qua non* for the abolition of the apartheid system that the forces that are fighting against this system should be kept in check by repressive means.

It therefore seems clear to us that the major Western powers have not departed from their old positions. According to these, the white minority regime is seen and treated as the defender and guarantor of the perceived interests of these powers. We, on the other hand, are viewed as a threat which must be dealt with in the appropriate manner.

In response to all this, the questions might be posed — what of the fact that the governments of the principal Western powers have, especially during the last twelve months, entered into direct contact with the ANC? And what of the fact that these governments have repeatedly called on the Pretoria regime to enter into negotiations with everybody concerned, including the ANC?

The Western powers entered into official contact with the ANC because the argument that they were seeking change by talking exclusively to the Botha regime could no longer be sustained. It had lost credibility. In addition, and as the Commonwealth Eminent Persons' Group understood and reported, it became clear to the Western governments that the majority of our people within South Africa recognized the ANC as their political representative. Hence it was inevitable that, if they were still interested in projecting themselves as brokers, honest or otherwise, these governments would have to be seen to be talking to the ANC.

However, the decisions taken in the various capitals, to relate to the ANC, did not in any way imply that there had been any change of attitude towards our policies, strategy and tactics. It is also obvious to us that in all the discussions we have held, by and large we have failed to move such major Western powers as the USA, the United Kingdom, and the Federal Republic of Germany, to view the South African situation from the perspective of the oppressed.

On all major questions pertaining to the issues we are discussing, the coincidence of views between the Pretoria regime and the powers that be in most of the West, persists. Where the racists describe us as a communist front, Western governments go so far as to order secret investigations of the ANC to establish the extent of this alleged communist domination.

Pretoria calls on us to renounce violence. The West calls on us to lay down arms. When the sole aggressor in southern Africa talks about so-called regional security, the Western powers condemn 'cross-border violence from all sides'. The white minority regime conducts a vigorous campaign against sanctions and is joined in that campaign by the Western powers.

We can go on *ad infinitum* and speak even about the questions of formulations and terminology. For example, our armed struggle is never that, but is either terrorism or violence. The limpet mines we use are never simply limpet mines, but are either of Soviet or communist origin. On the other hand, the guns and planes that Pretoria uses with such relish are never of British, American, French, Belgian or West German origin, but are mere guns or planes. The conclusions to draw from all this are obvious to all honest people.

ON NEGOTIATIONS

It is true that repeated calls have been made on the Botha regime to enter into negotiations with its opponents. However, nothing is said about how this regime will ultimately be brought to the negotiating table. At the end of the day, the call for negotiations turns out to be nothing more than a pious wish. It is not a desire that is translated into policy, accompanied by the necessary measures to ensure that it succeeds as a policy.

With regard to the possibility for negotiations, the Commonwealth Eminent Persons' Group observed correctly that 'the attitude of the South African government was clearly going to be the single most important determining factor'. At the end of their mission the EPG concluded that:

It is our considered view that, despite appearances and

statements to the contrary, the South African government is not yet ready to negotiate . . . (for the establishment of a non-racial and representative government) except on its own terms. Those terms, both in regard to objectives and modalities, fall far short of reasonable black expectations and well-accepted democratic norms and principles.

Later on in its Report the Group re-emphasized these points in the following manner:

The (government) is in truth not yet prepared to negotiate fundamental change, nor to countenance the creation of genuine democratic structures, nor to face the prospect of the end of white domination and white power in the foreseeable future. Its programme of reform does not end apartheid, but seeks to give it a less inhuman face. Its quest is power-sharing, but without surrendering overall white control.

Since the attitude of the Pretoria regime is the single most important factor determining the possibility for negotiations, and since that attitude is patently obvious, the test of the genuineness of the call for negotiations must necessarily turn on the willingness of those who make this call to change the attitude of the Pretoria regime towards these negotiations.

It is clear to us, as it was to the EPG and the Commonwealth mini-Summit to which the Group reported, that this cannot be done without pressure. As things stand, the Pretoria regime knows that it can continue to ignore the call for negotiations because the governments of the major Western countries have undertaken, almost as a matter of principle, that they will not act against the racist regime despite its continued failure to respond to the universal demand for an end to the apartheid system and its replacement by a democratic social order.

It was obvious from the very beginning that Sir Geoffrey Howe's mission to South Africa, last year, would not succeed, precisely for the reason that both the British government and the EEC were committed to avoiding any effective sanctions against apartheid South Africa. The experiences of both the EPG and the British Foreign and Commonwealth Secretary underline the central point that what both we and the international community must focus our attention on is action to end the apartheid system. Everything we do should be directed towards this end. We consider that any new international initiative seeking to bring about negotiations would be grossly misplaced and out of tune with reality exactly because the Botha regime is not prepared to address this fundamental question.

Nor indeed will it do to put the onus on the ANC to take such initiatives as it might be claimed would enable negotiations to take place; and neither will it do to fish around for such initiatives. If the key to negotiations were in our hands, we would long have used it to open the door. Such measures as have been proposed for us to adopt, namely, the cessation or suspension of our armed struggle or the unilateral proclamation of a moratorium, will do nothing to bring about negotiations. The Pretoria regime is refusing to negotiate not because there is an armed struggle, but because it is unwilling to give up white minority domination. Once again, it is instructive to look at the observations of the Eminent Persons' Group on these issues. The EPG said:

> To ask the ANC or other parties, all of them far weaker than the government, to renounce violence for all time, here and now, would be to put them in a position of having to rely absolutely on the government's intentions and determination to press through the process of negotiations. It was not a question of whether the Group believed in the sincerity of the South African government, but whether the parties would. It was neither possible nor reasonable to have people forswear the only power available to them should the government walk away from the negotiating table. For the government to attribute all violence to the ANC . . . was to overlook a situation in which the structures of society, dominated by a

relatively small group of people, were founded upon injustice which inevitably led to violence. In addition, in the light of recent events, the government of South Africa would need to give a firm commitment to desist from further aggression against neighbouring states.

On the specific question of the suspension of armed struggle, the EPG stated that 'a prior reduction in the level of violence before the government itself takes specific action in regard to the (Group's proposals) would not be feasible. A suspension of violence or a commitment to non-violence, if in the government's view the meaning is the same, would obviously in the present context require a commitment to suspend the violence arising from the administration of apartheid'.

Further, in one of its letters to the Pretoria regime, the EPG makes the point that 'the Lancaster House negotiations (on Zimbabwe) continued without the suspension of violence as have many others in situations of conflict'. This is a matter of historical fact with which we are all familiar. It makes no sense that we should be treated as an exception to this general practice.

We also need to reiterate the point that the source of violence in South Africa, Namibia and our region is the apartheid system and the racist regime. What must cease is, in the words of the EPG, the violence that arises from the administration of apartheid. For that to happen, the system of white minority domination must be brought to an end. It seems to us strange reasoning that we, the victims of violence, should be asked to respond to the continued terror of the Pretoria regime against the peoples of southern Africa by committing ourselves to cease our armed resistance, whether temporarily or permanently.

The Pretoria regime has blocked the path to negotiations. The recent whites-only elections in South Africa have confirmed P.W. Botha in his view that white South Africa stands with him in his determination to resist all change and further to entrench the apartheid system. The governments of the Western countries that awaited the results of this illegitimate electoral process now have their answer. The question we would like to ask is what then are they going to do?

Those who have always been opposed to effective sanctions against racist South Africa are already advancing arguments to justify their old positions. These claim that white South Africa has moved further to the right because of the sanctions that have been imposed. If it has not happened already, it will also be argued that the Botha regime has, as a result, become so strong that it will not be amenable to pressure — that all that can be done is to re-affirm the correctness of the policy of so-called constructive engagement.

All of this will, of course, come as music to the ears of the white supremacists in South Africa. Indeed, they will make certain that their friends state and re-state these arguments. We, on the other hand, are convinced that comprehensive and mandatory sanctions would succeed in breaking up this white power block. It is certainly our task to realize this objective and to achieve the transfer of power to the people through struggle.

NO TO REFORM

We say that apartheid cannot be reformed but has to be abolished in its entirety. Official Western policy towards South Africa will not change until this correct proposition is accepted, until the example set by Canon Collins is adopted as the only legitimate course open to those who say they want to see an end to apartheid.

This places the Western powers in the position in which they have to choose either to work for the total elimination of the apartheid system or, in fact, to connive at its perpetuation, as they do now. We are, however, certain that sooner or later they will come to realize that there has emerged an alternative democratic power within South Africa, an indigenous product of struggle which holds the future of South Africa in its hands.

The West will then have to decide whether it takes the side of this alternative power and the rest of the anti-colonial and anti-racist forces of the continent of Africa made up of nearly five hundred million people, or whether it ties itself to the doomed course followed by far less than five million Africans of European origin. It is no longer possible to run with the hares and hunt with the hounds.

The alternative power in our country is as real today as it is impossible to vanquish in the future. It is here to stay and will grow in strength despite all efforts to suppress it, until South Africa is liberated and peace returns to southern Africa. As a consequence of this development, it is becoming impossible to avoid confronting the question of the legitimacy of the powers which are contending with each other within our country. These two cannot co-exist, as fascism and democracy could not, but have to give way one to the other. Not even the best of conjurers can maintain an equidistant position between them. The times demand that you who are gathered in this hall should progress from opposition to apartheid to identification with and support for the democratic movement for national liberation in Namibia and South Africa. This evolution can no longer be avoided.

The broad perspectives of our country's democratic power are spelt out in the Freedom Charter. Organizationally, it is represented by many formations which recognize the leading role of the ANC in the struggle for a united, democratic and non-racial South Africa. Whether or not they support or engage in armed struggle, they are at one with us in seeking this outcome and are active in the struggle for its realization.

I should state here that when we say we are fighting for a united, democratic and non-racial South Africa, we mean what we say. It is very clear to us that unless our country becomes such an entity, we shall know no peace. To propose any so-called solutions which fall within the parameters of the apartheid system is no more than to prepare a recipe for a continuation of the conflict which has already claimed too many lives.

It is to ask for the continued murder and imprisonment of children, which has become a permanent feature of Pretoria's policy of repression. It is to prepare for the extension of the policy of the deliberate impoverishment of the masses of the black people, the forced removal and banishment of millions, the break-up of families and everything else that you know about the apartheid system.

As long as this system exists, whatever guise it assumes, so long will the frontline and neighbouring states be victims of aggression and destabilization. For all this to end, for these crimes to become a thing of the past, South Africa must become a democratic country, with guarantied liberties for all citizens, with equal rights for everybody regardless of colour, race or sex.

Given the changing balance of strength in our country and the shift of the strategic initiative into our hands, there is a sense in which the apartheid forces are becoming the opposition to the ascendant democratic movement rather than the other way round. The recent white elections demonstrate this point inasmuch as the Botha regime contested them on the specific platform of opposition to the ANC. Subsequent to its victory, this regime has not changed its tune but has continued with its threats to act vigorously against the democratic movement and has actually carried out these threats as well as murdering a young Zimbabwean woman who was married to the Administrative Secretary in our office in Harare.

In the recent period intense debates have arisen about the academic and cultural boycotts. In a critical sense these debates arise from the successes of our all-round struggle and reflect attempts to get to grips with new dimensions that the emergence of the alternative democratic power entails. The boycott campaigns, from their inception in the late fifties, were aimed at the total isolation of apartheid South Africa. This objective is inviolate and needs to be pursued with even greater vigour. At the same time we must take into account the changes that have taken place over time. In particular, as in almost every other field of human endeavour in South Africa, there has emerged a definable alternative democratic culture — the people's culture permeated with and giving expression to the deepest aspirations of our people in struggle, immersed in democratic and enduring human values.

This is a development, however, that is taking place within the context of the emergent alternative democratic power whose duty it is to draw on the academic and cultural resources and heritage of the world community to advance the democratic perspective in our country. For it is only with the realization of a non-racial, democratic and united South Africa that such a people's culture shall be able to flourish in full glory.

To a lesser or greater degree, there has always been a tradition of progressive culture which has struggled for survival and growth against colonial domination and commercialization. The change that has occurred is that this people's culture, despite the extreme hostility of the racist state, has grown into a mighty stream, distinct from and in opposition to the warped and moribund culture of racism. Its foremost exponents are today part of the democratic movement. The core of the cultural workers engaged in creating this people's culture are simultaneously engaged in developing our own institutions and structures which are aligned to mass democratic organizations in our country.

As in politics, trade unionism, education, sport, religion and many other fields, these developments at the cultural level both contributed to and are part of the emergent alternative democratic power at whose head stands the ANC.

Without doubt the developing and vibrant culture of our people in struggle and its structures need to be supported, strengthened and enhanced. In the same way as apartheid South Africa is being increasingly isolated internationally, within South Africa this people's culture is steadily isolating the intellectual and cultural apologists of apartheid.

Indeed, the moment is upon us when we shall have to deal with the alternative structures that our people have created and are creating through struggle and sacrifice, as the genuine representatives of these masses in all fields of human activity. Not only should these not be boycotted, but more, they should be supported, encouraged and treated as the democratic counterparts within South Africa of similar institutions and organizations internationally. This means that the ANC, the broad democratic movement in its various formations within South Africa, and the international solidarity movement need to act together.

On these questions John Collins entertained no doubts whatsoever. Having taken positions against racism, discrimination, oppression and war, he accepted that to bring these to an end he must march side by side with those of like mind, against the racists, the oppressors and the war-mongers. His example is eminently worthy of emulation.

Everywhere in our country, and after a year of national state of emergency, the democratic forces are at work to expand and strengthen their ranks and to raise the level and intensity of the offensive against the apartheid regime to new heights. For its part, this regime prepares itself for more atrocities, for the campaign of repression of which P.W. Botha boasts — as though to shoot and kill children, to imprison and torture them and their parents, to carry out one outrage after another against independent Africa, were the worthiest activities that one could ever imagine.

A terrible collision between ourselves and our opponents is inevitable. Many battles will be fought and many lives will be lost throughout our region. In preparation for this, the Pretoria regime has identified the defeat of the democratic movement as the centre-piece of state policy. Yet the outcome is not in doubt. Having reached the crossroads, the masses of our people have decided that our country must advance as rapidly as possible to the situation where they, black and white, will govern themselves together as equals. Whatever the cost, there is no doubt that we will win.

We cannot but regret that such titans of our struggle as John Collins will not be with us to celebrate the birth of democracy in our country. In a fortnight you, who are his compatriots, will be casting your votes to choose representatives to your parliament. How terrible it is that in the southern tip of Africa millions have to go through the furnace of violent struggle to win for themselves a right which you take for granted!

What a tragedy that many more will have to die simply

With Canon Collins, at the marriage of daughter, Tembi. *(L & S Photographic)*

because this, a democratic country, refused to heed Canon Collins's plea for his motherland to side with the oppressed and to declare war on the tyrants! What a tragedy that those who exercise power have become so bereft of vision that they have learnt to treat as no more than a slogan, the objective of the expansion of the frontiers of democracy to the black oppressed of Namibia and South Africa!

When freedom comes, what will they say then?

What will they do then?

Will they finally claim Canon Collins as one of their own?

LIST OF SOURCES

1.1 'Passive Resistance in South Africa', in J.A.Davis and J.K.Baker (eds) *Southern Africa in Transition*, Frederick A.Praeger, New York, 1966.

1.2 G.Carter, G.Gerhart and T.Karis, *From Protest to Challenge*, Volume III, Hoover, Stanford, 1977, pp223-228.

1.3 In possession of Adelaide Tambo.

2.1 In possession of Adelaide Tambo.

2.2 In possession of Adelaide Tambo.

2.3 'Southern Africa, South Africa and the ANC', *Sechaba*, April 1968.

2.4 'We Shall Win', *Sechaba*, December 1968.

2.5 'ANC Statement to the Preparatory Meeting of the Non-Aligned States', *Sechaba*, July 1970.

3.1 'Intensify the Revolution', *Sechaba*, July 1969.

3.2 'Bitter Battles to Come', *Sechaba*, February 1971.

3.3 'Message to the External Mission', *Sechaba*, March 1971.

3.4 'Increase our Striking Power', *Sechaba*, June/July 1975.

3.5 ANC document.

4.1 ANC document.

4.2 'The Seizure of Power', *Sechaba*, May 1975.

4.3 'A Future Free of Exploitation', *Sechaba*, second quarter 1978.

4.4 ANC document.

5.1 ANC document

5.2 'Oliver Tambo: Our Bases are Inside South Africa', *Journal of African Marxists*, February 1984.

5.3 'Church and Our Struggle', *Sechaba*, November 1980.

5.4 'India Pays Tribute to Mandela', *Sechaba*, February 1981.

5.5 'Our Alliance is a Living Organism that has grown out of the Struggle', *Sechaba*, September 1981.

6.1 'President O.R.Tambo's Address to the Nation', *Journal of African Marxists,* January 1986.

6.2 ANC document.

6.3.'Discussions with Gorbachev', *Sechaba,* February 1987

6.4 Riverside Church Disarmament Programme, 1987

6.5 ANC document.

6.6 ANC document.

LIST OF ABBREVIATIONS

AAC	All-African Convention
ANC	African National Congress
ANCYL	Congress Youth League
BPC	Black People's Convention
COSAS	Congress of South African Students
COSATU	Congress of South African Trade Unions
CPSA	Communist Party of South Africa
FSAW	Federation of South African Women
ICU	Industrial and Commercial Workers' Union
NEUM	Non-European Unity Movement
OAU	Organization of African Unity
PAC	Pan-Africanist Congress
SACOD	South African Congress of Democrats
SACPO	South African Coloured People's Organization
SACTU	South African Congress of Trade Unions
SAIC	South African Indian Congress
SANNC	South African Native National Congress
SASM	South African Students' Movement
SASO	South African Students' Organization
UDF	United Democratic Front
UNO	United Nations Organization
ZAPU	Zimbabwe African People's Union
WCC	World Council of Churches